YETIS, SASQUATCH & HAIRY GIANTS

Other books by David Hatcher Childress

The Mystery of the Olmecs
Technology of the Gods
Pirates & the Lost Templar Fleet
Lost Continents & the Hollow Earth
Lost Cities & Ancient Mysteries of the Southwest
Lost Cities of China, Central Asia & India
Lost Ciies & Ancient Mysteries of Africa & Arablia
Lost Ciies & Ancient Mysteries of South America
Lost Ciies of Ancient Lemuria & the Pacific
Lost Ciies of North and Central America
Lost Cities of Atlantis, Ancient Europe & the Mediterranean
Atlantis & the Power System of the Gods
Vimana Aircraft of Ancient India & Atlantis
The Crystal Skulls (with Stephen Mehler)

YETIS, SASQUATCH & HAIRY GIANTS

by
David Hatcher Childress

Yetis, Sasquatch & Hairy Giants

ISBN 978-1-931882-98-9

Copyright 2010

by David Hatcher Childress

Published by Adventures Unlimited Press
One Adventure Place
Kempton, Illinois 60946 USA

www.adventuresunlimitedpress.com
www.wexclub.com
www.treknepal.com

TABLE OF CONTENTS

PART ONE:

HAIRY GIANTS

CHAPTER 1

THE GIANTS OF YORE

There were giants in the earth in those days;
and also after that when the sons of God came
in unto the daughters of men, and they bare
children unto them, the same became mighty men
which were of old, men of renown.
—*Genesis 6:4*

The subject of yetis, bigfoot, hairy giants and wildmen is one that has managed to become extremely popular in modern culture. Tales of bigfoot, yetis, and living giants and wildmen are weekly fodder in the world's media. Press conferences are called, photos are shown, claims are made and bloggers weigh in with their ponderous opinions.

We will start this book with the subject of giants and wildmen because these subjects are a good precursor to the more controversial subjects of yeti and sasquatch. Giants and wildmen are very real, and no one really doubts that either exist. They both most certainly do. The question, though, is just how big these "giants" get? There can be no doubt that a good dose of exaggeration has come with stories of giants. Many, if not most, "professional" giants that worked in circuses and sideshows exaggerated their height as much as possible. Yet, no matter exactly how tall they were—or weren't—they were certainly people of considerable height, literal giants.

Since we know that modern giants often exaggerated their height, each struggling through his agent to be the tallest man in the world, it would seem that ancient chroniclers of giants were also told exaggerated stories, or made the exaggerations themselves. Still, we have to wonder at the core truth behind these tales. Were some of the men described really nine or ten feet tall? Did some of them genuinely have six fingers and six toes? What might be the limit for a full grown, proportional man to grow—12 or 14 feet tall? It is an amazing thought!

The word "giant" comes down to us from both ancient Greek and Latin. In Greek mythology, powerful giants called Titans—who were gods—ruled the earth during the legendary Golden Age. Their role as Elder Gods was overthrown by a race of younger gods, the Olympians. There are twelve Titans in their first literary appearance, in Hesiod's

10

Theogony. Later, a thirteenth Titan named Dione, a double of Theia, is mentioned by the Greek historian Pseudo-Apollodorus in *Bibliotheke*. The six male Titans are known as the Titanes, and the females as the Titanides ("Titanesses"). The Titans were associated with various primal concepts, from which their names largely derive. The original Titans were ruled by the youngest, Cronos (Saturn), who had overthrown their father, Oranos (Sky), at the urging of their mother, Gaia (Earth).

Several Titans produced offspring who are also known as Titans. These second-generation Titans include the children of Hyperion (Helios, Eos and Selene), the daughters of Coeus (Leto and Asteria), and the sons of Iapetus (Prometheus, Epimetheus, Atlas and Menoetius).

The Titans were of gigantic stature and enormous strength and, according to myth, they carried on wars with the gods and from them sprang the Gigantes, frightening beings with terrible faces and the tails of dragons. Eventually, the hero Hercules, himself said to be seven feet tall, slew the Gigantes and defeated the Titans with the aid of Zeus, who became the all-powerful god of the Greeks.[25]

Hercules also battled the giant Antaios in one of his adventures. A second-century BC Greek geographer named Pausanias tells us that the great walls of Mycenae, Tiryns and Argos were constructed by the giant race of Cyclopes. It is from this reference that archeologists get the term "cyclopean masonry" which is used to describe unusually gigantic rocks

11

within walls. The aforementioned Greek cities have such walls, but they are also found in Lebanon, Egypt, Peru, Bolivia, Mexico and many other places.

Homer describes the most famous Cyclops, a giant named Polyphemus, in *The Odyssey*. He dwelt in a cave on the coast of Sicily and lived on human flesh. He sought for victims with his mighty club which Homer describes:

The monster's club within the cave I spy'd
A tree of stateliest growth, and yet undry'ed,
Green from the wood; of height and bulk so vast,
The largest ship might claim it for a mast.

Giants of a previous civilization were said to have built the dolmens, trilithons and giant walls that are strewn throughout Europe, and are especially prevalent in France and the British Isles. The online encyclopedia, *Wikipedia* mentions that in Basque mythology, giants were said to have raised the dolmens and menhirs. Natural features like the basalt formation in Northern Ireland called the Giant's Causeway were similarly attributed to giants.

In Ireland, Wales, Scotland and England there are numerous tales featuring combat with giants. Giants were often noted for their stupidity. Some British and Irish stories relate how giants threw stones at each other—something that would explain many great menhirs and other mysterious gigantic stones on the landscape.

In Norse mythology, the giants are typically

12

An old print of a knight meeting a cyclops giant.

opposed to the gods and come in different types, such as mountain giants, fire giants, and frost giants. These giants are the origin of many of the monsters in Norse mythology, and it is foretold that in the eventual battle of Ragnarök the giants will storm Asgard and defeat the Gods.

Six-Fingered Giants of Renown

The Bible makes a number of references to races of people who are of great stature and actually names a number of individuals who were of abnormal height.

The first reference is in *Genesis* 6:4 which is about the Nephilim, the famous "Giants in the Earth" which married the daughters of men; these were the famous "Sons of God."

Then, in *Genesis* 14:5 we are told of the Rephaim, also giants, who were defeated by the hero-king Chedorloamer and the allied kings of Ashteroth. Also mentioned are the Emims, who dwelt in the wilderness of Moab, "a people great, and many, and tall as the Anakims, which also were accounted giants as the Anakims." (*Deut.* 2:10)

British scholar C.J.S.Thompson mentions the Anakims in his 1930 book *The History and Lore of Freaks*. He says this race of giants dwelt at Hebron, and were the same giants who excited the wonder and alarm of the spies sent by Moses in Canaan. These giants are variously described as the sons of Anak, or

14

David and Goliath do battle.

Anakim, and the descendants of Anak. They were "men of great stature" and according to *Numbers* 13:32, "And there we saw the giants, the sons of Anak which come of the giants; and we were in our own sight as grasshoppers, and so we were in their sight."[25] In *Deuteronomy* 9:2 they are described as, "A people great and tall, the children of the Anakims, whom thou knowest and of whom thou hast heard say, 'Who can stand before the children of Anak?'"

The land of Ammon "also was accounted a land of giants; giants dwelt therein in old time; and the Ammonites called them Zamzumminms, a people

15

A Doré engraving of David holding up the head of the slain Goliath.

great and many and tall as the Anakims." (*Genesis* 12:12)

Og, King of Bashan, was the last of the race of these giants we are told in the book of *Joshua*. "All the Kingdom of Og in Bashan, which reigned in Ashtaroth and in Edrei, who remained of the remnant of the giants; for these did Moses smite and cast them out."

According to *Deuteronomy* 3:11, his bed could still be seen on display in the city of Rabbah: "It is nine cubits long and four cubits wide, according to the ordinary cubit." This translates to a bed that is 13.5 feet long and six feet wide. Indeed a bed big enough for a giant!

Says C.J.S. Thompson, "It is probable that Og, whose story survived in many Eastern legends, was about nine feet in height, although in some accounts he is said to have been taller, and according to the *Targum*, he was 'several miles' in height."[25]

The Bible relates the familiar tales of how giants joined the Philistines and fought against the Hebrews in the second book of *Samuel* (21:20) and says that "there was a battle in Gath, where was a man of great stature, that had on every hand six fingers, and on every foot six toes, four and twenty in number, and he also was born a giant. And when he defied Israel, Jonathan the son of Shimeah the brother of David slew him."

Goliath, whom David slew with his slingshot, may also have had six fingers and toes and was said to stand six cubits and a span in height. This is about

17

nine feet, nine inches, a considerable height by any standards. He may have been under seven feet, as *Wikipedia* says that the original Septuagint Hebrew Bible as well as the historian Josephus (and the Dead Sea Scrolls) give Goliath's height as "four cubits and a span," which would make him approximately six feet seven inches. He was certainly a big man whose coat of mail weighed 5,000 shekels of brass, computed to be about 208 pounds.

The prophet Amos testifies that the land of Canaan was originally inhabited by giants, destroyed by Yahweh in the Israelite conquest. Amos says in a divine oracle: "I destroyed the Amorites before them, whose height was the height of cedar trees, and whose strength was like an oak" (*Amos* 2:9).

A little known apocryphal book of the Old Testament is called *Ogias the Giant*, also known as the *Book of Giants*. According to *Wikipedia* the text relates how, before the Biblical deluge, a giant named Ogias fought a great dragon. A brief mention of this giant, "Ohia" is found in the Babylonian Talmud (*Nidah*, Ch 9) which says, "Sihon and Og [from the book of *Numbers*] were brothers, as they were the sons of Ohia the son of Samhazai [one of the leaders of the fallen angels in the book of *Enoch*]".

Ogias the Giant is thought to have been based on the book of *Enoch* which elaborates on an obscure passage from *Genesis* (6:1-4) concerning the Nephilim, which became "fallen angels." The *Book of Giants* concerns itself with filling in details about the giants and their offspring that are missing from

18

the book of *Enoch*. *Wikipedia* says that a version of the *Book of Giants* was spread by the Manichaean religion; it reached deep into Central Asia and exists in Syriac, Greek, Persian, Sogdian, Uighur and Arabic, although "each version is somewhat distorted, incorporating more local myths."

The Jewish-Roman historian Josephus mentions two pillars, one of stone and one of very hard brick, that were placed by giant men to stand as a monument to their architectural wisdom in the event of a cataclysmic flood such as those in legends. These giants were known as the children of Seth (identified by British author H.T. Wilkins as "giants of the kingdom of Thoth, or Taut of Atlantis..."[87]) and they had erected the two pillars so that at least one might survive the flood.

Says Josephus, "Now, these pillars remain in the land of Siriad to this day... Noah quitted the land of Seth for fear that his family might be annihilated by the giants. Their span of life had been reduced to 120 years... and Jah turned dry land into sea to destroy the earth... The food of the antediluvians was fitted to maintain a long life, and they observed the stars over the period of the Great Year, that is 600 years... Ephorus and Nicolaus say that the antediluvians had a span of life of 1,000 years. As late as the days of Joshua, son of Nun, there were still giants of Hebron, who had bodies so large and faces so entirely different from other men, that they were surprising to the sight and terrible to the hearing. The bones of these giant men are still shown to this day."[36]

19

Josephus is affirming to us what the ancient traditions tell: that in antiquity, men in general were larger than men today, and they were longer lived, though their lifespans had been shortened from hundreds of years to only 120. As we read in the Bible:

> My spirit shall not always strive with man,
> for that he also is flesh:
> yet his days shall be
> a hundred and twenty years.
> —*Genesis* 6:3

The Giants of Patagonia

The British author and excellent researcher Harold T. Wilkins discusses many tales of giants in his 1952 book *Secret Cities of Old South America.*[87] Says Wilkins, "One tradition in ancient Mexico says that the pyramid of Cholula was built by an antediluvian man, the giant Xelhua, who emerged from the mountain Tlaloc. ...In old Peru, the Quechuas say that the pucaras (forts and prehistoric strongholds, such as Chanchayillo, and Quellantana, overlooking Lago de Titicaca, near the pueblo of Vilcachico), were 'erected by giants before the sun shone'..."

Wilkins mentions a curious incident in northern Mexico: "In the fall of 1929, Dean Byron Cummings of Arizona University and Professor Manuel San Domingo, a Mexican Government scientist of

20

Sonora went to a dangerous spot 160 miles from the international border where the turbulent Yaquis smash excavation work with rifle butts and menace intruders with sudden death. They found three giant skeletons of two men and one woman eight feet tall. The skulls were a foot long and ten inches wide, and there were remains of six children, all six feet tall. In tall ollas were human ashes suggesting either cremation or human sacrifices. The remains were in an ancient burial ground called the 'Cyclopes necropolis.' Beautiful ceramics were buried with the giants' remains which were also covered with fine jewels."[87]

Wilkins goes on to say, "Earlier in the same year (1929) Mr. Paxon Hayes found mummies of a peculiar race of Mongoloid giants in dry caves in the sierras of New Mexico, USA. He got out 34 of these mummies, and did four years' hard work in the region. He says facial angles of these and their burial customs are different from those of Indians. They have slanting eyes and sloping foreheads, and the adults are about seven feet high, though their feet are only seven inches long. Their hair is black, with a peculiarly sunburnt tinge when closely examined. The remains were preserved in asphaltum, or resin, and wrapped in burial clothes bound with fibre."[87]

Wilkins also notes, "Telegrams from Casas Grandes, Mexico, in 1923, announced the discovery of several skeletons of Indians *fifteen feet tall,* buried side by side, with vases of precious stones. The news came from Ciudad Juarez." (Italics in this and the following paragraphs are by Wilkins)

21

Elsewhere, Wilkins mentions a discovery made in a cavern in a coal mine, in Pas de Calais, France. In January 1884, "six fossilized human bodies were found with remains of arms and utensils, in petrified wood and stone. In a second cave were eleven *giant human bodies,* animals, and even precious stones. The walls of this cave were decorated with pictures of combat between *giant men and beasts of gigantic size.*" [87]

On page 430 he mentions that an "amazing discovery was made, in 1577, near Reyden, in Switzerland, when, in a cave revealed by the fall of a very ancient decayed oak, there were found the bones of a giant man, *16 feet tall!* The remains were sent to the senate of Luzern, and a well known physician of Basel, Felix Plater, reconstituted missing parts of the skeleton structure of the giant, which was then painted by an artist of Basel, Joannes Bock..."[87]

One of the great mysteries of history involves the tales of a race of giants in southern Argentina and Chile, which were told by the first European explorers into the region. The northern part of Argentina is the swampy and partly wooded area known as the Gran Chaco, while the southern area is the cool, arid plateau of Patagonia. Geographically, Patagonia is formed by a plain which rises west from the Atlantic to the Chilean border in the towering peaks of the Andes.

The population density over the 450,000 square miles of Patagonia is one person per square mile, kept company by 40 sheep. Quite a few Welsh arrived in

22

Patagonia in the 1800s to tend these sheep, founding a number of Welsh towns that are still there today. Patagonia itself means, "the land of the people with long feet," a title which refers to the stories of the Patagonian Giants.

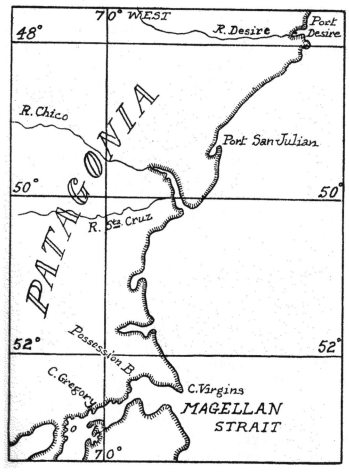

When Ferdinand Magellan discovered Patagonia in 1520, on his way around the world, he anchored at Port San Julian, just north of Tierra del Fuego ("the land of fire"). While Magellan's fleet laid at anchor in the natural bay, a native of extremely large proportions appeared on the beach. "This man," wrote Pigafetta, a companion of Magellan, "was so tall that our heads scarcely came up to his waist, and his voice was like that of a bull." Other natives emerged, and according to a historian in Spain, the smallest of them was taller and bulkier than any Spaniard. So was born the story of the Patagonian Giants, appearing to vindicate those historians who had insisted that such a race must exist.[45]

Sir Francis Drake anchored in the same harbor in 1578, also reporting men of great stature, whom he described as being well over seven feet tall. Anthony Knyvet, who took part in an expedition to the Strait of Magellan in 1592, wrote of having seen Patagonians from ten to twelve feet in height, and of having measured several bodies of the same size at Port Desire. Several skeletons ten or eleven feet long were discovered in 1615 by two crewman from the Dutch schooner *Wilhelm Schouten*.[45]

By this time, the existence of a race of giants seemed well established, however, for nearly one hundred fifty years after this last sighting, no other reports were made of these Patagonian Giants. Other natives of Patagonia were of normal size, but they did insist that giants lived in the interior of the land.

When Commodore Byron visited the Strait of

A historic drawing of Lord Byron and the Patagonian giants.

Magellan in 1764, he reported sighting some natives on horseback who waved at his party. Byron later wrote in his log that the chief of these natives "was of a gigantic stature and seemed to realize the tales of monsters in a human shape: he had the skin of some wild beast thrown over his shoulder."[45]

Upon meeting with five hundred more of these giants, each taller than the tallest of the British, one of Byron's officers wrote, "…some of them are certainly nine feet, if they do not exceed it. The commodore, who is very near six feet, could but just reach the top of one of their heads, which he attempted, on tip-toe; and there were several taller than him on whom the experiment was tried."[45] Although most people overestimate the height of a person who is taller than

25

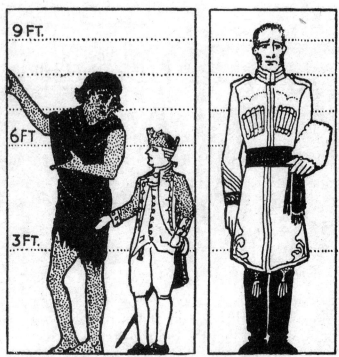

A Patagonian giant compared with Byron and Fedor Machnov.

they are, and a man of Byron's height could probably only reach up to about eight feet, the race his group encountered was definitely of incredible height.

These sightings were the last recorded of the Patagonian Giants. To this day, no one has identified who these giants were, and some doubt that they even existed. Some who believe the stories feel that they lived somewhere in the interior of Patagonia, rarely coming to the coast.

It is interesting to note that in 1895 a discovery

26

was made of the reportedly fresh skin of a giant ground sloth (Mylodon) in a cave at Consuelo cove at Last Hope Inlet, on the western coast of Patagonia. These creatures stood about fifteen feet tall, and were thought to have been extinct for 30,000 years. But this skin was rolled up and carefully buried in a cave which also contained human remains, including a mummy![32] Evidence suggested that ground sloths were actually penned in in the cave, fed and later slaughtered. Did ancient (or not-so-ancient) man actually domesticate giant ground sloths in Patagonia? What sort of man would do this—perhaps one of great stature?

One interesting tribe that lived in Tierra del Fuego at the time of the European discovery was the Onas. They were quite an unusual bunch, wearing no clothes, but covering themselves with mud to keep warm. Somewhat taller than average Indians at nearly six feet, they often wore a piece of wood on the top of their head, giving them extra height. This custom may have started in imitation of the Patagonian Giants, but their tradition claims they dressed like this to frighten their own women, to keep them in line.

According to an ancient legend among the Onas, in an earlier time, the tribe's women managed the society and educated the children. There was a conspiracy among the women to keep the men afraid of them and their power, until one man discovered the women's trick, and the tables were turned. Now it is the men who keep the women in fear.

But back to the actual giants: did they really exist? In 1925 a group of amateur "investigators" destroyed

27

one of the most important finds of its kind. Digging into an Indian mound at Walkerton, Indiana, they had unearthed the skeletons of eight prehistoric humans, ranging from eight to almost nine feet tall, all wearing substantial copper armor. Unfortunately, the evidence was scattered and lost.[53]

Author Ivan T. Sanderson relates a story from a letter he received from an engineer who was stationed on the Aleutian island of Shemya during World War Two. While building an airstrip, his crew bulldozed a group of hills, discovering under several sedimentary layers what appeared to be a graveyard of seemingly human remains, consisting of crania and long leg bones. The crania measured from 22 to 24 inches from base to crown. Since an adult skull normally measures about eight inches from back to front, such a large crania would imply an immense size for a normally proportioned human. Furthermore, every skull was said to have been neatly trepanned![69]

Sanderson tried to gather further proof, eventually receiving a letter from another member of the unit who confirmed the report. The letters both indicated that the Smithsonian Institution had collected the remains, yet nothing else was heard. Sanderson seems to be convinced that it was not a hoax, but wondered why the Smithsonian would not release the data. To quote him, "…is it that these people cannot face rewriting all the textbooks?"

In 1833, soldiers digging a pit for a powder magazine at Lompoc Rancho, California, hacked their way through a layer of cemented gravel and came up with the skeleton of a man about twelve feet tall. The skeleton was surrounded by carved shells, huge stone axes, and blocks of porphyry covered with unintelligible symbols. The giant was also noteworthy in another respect: he had a double row of teeth, both upper and lower.[52] When local Indians began to attach a religious significance to the skeleton and artifacts, the authorities ordered it secretly buried; it is now lost to science.

Researchers Brad Steiger and Ron Calais report in their book *Mysteries of Time and Space*[94] that in 1895, a party of miners working near Bridalveil Falls, California, found the tomb of a woman whose skeletal remains indicated that she had stood six feet, eight inches in height. The corpse had been wrapped in animal skins and covered with a fine gray powder. She was clutching a child to her breast.

They also report that in 1898, scientists excavating in Death Valley found the fossilized remains of a giant female who stood seven feet, six inches and whose spine bore several extra "buttons" at its base, indicating that the woman and her unknown people were endowed with a tail-like appendage.[94]

Steiger and Calais also relate that the *Dallas Morning News* on July 30, 1974, carried a story of the discovery of the skeleton of a seven-foot woman sealed in a cave at the crest of a high mesa near the hamlet of Chalk Mountain, Texas.[94]

Also in Texas, at the Paluxy River site, creationist researcher Dr. Clifford Burdick claims to have found evidence of dinosaurs and man walking together

29

in the many fossilized footprints in the sandstone of the river. The human tracks, found in situ with the tracks of a tyrannosaurus rex, are said by conservative geologists to be over 80 million years old. The creationists feel that these, and all fossils, are only five to six thousand years old (and the truth is probably somewhere between these two figures). The fossilized "human" footprints are of an enormous size, indicating that these ancient people were literal giants. They may have been over 10 feet tall, and there can be no doubt that they had very big feet! [94]

There are legends of giants all over the world, from China and Pacific Islands to Africa and the Americas, but what we really require is proof. Perhaps the bones of giants have been found, or even better, perhaps giants exist even today!

GIANT
HUMAN
FOOT
PRINT

FOUND:
PULUXY
RIVER
BED
GLEN
ROSE
TEXAS

An old print of of the English giant William Evans.

CHAPTER 2

GIANTS AMONG US

The difference between ordinary
and extraordinary is that little extra.
—*Jimmy Johnson*

᳁ —₥— ᳁

There are Giants in the Earth

Giants have long caught the fascination of mankind, with a revival of "giant consciousness" in Europe taking place in the middle ages. Some scientists and historians at that time argued that there must still be a race of giants somewhere in the world, since the legends were so numerous. When early settlers began to excavate some of the mounds found in the Ohio and Mississippi River Valleys, they discovered bones of what they deemed a former race of giants.

A race of giants became associated with the

huge North American pyramids at the Illinois site of Cahokia along the Mississippi River. Cahokia is only one of hundreds, even thousands of pyramids throughout the central United States.

At Cahokia, sheets of copper, plates of mica, shells and turquoise have all been found at burials. These various materials all originate from vastly separated areas of the Midwest.

Furthermore, some rather interesting skeletons and artifacts have been discovered in many mounds throughout the Midwest:

•In his book, *The Natural and Aboriginal History of Tennessee,* author John Haywood describes "very large" bones found in stone graves in Williamson County, Tennessee, in 1821. In White County, an "ancient fortification" contained skeletons of gigantic stature averaging at least seven feet in length.

•Giant skeletons were found in the mid-1800s near Rutland and Rodman, New York. J.N. DeHart, M.D., found vertebrae "larger than those of the present type" in Wisconsin mounds in 1876. W.H.R. Lykins uncovered skull bones "of great size and thickness" in mounds of the Kansas City area in 1877.

•George W. Hill, M.D., dug out a skeleton "of unusual size" in a mound of Ashland County, Ohio. In 1879, a nine-foot, eight-inch skeleton was excavated from a mound near Brewersville, Indiana. (*Indianapolis News,* Nov. 10, 1975)

•A six-foot, six-inch skeleton was found in a Utah mound. This was at least a foot taller than the average Indian height in the area, and these natives—what

34

few there were of them—were not mound builders.

•"A skeleton which is reported to have been of enormous dimensions" was found in a clay coffin, with a sandstone slab containing hieroglyphics, during mound explorations by a Dr. Everhart near Zanesville, Ohio. (*American Antiquarian,* v.3, 1880, page 61)

•Ten skeletons "of both sexes and of gigantic size" were taken from a mound at Warren, Minnesota, in 1883. (St. Paul *Pioneer Press,* May 23, 1883)

•A skeleton "seven feet six inches long, and nineteen inches across the chest" was removed from a massive stone structure that was likened to a temple chamber within a mound in Kanawha County, West Virginia, in 1884. (*American Antiquarian,* v. 6, 1884, 133f. Cyrus Thomas, *Report on Mound Explorations of the Bureau of Ethnology,* 12th Annual Report, Smithsonian Bureau of Ethnology, 1890-91)

•A large mound near Gastersville, Pennsylvania, contained "a kind of vault... in which was discovered the skeleton of a giant measuring seven feet two inches ... On the stones which covered the vault were carved inscriptions..." (*American Antiquarian,* v. 7, 1885, 52f)

•In Minnesota, in 1888, remains were discovered of seven skeletons "seven to eight feet tall." (St. Paul *Pioneer Press,* June 29, 1888)

•A mound near Toledo, Ohio, held 20 skeletons, seated and facing east, with jaws and teeth "twice as large as those of present day people," and beside each was a large bowl with "curiously wrought hieroglyphical figures." (Chicago *Record*, Oct. 24, 1895; cited by Ron G. Dobbins, *NEARA Journal*, v. 13, fall 1978)

•The skeleton of "a huge man" was uncovered at the Beckley farm, Lake Koronis, Minnesota; while at Moose Island and Pine City, bones of other giants came to light. (St. Paul *Globe*, Aug. 12, 1896)[36, 58, 60,]

•A decayed human skeleton claimed by eyewitnesses to measure around 3.28 metres (10 feet 9 inches tall), was unearthed by laborers while ploughing a vineyard in November 1856 in East Wheeling, now in West Virginia. (*The Forbidden Land*, 1971, Robert Lyman)

•A 9' 11" (3.02 meters) skeleton was unearthed in 1928 by a farmer digging a pit to bury trash in Tensas Parish, Louisiana near Waterproof. In 1931 a 10' 2" (3.1 meters) skeleton was unearthed by a boy burying his dog in 1933 in nearby Madison Parish. (*The Forbidden Land*, 1971, Robert Lyman)

A curious statement about the Susquehannock Indians was made by Captain John Smith in the 1694 edition of his book *The General History of Virginia, New England and the Summer Isles* (and quoted in the 1936 book *Archaeological Studies of the Susquehannock Indians of Pennsylvania* by Donald Kudzow) who says:

> Sixty of those Susquehannocks [an English name for the Andastes] came to us… [S]uch great and well proportioned men are seldom

seen, for they seemed like giants to the English. ...These are the strangest people of all those countries both in language and attire. As for their language, it well matched their proportions, sounding from them like a voice in a vault. Their attire is the skins of bears and wolves, some have cassocks made of bears heads and skins... The half sleeves coming to the elbows were the heads of bears, with their arms coming through the open mouth. ...[F]or a jewel, one had the head of a wolf hanging from a chain... with a club suitable to his greatness sufficient to beat out ones' brains. Five of their chief wereowances [leading chiefs] came aboard us... the greatest of them his hair, the one side was long and the other shorn close with a ridge over his crown like a cock's comb. ...The calf of whose leg was of a yard around, and all the rest of his limbs so comparable to that proportion that he seemed the goodliest man we ever beheld!

The Susquehannocks lived in farming villages and used canoes to fish and navigate the Susquehanna River, which is named after them. They had a series of wars with the Iroquois League and their population diminished and, ultimately, their tribal identity vanished. Today we know little about them and it is thought that surviving Susquehannock merged with the Delaware, Tuscarora, Oneida, and the Oklahoma Seneca.

꙼ —៳៳— ꙼

Giants Discovered Out in the Wild West

A large number of reports of giant skeletons being excavated or discovered in the western United States and Mexico were published in newspapers of magazines of the 1800s and 1900s.

Nebraska was the burial site of other giant bones. In William Cody's 1879 autobiography, *Buffalo Bill*,[46] Cody tells a very interesting story. He and his companions were five miles above Ogallala on the South Platte when a Pawnee Indian came to the camp with the bones of a giant. The surgeon of the group pronounced one of the giant bones to be a human thighbone, and the Pawnee then told a curious legend.

According to Buffalo Bill's own account, "The Indians claimed that the bones they had found were those of a person belonging to a race of people who a long time ago lived in this country. That there was once a race of men on the earth whose size was about three times that of an ordinary man, and they were so swift and powerful that they could run along-side of a buffalo, and taking the animal in one arm could tear off a leg and eat the meat as they walked.

"These giants denied the existence of a Great Spirit so he caused a great rain-storm to come, and the water kept rising higher and higher so that it drove those proud and conceited giants from the low grounds to the hills, and thence to the mountains, but

38

at last even the mountain tops were submerged, and then those mammoth men were all drowned. After the flood had subsided, the Great Spirit came to the conclusion that he had made man too large and powerful, and that he would therefore correct the mistake by creating a race of men of smaller size and less strength. This is the reason, say the Indians, that modern men are small and not like the giants of old, and they claim that this story is a matter of Indian history, which has been handed down among them from time immemorial."[46]

A Giant with a Double Row of Teeth

In his book *Stranger Than Science,*[52] Frank Edwards describes how, in 1833, soldiers digging a pit for a powder magazine at Lompock Rancho (near San Luis Obispo) hacked their way through a layer of cemented gravel and came up with the skeleton of a man about twelve feet tall. The skeleton was surrounded by carved shells, huge stone axes, and blocks of porphyry covered with unintelligible symbols. The giant was noteworthy in still another respect: he had a double row of teeth, both upper and lower.[52] When local Indians began to attach a religious significance to the skeleton and artifacts, the authorities ordered it secretly buried, so it is lost to science.

Edwards also mentions that another giant man was found off the California coast on Santa Rosa Island in the 1800s. He also had a double row of teeth. These giants may have been the ones who roasted the dwarf

39

Two turbaned giants in India (unknown height).

mammoths on the island thousands of years ago.[52]

Early reports from Jesuit missionaries along the Colorado River described the Yuma Indians as literal giants. In September of 1700, Father Kino was exploring the area and was hailed by thousands of Yumans, who greeted him in peace as he rode along the southern section of the Colorado River.

Mongolian giant, circa 1922.

Says Charles Polzer in his book *A Kino Guide*, "The Yumans were gigantic in stature, and one of them was the largest Indian (the famed priest who built early missions from northern Mexico to California) had ever seen. It must have been a little nerve-wracking to be the willing captive of such giants. But Padre Kino's own good will and understanding of the Indian ways won a whole new nation in friendship."[61]

In the theory that mankind has been getting progressively shorter over history, mainly due to constant warfare, the Yumans may have been the descendents of a race of giants, and by the 1700s were still quite tall by normal standards of the time. Today the Yumans are of normal height, as far as I know.

Another interesting tale of California giants comes

41

from Choral Pepper. Choral, with her husband Jack, published *Desert Magazine* in the 1960s and wrote books up until the 1980s. She was also a friend of Erle Stanley Gardner who wrote many of the Perry Mason novels, as well as many of the scripts for the television show starring Raymond Burr.

Choral and Jack accompanied Gardner on some of his expeditions into Baja California, and she chronicled their adventures in her 1973 book *Baja California: Vanished Missions, Lost Treasures, Strange Stories Tall and True.*[62] In her chapter on central Baja missions, she mentions a curious story from Mission San Ignacio de Kadakaman, known usually as simply San Ignacio, an oasis of the Cochimi Indians. The Jesuit priest Juan Bautista Luyando, a wealthy man in his own right, donated dozens of Arabian date palms to the oasis, where they still thrive today.

Pepper says that the village became alarmed when sometime after 1752, Padre George Retz "dug up a gigantic skeleton at Rancho san Joaquin, about ten miles to the south. He reported that the bones exactly resembled those of a human being, with the dimensions of the skull, vertebrae and leg bones representative of a man over eleven feet tall. This find caused the missionaries to have second thoughts about the natives' report that the cave paintings in the region's canyons were executed by giants."[62]

The Giants of Arizona and Sonora

A curious story is told by Frank Edwards about the discovery of a sarcophagus of a giant that was unearthed by workmen in Fort Crittenden, in southern Arizona, southwest of Tombstone. Originally known as Casa Blanca, Fort Crittenden, also called just Crittenden, was a town that had its origin in the 1860s. There was a rail depot and much mining activity from the mid- to late 1800s. Currently it is a ghost town listed on maps as Fort Crittenden Ruin, and the only standing building is a hotel built in 1885. In 1887, an earthquake damaged the hotel and the second story was removed and that is how it stands today. By 1900, most residents had moved elsewhere as the mines played out. An abandoned railroad line runs just south of the ghost town and the San Ignacio del Babocomari reservation is just to the east. In 1891 workmen were digging the foundation of a house when they unearthed a stone coffin that once held the body of a man approximately 12 feet tall. A carving on the granite case indicated that he had twelve toes.[52, 101]

According to Brad Steiger, *The New York Times* of December 2, 1930 carried an item that told of the discovery of the remains of an apparent race of giants who once lived at Sayopa, Sonora. Sayopa is a mining town three hundred miles south of the Mexican border, south of Crittenden. Steiger says that J. E. Coker, a mining engineer, stated that laborers clearing ranchland near the Yazui River had dug into a very old cemetery and had found "bodies of men,

43

averaging eight feet in height, buried tier by tier."[102]

The skeletal remains of seven giants was featured in a curious story about a sealed cave with a door cut into the rock that was published in the *Phoenix Herald* in 1892. The article is quoted in a chapter entitled "Royal Treasure?," published in a book entitled *Arizona Cavalcade*[103] by Joseph Miller. The book is a compilation of old newspaper reports and it contains several very curious articles.

The 1892 article is about a man named Andrew Pauly who claimed to have made a discovery around 1889 while searching for some stolen horses. He saw a "most peculiar appearance of the face of the rock in one of the remote recesses or clefts of the cliff up which I had gone looking for water, which gave me the impression of the work of some human hand. It looked like a small door cut in the rock and again skillfully closed by some dusty material. I was too thirsty to have any curiosity then, so I pulled on for the top of the range."

Andrew Pauly then returned to the place in 1892, believing that the sealed cave entrance was a door to a treasure chamber. Says the *Phoenix Herald:*

> As was noted last week that he was about to go out in search of what he considered a very peculiar artificial opening in the rocks among the mountain which now prove to be not very remote from the orchard of the upper valley, Pauly started out with a prospector's outfit and succeeded in finding the object of his search,

and furthermore, that it was a genuine piece of masonry in a cut opening in the solid rock and of such thickness and consistency that with a prospecting pick, hammer, and other tools, he was five days in making an opening though the cement and rock that packed the opening which is not now much larger than a man can crawl through.

Pauly tells a wonderful story of his discovery in the chamber behind the barricade through which he has worked his way. He found a chamber apparently cut from solid rock not less than twenty by forty feet in dimensions and about ten feet in height. The floor was covered by seven immense skeletons of men who in life must have been not less than seven feet in height, and there was further evidence that they must have been warriors as the remains of what were copper shields, copper spear heads, and battle axes and other artifacts were found with the skeletons.

A most interesting discovery was a small ornament, a crude amulet apparently, of gold, a metal that has never before been found in all the searches that have been made of the ancient Aztec mounds and ruins so plentifully distributed through this region of country. A yet more important and startling discovery was an opening at the farther end of the chamber also closed with what appears to be a sort of rude bronze door. So neatly and accurately filled

45

into the solid rock that barring a jut of the rock over and at the sides of the door it might have grown there, so solid does it appear. It is about two by three feet in dimensions and of unknown thickness, but when struck sounds as though it either lay against solid rock or was of great thickness.

The mystery of this second discovery now occupies Pauly's attention and he provided himself with the necessary means to remove the door or heavy bronze plate set in the side of the cave, or whatever it may be. As we have above indicated, the place may prove the treasure house of the Aztec tribes or it may prove nothing more than has been found, but at any rate the discovery is a startling and interesting one. Pauly, who works entirely alone, so far, traveled to town on foot yesterday, and guards his treasure with the greatest secrecy so far as its location is concerned, though he talked very freely with a *Herald* representative as to what he had found and what he thinks he may find which he believes to be nothing less than the treasure vault of an ancient royalty.[58, 102]

Nothing more was ever heard about this astonishing find. The seven-foot skeletons on the floor are very intriguing, but no further information is known about the amazing discovery. Like many mummies and other artifacts, they probably vanished early into private or other collections, likely never to be seen again.

The Strange Giants of Nevada

Geologists agree that in ancient times, most of Nevada was an inland sea, known geologically as the Lahontan Sea or Lake. This water has been drying up for thousands of years, and such lakes as Tahoe, Walker and Pyramid are the last remains of the Lahontan Sea. Nevada was a different place back then, a lush lake district with plenty of animals, including huge ground sloths, mastodons and rhinos. Man lived there, too. In 1930, the still-decomposing remains of a giant ground sloth were found in Gypsum Cave, Nevada, by the archaeologist Mark Harrington working for the Southwest Museum of Los Angeles.[64] As was the case with the Patagonian find, there was an indication that the sloths were domesticated, or held captive, in the cave. What but a giant man could domesticate a twelve-foot-tall ground sloth?

I went to Nevada to investigate the strange stories of red-haired giants found in a cave which had been studied by scientists from the University of California at Berkeley. In 1911, miners began to work the rich guano deposits in Lovelock Cave, 22 miles southwest of the town of Lovelock. They had removed several carloads of guano when they came upon some Indian relics. Soon afterward a mummy was also found; reportedly it was that of a six-and-a-half-foot-tall

47

person with "distinctly red" hair.

Legend relates that a race of giant "freckle-faced redheads" once roamed the Humboldt Sink area of northern Nevada. According to legends of the local Piute Indians, a tribe of cannibalistic, red-haired giants called the Si-te-cahs were once the mortal enemies of the Indians in the area, who had joined forces to drive them out. It was said that the giants came in boats to the Lovelock-Winnemucca area and were then chased into a cave where they had their camp. The Paiutes stacked huge piles of wood at the entrance to the cave, lit a bonfire and suffocated the giants.

The strange legends of red-haired giants in Nevada are even told in the first book ever written by a Native American woman. The author was Sarah Winnemucca, the daughter of Chief Winnemucca, and the book was *Life Among the Paiutes,* published in 1882. This was thirty years before the astonishing discoveries were to be made in Lovelock.

The discovery of the vast remains at Lovelock are well told in an article from the *Humboldt Star* which ran on May 13, 1929. The article details the circumstances of the discovery, and then goes on to mention the curious fate of one of the red-haired skeletons under the heading *Mummy Used by Lodge:* "But money was temporarily lacking, and before an expedition could be sent much valuable material was destroyed. The best specimen of the adult mummies found, reported to be six feet six inches in height, went to a fraternal lodge for initiation purposes.

48

"Finally, in 1912, finances having been arranged, the University of California sent Llewellyn L. Loud of the museum of anthropology to the scene. In spite of the work that had been done on the guano, Loud managed to accumulate 10,000 specimens single-handed. An outstanding feature of this collection was the profuse textile material, including over 1,500 fragments of basketry and 1,400 of matting. The climatic conditions are so fine for preservation of even delicate material that Professors A.L. Kroeber and R.W. Lowie, in a preface to the report just published by the University Press, state that the situation recalls those in Egypt and Peru and is rivaled by few other archaeological sites in North America...

"Some of the human material was found buried in pits, as if left by the former inhabitants for safe-keeping. The guano diggers reported that they had uncovered thirteen buried bodies, and Loud found 32 more. Some of these were represented by fragments of bones, some by complete skeletons, and some by remarkably preserved mummies." [65]

University of California archaeologist Llewellyn Loud gave an account of his return to Lovelock Cave at the end of 1924, this time with Mark Harrington, and they published their definitive work on the cave in 1929, entitled simply *The Lovelock Cave*.[65] In systematic excavations, the cave was found to contain the remains of 12 more bodies, making the total of bodies recovered from the cave almost 60. Harrington estimates the age of the cave as 4,000 years old, occupied by at least 1,000 B.C. [65]

49

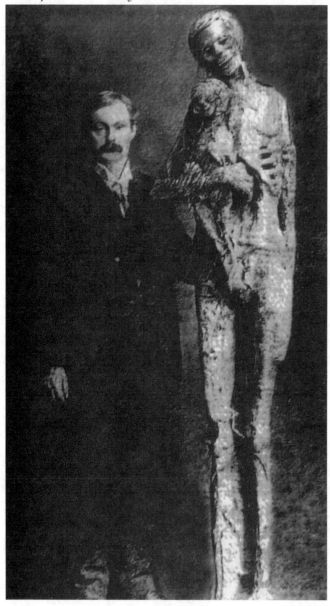

Rare photo of a giant woman and child found at Yosemite.

Today some of the bones, including a giant skull and some femurs, can be seen at the museums in Winnemucca and Lovelock. I stopped in at the Lovelock museum to look at the bones and other artifacts. The ladies who ran the museum were friendly and helpful, and very familiar with the stories of the red-haired mummies.

"I remember this photo," said Wanda, the director of the Chamber of Commerce, "of a man holding a skeleton by the hair and standing on a big crate. He was holding this skeleton over his head and this skeleton was tall. At least seven feet tall if not more. And it had long red hair. That is the story, and the photo is real. I think that Wilbur Green has that photo."

"We don't have much of that stuff around here anymore," continued Wanda. "Some of the duck decoys and a few skulls. We don't know where the red-haired mummies are. Maybe in Carson City with some of the other things. Many of the artifacts are there. We are trying to get some of it back here for our museum."

Sadly, I was informed that many odd relics, including skeletons, were destroyed when some years back, a shed containing many of the artifacts caught fire and burned to the ground. The shed had also contained carvings on marine shells and articles laboriously made of colored feathers.

Other bones and artifacts of "giants" have turned up in the Lovelock-Winnemucca area. In February and June of 1931, skeletons were found in the Humboldt lakebed near the cave. The first of these

51

was eight and one-half feet long and appeared to have been wrapped in a gum-covered fabric somewhat after the Egyptian manner. The second was almost 10 feet long according to the *Lovelock Review-Miner's* article of June 19, 1931. On September 29, 1939, the *Review-Miner* reported the discovery of a seven-foot-seven-inch skeleton on the Friedman Ranch near that town.[36, 104]

The rancher, a man named Reid, decided to collect as much information as he could on mummies, giants and whatnot in the Lovelock area. Some Paiute Indians told him that they had encountered, but hadn't disturbed, petrified bodies of the peculiar giants lying in the open in a wilderness area south of Lovelock Cave. One of the most fascinating objects attributed by the Indians to these people is a stone pyramid in New York Canyon near Job's Peak on the east side of the East Humboldt Range, 215 miles southeast of Lovelock in Churchill County. Unfortunately, this has been somewhat disarranged by earthquakes in recent decades.[36, 104]

Another strange report was made of Nevada giants in July of 1877. Four prospectors were moving along the hills of Spring Valley near Eureka, Nevada, in search of precious metals when one spotted something sticking out of a ledge of rock. What he found wasn't gold, but evidence of an ancient giant.

Using their picks, the prospectors soon chipped out human leg and foot bones that had been encased in solid quartzite. The black bones, which had been broken off just above the knee, included the knee

52

joint, kneecap, lower leg bones, and a complete set of foot bones. The man who had once walked on this leg was obviously huge—from knee to heel, the bone was 39 inches long.

The men quickly took their find to Eureka, where local physicians examined it. The doctors ruled that the bones were human, and extremely old. After the Eureka newspaper wrote articles about the giant leg bone, several museums sent archaeologists to look for the rest of the remarkable man's skeleton—but no further traces were discovered.[84, 104]

Tales of giants, giant tools and constructions by giants are commonplace all over the world. Though skeletons and mummies of "giant" people have been found, even fairly recently, little solid evidence remains. Do these skeletons just crumble to dust when exposed to the air? Some discoveries appear to be suppressed, as in the Lovelock case, while other discoveries—and subsequent loss of evidence—appear to be the result of negligence or carelessness. In any event, the quest for giants in the earth continues.

The Search for Modern Giants

Giants have been reported throughout history and they continue to live among us even today. A curious drawing, supposedly from Italy, circa 1856, shows four men around the skeleton of a giant man who was allegedly eleven and a half feet tall. Little is

53

An old illustration of a huge skeleton supposedly discovered in Italy, circa 1856.

known of the origin of this old drawing (some claim it is actually a photograph), including where it was originally published. It seems to have been dug up by some folks whose main interest is in proving that the Bible is the literal word of God and that the stories of giants in the Bible are literally true. One site says: "A miner fell through a hole in a mine in Italy and found this 11' 6" skeleton."

If authenticated, this would make the skeleton that of the tallest man ever to have been known to exist. According to *The Guinness Book of Records*, the tallest human being ever authenticated was Robert Wadlow, the "Alton giant," who was only 8' 11" tall, and who died of a septic blister caused by the way his ankle brace rubbed against his right ankle. Wadlow was so tall, he had to wear braces to support his own body!

54

Robert Wadlow with his father.

Fedor Machnov with midget, circa 1900.

Wadlow was born on February 22, 1918 in Alton, Illinois, near St. Louis. Wadlow had the pituitary gland syndrome known as hypertrophy, and he continued to grow in size throughout his short life. This is sometimes equated with acromegaly, and it is essentially a prepubertal excess of growth hormone which leads to "pituitary gigantism" (vertical growth). Many modern day giants, however seem to have a normal pituitary gland.

Wadlow's size began to take its toll as he continued to grow and, as noted above, he required leg braces to walk. He had little feeling in his legs and feet. Despite the braces and difficulty with his legs and feet, Wadlow was never confined to a wheelchair. On June 27, 1940 (eighteen days before his death), he was measured at 8 feet 11.1 inches (2.72 m) by doctors C. M. Charles and Cyril MacBryde of Washington University School of Medicine in St. Louis. He is still officially the tallest man who ever lived.

It has been said that the Russian giant Fedor Machnov was nine feet tall, making him one inch taller than Wadlow. Machnov was well proportioned, though like Wadlow, he had unusually long legs.

Born in Vitebsk, Russia, in 1881, Machnov caused a

Fedor Machnov.

57

sensation wherever he went, particularly in Paris, where almost all the members of the anthropological society took a keen interest in his extraordinary physique. The Paris anthropological society would have liked to examine him in intimate detail, but Machnov refused throughout his entire life to undress in front of doctors. He did allow them to measure his feet, however, which were eighteen inches long, and his hands, which measured almost thirteen inches.

"This Russian," they observed, "is all legs." In fact, if he had been born legless, he would have been of normal height! His head, which was too small for his body, made him look a bit comical and he unsuccessfully tried to overcome this by wearing a richly embroidered Cossack uniform. His ears were six inches long, and his mouth four inches wide. He was married to a Russian woman who was of normal height.

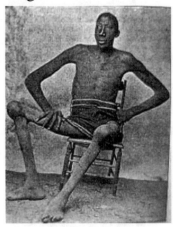

John "Bud" Rogan.

After a few days of rest he was generally a couple of inches taller than at the end of a particularly strenuous day, which could result in significant compression of his spine. Machnov ate four meals a day. His breakfast alone would have fed an entire family for two days. Every morning at nine, he downed two quarts of tea, twenty eggs and eight round

58

loaves of bread with butter. Lunch consisted of five and a half pounds of meat, two pounds of potatoes and three loaves of bread and another quart of tea. Before going to bed he would put away fifteen eggs, more bread and another quart of tea! Machnov died in his bed in October 1905.

Trijntje Keever, circa 1630.

Only 12 people are officially credited with having been over 8 feet tall, and Machnov is not one of them. The second tallest person in modern history, nearly as tall as Wadlow, was John "Bud" Rogan. Rogan was born in 1868 and he grew normally until the age of 13. He began to grow very rapidly at that age, and developed Ankylosis, a condition in which the joints stiffen and become immoble. Eventually Rogan could not stand or walk. His height was measured while he was in a sitting position. His exact height was not officially recorded until his death, at which point he was 8'9" tall. Due to illness he weighed only 175 pounds. He is the tallest

African American ever recorded. He died in 1905 due to complications from his illness.

The tallest woman on record was Trijntje Cornelisdochter Keever, born in 1616 in Edam, Holland. Nicknamed De Groote Meid (in English, The Big Girl), Keever stood nine Amsterdam feet or 2.54 meters (8 ft 4 in) tall at the time of her death at age seventeen.

Trijntje first received public attention when she was nine years old and had reached the height of two meters (6 ft 7 in). Her parents took her to carnivals to earn some money by letting people view her. She died of cancer and was buried on July 7, 1633 in Edam, her town of birth.

The tallest person currently alive is Zhao Liang, a circus performer from Henan in China. In April 2009, doctors in Tianjin measured his height at 2.46 meters (8 ft 1 in). Zhao played basketball until liga-

"Big Gust" the giant.

An old photo of a Mongol giant who was sent to Moscow as a tribute.

Zhao Liang.

ment damage to his left foot in 2001. In 2009 he visited a hospital because of this injury; he said he was too poor to have it treated sooner. Despite advising Zhao against any intense physical exercise, Zhao's surgeon has declared that he has no health issues related to his height. His parents and siblings are average height, though his grandfather was 2 meters tall (6 ft 6 1/2 in). Zhao grew 10 centimeters (about 4 inches) a year till age 23.

According to Wikipedia, Zhoa joined a circus in Jilin province in 2006. Though he was recruited for his height, he now also does magic tricks and plays the saxophone and cucurbit flute. Until someone bigger comes along, he is officially the tallest person in the world.

⚭ ⎯⤳⎯ ⚭

Wikipedia gives us this list of the tallest men and women officially known to history:

Tallest male

Robert Wadlow — Confirmed tallest male and person by Guinness World Records at 8'11." (272 cm). (b.1918, d.1940)

John Rogan — Second tallest male in recorded

history at 8'9 ½" (268 cm). Tallest African American. (b.1868, d. 1905)

Don Koehler — 8' 2" (2.49 m), Tallest in World for most of 1970s. Had 5'10" twin sister. (September 1, 1925 — February 26, 1981)

Zhao Liang — 8' 1.1" (2.48 m)

Väinö Myllyrinne — Tallest Finn, standing 8'1" (247 cm). Myllyrinne was born in 1909 and died April 13, 1963.

Gabriel Estêvão Monjane — Guinness World Records listed him as tallest man from 1988 to 1990 at 8'1" (246 cm). (b.1944, d.1990)

Suleiman Ali Nashnush — Libyan who may be the tallest basketball player at 8'½" (245 cm). (b.1943 d.1991)

Rigardus Rijnhout — Tallest Dutchman at 7'9" (2.37 m), nicknamed 'Reus van Rotterdam' (Giant from Rotterdam), (b. Rotterdam, 21 April 1922 —d. Leiden, 13 April 1959)

Gogea Mitu (b. Gogu Stefanescu) — Romanian boxer at 7'9" (2.36 m). (b. 14 July 1914—d.22 June 1936).

Bao Xishun — Former Guinness World Record holder for tallest living person at 7'9" (236 cm). (b.1951)

Sun Ming-Ming — Chinese basketball player. Formerly second tallest living person at 7'9", currently third tallest living person.

Radhouane Charbib — Listed by Guinness World Records as tallest man before Bao Xishun and Sun Ming Ming at 7'8¾" (235 cm).

63

Hussein Bisad in London.

Ri Myung Hun — Former basketball player with the North Korean national team. 7'8½" tall.

George Bell — Tallest living American at 7'8" (234 cm).

Yasutaka Okayama — Tallest basketball player drafted in National Basketball Association history at 7'8" (234 cm).

Neil Fingleton — Tallest person born in UK at 7'7½" (233 cm).

Romanian boxer Gogea Mitu.

Hussein Bisad — Somali, considered to be one of the tallest living men at 232 cm.

Alam Channa — Pakistani, considered to be the tallest living man when he died in 1998 at 7'7¼" (232 cm).

Manute Bol — Tied for tallest in NBA history at 7'7" (231 cm).

Gheorghe Muresan — Tied for tallest in NBA history at 7'7" (231 cm).

Kenny George — Tallest Division I basketball player at 7'7" (231 cm).

Jorge Gonzalez — Tallest wrestler in WWE history at 7'10" (229 cm).

Yao Ming — Yao is currently the tallest player in

65

the NBA at 7'6" (229 cm).

Matthew McGrory — tallest actor at 7'6" (229 cm) when he died.

Tallest female

Trijntje Keever — Tallest recorded woman at 8'4" (254 cm). Died in 1633 at age 17.

Zeng Jinlian — Tallest woman at 8'2.75" (249 cm). Suffered from spine curvature and could not stand at full height. Died in 1982 at age 17.

Jane Bunford — Former world's tallest woman (until Zeng Jinlian) and possibly the world's tallest person at the time of her death in April 1922 at 7'8" (234 cm), but due to a curved spine she could not stand up straight. However, if her spine had normal curvature, she would have stood 8'0 (244 cm).

Yao Defen — Claimant as tallest living female at 7'9" (234 cm). Not confirmed by Guinness World Records.

Sandy Allen – Listed as tallest living female by Guinness World Records at 7'7¼" (232 cm), until her death on August 13, 2008.

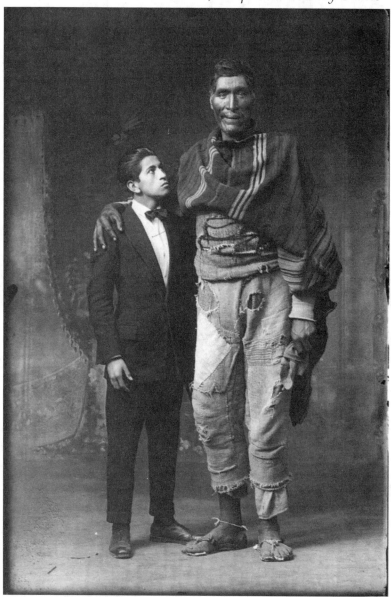

The famous giant of Cuzco, Peru (unknown height).

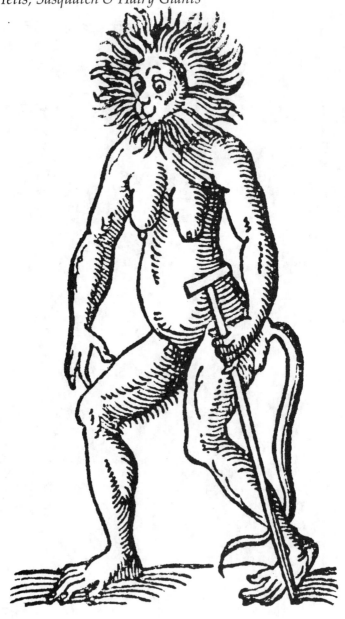

An old print of a wildman or wildwoman.

CHAPTER 3

WILDMEN AND HAIRY GIANTS

I think that only daring speculation can lead us further,
and not accumulation of facts.
—*Albert Einstein*

⚜ —⚊— ⚜

Wild hairy men have been popular in literature for thousands of years. The original boogey man was essentially the wild Hairy Man. Often, they were described as giants as well, as if being hairy and wild wasn't scary enough.

According to *Wikipedia*, the wildman or woodwose, in old English, is a mythological figure that appears in the artwork and literature of medieval Europe. "Images of wild men appear in the carved and painted roof bosses where intersecting ogee vaults meet in the Canterbury Cathedral, in positions where

A wildman from olden days.

one is also likely to encounter the vegetal Green Man." The wildman was often armed with a club, and was a link between civilized humans and the dangerous elf-like spirits of natural woodland, such as Shakespeare's character Puck in *A Midsummer Night's Dream*. The image of the wild man survived to appear as a support image on heraldic coats-of-arms, especially in Germany, well into the 16th century. Early engravers in Germany and Italy were particularly fond of wild men, wild women, and wild families, and many examples of such characters are found in the art of from Albrecht Dürer, Martin

70

Schongauer and others.

Both folklorists and cryptozoologists apply the term "wildmen" to the European wild human. The term is also used in worldwide reports of hair-covered bipeds resembling bigfoot, but tends to be most often applied to beings that seem more human than ape, or to people who live on the fringe of civilization and have developed supernatural overtones, such as the ability to predict the future or mysteriously vanish.

As one would easily imagine, the key characteristic of the wildman is his wildness. Wildmen, often imagined at giants (whether they were or not) were seen as beings of the remote wilderness, and as such represented the antithesis of civilization and civilized people who were no longer "wild."

From the earliest times wildmen were associated

A wildman appears on this 1629 coin.

An old print of a fight in the forest with a wildman.

with hairiness and by the 12th century they were almost invariably described as having a coat of hair covering their entire bodies except for their hands, feet and faces above their long beards; the breasts and chins of the females were also hairless. With today's abundant stories of yetis, sasquatch, yowies (in Australia), and bigfoot reported all over the world, one cannot help but think that there is a connection between the large hairy wildmen of the Middle Ages and the sasquatch-yeti.

Some humans do have a hormonal disorder called Hypertrichosis that causes an overproduction of male hormones and a subsequent acute hairiness. Hypertrichosis is thought to occur because of tumors near glands or because of some genetic chromosome defect. Perhaps some men and women in ancient times had this disorder and became outcasts of society, ultimately becoming wild men (and women). But this disorder does not seem to be the origin of most wild-men.

In many medieval stories of the wild-man, he was a nor-mal human who had gone wild, becom-ing something of a misfit holy man. In the 7th-century Irish tale *Buile Shuibhne*

Prussian coat of arms featuring two wildmen.

(translated as "Frenzy of Shuibhne" or *The Madness of Sweeney*) which describes how Sweeney, the pagan king of the Dál nAraidi of Ulster, assaults the Christian bish-op Ronan Finn and is cursed with madness as a result. Sweeney spends many years roaming naked through the woods, composing verse. A similar Welsh story is about Myrddin Wyllt (the origin of the name Merlin of later romance). In the various versions of this story, Myrddin is a warrior in the service of King Gwend-doleu ap Ceidio at the time of the Battle of Arfderydd. When his lord is killed at the battle, Myrddin takes to the Caledonian Forest in a fit of madness that also gives him the ability to compose prophetic poetry.

Another version of this story comes from Geoffrey of Monmouth in his Latin *Vita Merlini* of around 1150, though here the figure has been renamed "Merlin." According to *Wikipedia*, Geoffrey says that after Merlin witnessed the horrors of the battle:

> ...a strange madness came upon him. He crept away and fled to the woods, unwilling that any should see his going. Into the forest he went, glad to lie hidden beneath the ash trees. He watched the wild creatures grazing on the pasture of the glades. Sometimes he would follow them, sometimes pass them in his course. He made use of the roots of plants and of grasses, of fruit from trees and of the blackberries in the thicket. He became a Man of the Woods, as if dedicated to the woods. So for a whole summer he stayed hidden in the woods, discovered by none, forgetful of himself and of his own, lurking like a wild thing.

So, what we see here is that the classic wildman is a crossover between the worlds of bigfoot and humans. Some wildmen were humans who had just always lived in the deep woods, shunning civilization; others were people who had "gone crazy," and were now living off roots, berries and wild game in the woods, just like bears or sasquatch. In some ways, they were the "village idiots" who had left their village and were living in the forest.

Two views of wildmen from A. Durer, 1499.

However, it also seems clear that some wildmen, especially the giant hairy ones, might have more in common with yeti and sasquatch than with normal human beings with anti-social tendencies. For instance, *Wikipedia* mentions that a wildman is described in *Konungs Skuggsjá* (*Speculum Regale* or "the King's Mirror"), a book written in Norway around 1250 AD:

> It once happened in that country (and this seems indeed strange) that a living creature was caught in the forest as to which no one could say definitely whether it was a man or some other animal; for no one could get a word from it or be sure that it understood human speech. It had the human shape, however, in every detail, both as to hands and face and feet; but the entire body was covered with hair as the beasts are, and down the back it had a long coarse mane like that of a horse, which fell to both sides and trailed along the ground when the creature stooped in walking.

This wildman would seem to be of the bigfoot type, though he would appear to be a sasquatch of smaller size, or perhaps one that was not yet fully grown. There seems to be little doubt the wildman did indeed exist in Europe and other parts of the world, but is the wildman a human being, or an ape-creature? As we have seen, he could be either.

Hairy Apemen of South America
Let us look at some of the early curious reports of wildmen. Some years ago, while researching a book

on pirates and the Knights Templar, I came across a curious aside in one of the books I was reading, a 1678 book entitled *The Buccaneers of America*[26] by Alexander O. Exquemelin (the book was translated from the French by Alexis Brown). Exquemelin's book was a bestseller in its own time, and has been reprinted by Penguin Books in 1969 and Dover Books in 2000.

The former pirate Exquemelin goes on about various buccaneers that he sailed under, and at one point includes several chapters about the French buccaneer named Francois l'Olonais and his raid (with 660 men) of the Spanish port of Maracaibo in Venezuela. After describing the journey of the buccaneers from their base on Tortuga to Venezuela, he describes Maracaibo bay (which he calls a lake) and the land—and inserts a strange note about apemen in the mountains:

> On Pigeon Island stands a fort guarding the strait, as any ship wishing to enter the lake must pass close to the island. For at the mouth is a bar, or sandbank, in fourteen feet of water, and about a league inwards is another sandbank called El Tablazo, where there is only ten feet of water. Thereafter, as far as Rio de las Espinas (about forty leagues along the lake) the water is six, seven and eight fathoms deep.
>
> Some six leagues along the lake shore, on the western side, lies Maracaibo, a very

77

handsome city with fine-looking houses along the waterfront. The population is considerable: counting the slaves, it is reckoned that three or four thousand souls live there, and among them 800 men capable of bearing arms, all Spaniards...

There are tribes of Indians living along the western shore, still unconquered, whom the Spaniards call Indios Bravos. They will have no dealings with the Spaniards. They build their houses high up in the trees which grow in the water, so as to be less plagued by the mosquitoes. On the eastern side of the lake are Spanish fishing villages, built on piles above the water. The surrounding land is so low and swampy the mosquitoes make life intolerable, and there is danger of floods. The lake is fed by seventy-five rivers and streams, and when it rains hard the land may be flooded for a distance of two or three leagues. The village of Gibraltar often lies so deep under water that the inhabitants are forced to abandon their houses and retreat inland to the plantations...

Beautiful rivers flow through all the surrounding countryside. Cacao plantations grow beside the rivers, and in time of drought they channel water into these plantations along ditches, which have sluices to check the flow when they have sufficient. Considerable quantities of tobacco are also produced, of a kind highly esteemed in Europe; this is the genuine Virginian tobacco, known as Pope's Tobacco.

The fertile land stretches some twenty leagues, being bounded on the lake side by swamps and on the other by high mountains, always covered with snow. On the far side of the mountains is a large town called Merida, having authority over the village of Gibraltar. Merchandise from Gibraltar is taken there over the mountains — on pack-mules — and this only once a year, because the journey is so cold as to be almost unbearable. On the return journey from Merida they bring back meal, sent from Peru by way of Santa Fe.

A Spaniard told me of a sort of people who live in these mountains, of the same stature as the Indians, but with short curly hair and with long claws on their feet, like apes. Their skin resists arrows, and all sharp instruments, and they are very agile climbers, having tremendous strength. The Spaniards attempted to kill some of the tribe with their lances, but the iron could not pierce their tough skin. These wild men managed to seize some of the Spaniards, carrying them up to the tree-tops and hurling them to the ground. These people have never been heard to speak. Sometimes they come down to the plantations at the foot of the mountains and carry off any women slaves they can capture.

I have read various descriptions of

America, but never found any mention of such people, so I believe they must be a sort of Barbary ape living in those parts, for I have seen many apes in the forest. Nevertheless, several Spaniards have assured me that these creatures are human, and that they have seen them frequently: I give it here for what it's worth. Truly, God's works are great, and these things may well be.[26]

This curious tale of apemen living in the jungle-covered mountains of western Venezuela is an odd one. They sound like some sort of bigfoot or yeti. They are men, but wildmen covered with hair who kidnap women. Stories of wildmen and yetis in the Himalayas, China and Central Asia have also mentioned the occasional kidnapping of human women.

The first reports that came out of South America came from the northernmost tip of the Andes. A member of a Spanish gold-hunting expedition in the late seventeenth century wrote back to Sevilla that his group had fought with and killed fourteen giant beasts, in a section of jungle near the Colombia-Panama border. Subsequent stories of "man-apes" drifted back to Europe from time to time, as the tropical forests and mountain slopes were crossed by Spaniards, Portuguese and Englishmen intent on pulling precious minerals out of the earth and sticky resins out of the bush. The names given to the beasts they encountered were numerous—the creatures were

80

The photograph taken by Francois de Loy.

known as the mapinguary, capelobo or pelobo in the jungle vocabularies of the south (across the Amazon delta through Brazil), or as the di-di or Mono Grande in the northern countries of Ecuador, Colombia and Venezuela.

Richard Oglesby Marsh writes of an American prospector named Shea, who in 1920 arrived in Panama with a tale he'd brought up from the Andes, a tale centering on his encounter with an animal "six feet tall, which walked erect, weighed possibly three hundred pounds, and was covered with long black hair." Shea's encounter went thus: he was surprised by the animal standing upright before him on a mountain ridge, chattering at him angrily; he pulled out his revolver and promptly shot it through the head. Examining the dead animal where it lay before him, Shea noticed that the big toes on its feet were parallel with the other toes, as they would be on a human being, and not opposable and thumb-like as they would have been on the foot of any monkey or ape.[32]

In 1924 in another part of the South American forest, another man met up with his own furious primate. Swiss geologist Francois de Loys was returning with his expedition from the Sierra de Peija in the northern tip of Colombia and was making his way along the Sierra de Unturan, near the Brazilian border of Venezuela. Not far from a small river, he came upon a pair of screaming monkeys who were so beside themselves with the rage of being discovered they filled their hands with their own excrement and

A comparison of de Loys' Ape with a human.

threw it at the party of intruders. In response, the men shot the nearest animal, as the other escaped into the brush. The corpse of what turned out to be the female of the pair was propped up on a fuel crate and photographed by the geologist; the photograph of the dead female survives today.[32]

This photograph shows an animal not much over five feet tall, yet in a hemisphere where the largest monkeys are never more than three foot seven, this specimen does seem to be a rather curious savage. De Loys counted thirty-two teeth in the animal's mouth, which is a surprising number for any New World primate; platyrrhinians, or New World monkeys, without exception have thirty-six teeth in their heads, while catarrhinians, or Old World monkeys, have thirty-two. (This is not just a question of existing canines and molars, with the possibility of decay or other loss; it concerns jaw structure and tooth placement just as much as tooth number.) This means that the animal was essentially an Asian, or

83

The "monkey woman" from Minas Gerais, Brazil, circa 1968.

Old World ape. If this was the case, then these giant apes—bigfoot—may have come from Asia across the Bering Straits into Alaska and down through North America many tens of thousands of years ago, if not hundreds of thousands of years ago.

The Italian archaeologist and explorer Count Pino Turolla heard about the legendary Mono Grande on

84

his many expeditions to South America in the 1960s. In April 1968 Turolla's Zapes Indian guide, Antonio, described his own exposure to the animal and the tragic death of his own son. Antonio had gone with his two sons to the Forbidden Range of Pacanaima, and as the three men approached the savannah, they met up with three enormous creatures. Described by Antonio as huge lumbering beasts with smallish heads and extremely long arms, the three set upon Antonio and his sons with clubs. During this attack, the younger son was killed.

Six months after hearing this story, Turolla returned to Venezuela and convinced Antonio to guide him to the Forbidden Range where the attack had occurred. This time, though, there was no confrontation; close to the Pacanaima ruins the animals circled the party through the bush, but did not attack. Instead they sent up a howl that Turolla described as being in volume like the roar of a lion, but in pitch higher and more shrill. The three Indians in the party became nervous, and then alarmed, as this howl continued, and after a few moments they turned and ran back along the trail. The howl persisted, a terrifying sound that seemed to come from all around them at once, drowning out all other noises, rising again and again as Turolla advanced toward the savannah in the distance.

But nothing happened. After a stillness between the howls, the animals—this time there seemed to be only two—loped off through the foliage, and the one image that Turolla retains is of their enormous shadows moving across the boulders before him in

85

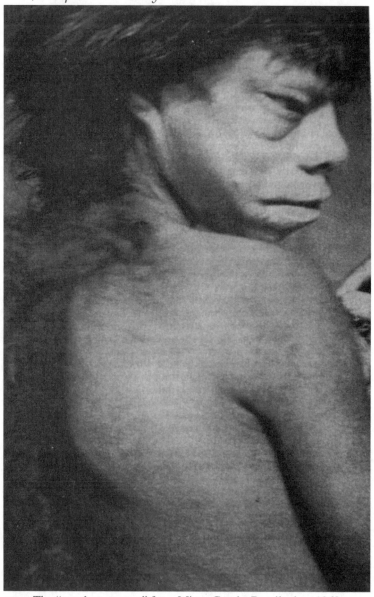

The "monkey woman" from Minas Gerais, Brazil, circa 1968.

the dusk. No longer howling, they soon became a blur against the rocks. The impression he had was of two hairy apelike creatures, well over six feet tall, who ran and leapt in an erect posture. He described them as two perfectly straightforward giant apes, howling like two devils. He estimated their height as being between six and eight feet, but stressed that he was over fifty feet away from where they were silhouetted against the rock. There were no other Indians and no prospectors in the area at the time. After the animals had disappeared, he shot his rifle into the air to call back the men who'd run off, and the group made their way to La Esmeralda. There, locals assured him that the "Monos" were not uncommon. One prospector recounted how his small mule had been carried off by one. The mule was found several kilometers away; it had been ripped open and torn apart.[6]

Turolla had brought with him in his wallet a copy of the photograph of the large monkey, or ape, shot by Francois de Loys, and found that those he talked to who had seen the local animals identified them closely with the animal in the photo.[6, 28]

Michael Grumley writes in his book *There Are Giants in the Earth*[6] that during Sir Walter Raleigh's South American expedition in 1595 and 1596 the explorer reported that although he came face to face with none of the animals, he was convinced of their existence by the many tales of those people who had encountered them.

In 1796, Bernard Heuvelmans reports in *On the Track of Unknown Animals*, Dr. Edward Bancroft brought back from Guiana a tale of an "apeman":

> ... much larger than either the African [the chimpanzee] or Oriental, if the accounts of the natives may be relied on. ...They are represented by the Indians as being near five feet in height, maintaining an erect posture, and having a human form, thickly covered with short black hair; but I suspect that their height has been augmented by the fear of the Indians who greatly dread them.[32]

Five feet, again, is not so very large, except when measured against the height of all other South American monkeys, who stretch no further skyward than three and a half feet. And there are no known apes in all of South America—only the many species of platyrrhinian, or "broad-nosed" monkey, known commonly as spider monkeys.

Turolla describes his December 1970 archaeological expedition in the Guacamayo Range, not far from the River Chancis in Ecuador, in his book *Beyond the Andes*.[28] He says that the territory that he and his South American assistant, Oswaldo, were exploring was neither specifically Ecuadorian nor Colombian, but belonged instead within the province of the Aucas tribe between the two countries. An Indian shaman from the Amazon gave him a lead, describing to him the entrance to a particular cave in which he assured Turolla he would find evidence to support his theory concerning the real beginnings of world culture, and of South American culture specifically. The men were able to find the cave and entered it with great excitement. Inside the cave, they encountered what seemed to be a giant apeman that gave a great roar and threw boulders at the two explorers. They ran for the mouth of the cave, Oswaldo shooting his rifle blindly into the darkness behind them. They were glad that the animal did not follow them to the mouth of the cave, but they were too afraid to go back inside and investigate further.

Nguoi Rung: The Vietnamese Hairy Wildman

Like Europe and the Americas, Southeast Asia, especially Vietnam, has traditions of a wildman who lives in the forest. Known as the Nguoi Rung, the Vietnamese wildman is said to inhabit remote mountain forest areas, particularly in Kontum Province, along the border with Cambodia.

The Nguoi Rung ("forest people" in Vietnamese) is also known in other wilderness areas of Laos and northern Borneo, where it is called the Batutut or Ujit. Perhaps encounters with the Batutut gave rise to the popular expression "wildman of Borneo." All of these "wild hairy men" are described as being approximately the size of a tall man—about six feet in height—and their bodies are completely covered with hair except for the face, knees, the soles of the feet and the hands. The hair of the Nguoi Rung ranges from black to gray to brown. The creature walks on

89

Chinese officials examine casts of Chinese wildman footprints.

two legs and has been reported both solitary and moving in small groups.

According to *Wikipedia*, as early as 1947 a French colonist sighted one of the cryptids and referred to it as a *L'Homme Sauvage* ("wild man"). Then, in 1970, Dr. John Mackinnon claimed to have observed tracks of a similar wildman in Sabah, northern Borneo. Dr. Mackinnon says that he believes that this hominid is similar to the *Meganthropus,* and it also lives in Vietnam's Vu Quang nature preserve, the home to a number of newly discovered animals. In the 1990s,

Mackinnon and his colleagues found two new species in the Vu Quang nature preserve: a goat-like animal dubbed the *saola* from its long spindle-shaped horns, and a robust muntjac deer. These are the first new large mammals discovered by science since the early decades of the 20th century.

Wikipedia also mentions that two Nguoi Rungs were reportedly captured by tribesmen near Dak Lak Province, Vietnam, in 1971. Then, in 1974 a North Vietnamese general, Hoang Minh Thao, requested an expedition to find evidence of the creatures, but it was unsuccessful.

In 1982 Professor Tran Hong Viet, now at the Pedagogic University of Hanoi, discovered in Kontum

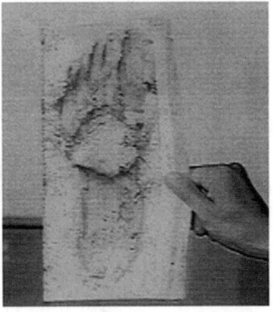

Vietnamese wildman footprint made in 1982.

Province a Nguoi Rung footprint. He made a cast of it that measured 28 by 16 centimeters. The footprint is said to be similar to a very large human's, though much wider and with toes much longer than those of a human. Professor Viet only recently returned to his research on this subject, inspired by a Japanese television show on the Vietnamese apemen broadcast in March of 1996.

Some recent studies on the Nguoi Rung are from Professor Dang Nghiem Van, Director of Hanoi's Institute for Religious Studies, who has collected many stories of Nguoi Rung in the mountains of central and northern Vietnam. Professor Van says that the Nguoi Rung will come at night to places where people have fires. They sit beside men but do not speak or make any sounds. There are stories of couples of Nguoi Rung moving rapidly, easily climbing trees, shaking trees for insects and sleeping in grottos on mountain slopes. Professor Van's detailed notes have yet to be published.

The May 1969 cover of *Argosy*.

Online discussions of the Nguoi Rung also tends to speculate on the possibility that the famous Minnesota Iceman might have originally been from Vietnam, and therefore would have been a frozen Nguoi Rung. The

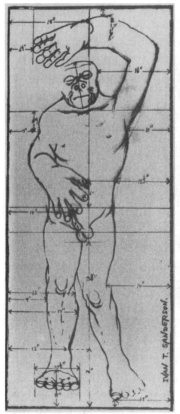

The Minnesota Iceman
drawn by Sanderson.

Minnesota Iceman was an ape-like creature about six feet tall, encased in a block of ice that was exhibited at state fairs or carnivals in Minnesota and Wisconsin starting around December 1968. It vanished by 1974, and no one knows what became of it.

The mysterious owner had been based in California, and had suddenly withdrawn the Iceman and replaced it with a different exhibit that was clearly a model and looked different from the original. The original was extremely realistic, if it was a fake. One of its arms appeared to be broken and one of its eyes appeared to have been knocked out of its socket, allegedly by a bullet that was supposed to have entered the animal's head from behind. If the Minnesota Iceman was a genuine animal, the specimen would be a significant zoological discovery. Many now think it was an elaborate hoax, but it truly remains a mystery.

Both Ivan T. Sanderson and Bernard Heuvelmans believed that the Minnesota Iceman was the real deal: a genuine abominable snowman encased in ice. Heuvelmans consistently claimed that the Iceman was a genuine specimen and that it was originally from Vietnam. Sanderson and Heuvelmans gave the Iceman the name *Homo pongoides,* having examined the specimen and concluding it was a genuine creature, noting "putrefaction where some of the flesh had been exposed from the melted ice." [32, 69, 74]

Heuvelmans wrote a scientific paper about the Iceman and theorized that it was shot and killed in Vietnam during the Vietnam War. Sanderson wrote an article for *Argosy* magazine and spoke about the frozen sasquatch-cicle on *The Tonight Show* with Johnny Carson. The Smithsonian Institution was reportedly briefly interested in the Iceman, asking the famous bigfoot scholar John Napier to investigate the matter. Later, the Smithsonian suggested the FBI investigate, due to reports that the creature had been shot through one of its eyes and killed. Shortly thereafter, the Iceman disappeared, withdrawn from public display. [74, 69]

94

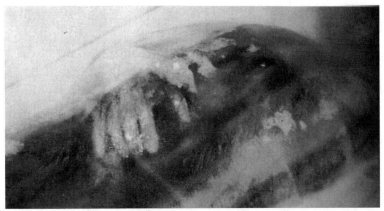

The Minnesota Iceman photographed by Ivan T. Sanderson in 1968.

Sanderson called the Minnesota Iceman "Bozo" in the May 1969 issue of *Argosy*:

Bozo's face is his most startling feature, both to anthropologists and anyone else±and for several reasons. Unfortunately, both eyeballs have been blown out of their sockets. One appears to be missing, but the other seems (to some, at least) to be just visible under the ice. This gives Bozo a gruesome appearance, which is enhanced by a considerable amount of blood diffused from the sockets through the ice. The most arresting feature of the face is the nose. This is large but only fairly wide, and is distinctly pugged, rather like that of a Pekinese dog but not like that of a gorilla, which actually doesn't have a nose, per se. The nostrils are large, circular and point straight

95

forward, which is very odd. The mouth is only fairly wide and there is no aversion of the lips; in fact, the average person would say he had no lips at all. His muzzle is no more bulging, prominent, or pushed forward than is our own; not at all prognathous like that of a chimp. One side of the mouth is slightly agape and two small teeth can be seen. These should be the right upper canine and the first premolar. The canine or eye-tooth is very small and in no way exaggerated into a tusk, or similar to that of a gorilla or a chimp. But to me, at least the most interesting features of all are some folds and wrinkle lines around the mouth just below the cheeks. These are absolutely human, and are like those seen in a heavy-jowled, older white man.

Both American and Vietnamese veterans from northern Vietnam had reported tales of apemen. The Vietnamese zoologist Professor Quy, interviewed for a popular article in early 1995, said that he had gotten a letter from a former Vietnamese soldier who saw the body of an ape being loaded on to a helicopter at a highlands airfield in the mid-1960s. It is possible that this was the Vietnamese wildman that later became the Minnesota Iceman? And where is the Minnesota Iceman now? In some private walk-in freezer somewhere in the suburbs of Los Angeles? Or perhaps in a government vault where its DNA has long been analyzed and cloned by military specialists. [16]

Is this perhaps the answer to some reports of bigfoot and flying saucers being seen together? Though such incidents are a very small subsection of bigfoot reports, they are intriguing, even if some of them are hoaxes. Could it be that the US Army at its Area 51 flying saucer manufacturing facility is also experimenting with and cloning genuine sasquatch DNA that came from the Minnesota Iceman? It is reminiscent of a scene from Steven Spielberg's *Men in Black* movies where the humans walk past aliens, bigfoot and genetic oddities as they tour an underground base. Does the military occasionally drop off a cloned bigfoot with one of its flying saucers just to muddle the already muddled world of these phenomena? As we are beginning to see in this book, many strange things are very possible!

PART TWO:

YETIS

CHAPTER 4

THE CALL OF THE YETI

Our coolies at once jumped at the
conclusion that this must be the "Wild
Man of the snows," to which they
gave the name of Metohkangmi, "the
abominable snow man," who interested
the newspapers so much.
—*Himalayan Explorer C. K. Howard-Bury*

〜 —᰾— 〜

Call of the Yeti

Hopefully we won't have to worry about cloned
abominable snowmen running amok (a Malaysian
word, by-the-way) through Singapore, Bangkok or
Kathmandu in the very near future. For the time being,
there is plenty of danger and adventure in remote
parts of the Himalayas. Climbing and exploring in
the Himalayas of Tibet, India, Bhutan and Nepal is
hazardous enough for any adventurer—and if you
were to stumble onto a yeti cave, either purposely

or by accident, you would want to have your pepper spray and ice axe handy. You're miles from nowhere in steep, unknown country, when you could come face-to-face with some hairy man-ape who has the strength of Mighty Joe Young.

At 19, my fascination with the Himalayas and the yeti had so consumed me that I dropped out of college and went to the Far East to teach English. Eventually my trail led to Kathmandu where I began to trek all over the Himalayas in an effort to photograph the creature or get hair samples. I wrote about these experiences in my book *Lost Cities of China, Central Asia & India*.[58]

Eventually, I trekked to the remote Rowaling Himalayas, where one night I lay in my sleeping bag on a high mountain pass that stretched north into Tibet. As I drifted off to sleep I thought about the combinations of rumors, expedition accounts, Sherpa stories and photographic evidence that had made up the yeti legend. Visions of the strange creature—Neanderthal man or savage giant ape—drifted through my mind as the cold mountain winds howled against the mountain peaks outside. Then in the distance there was a strange sound, a high-pitched wail that sent a chill down my spine. Was it the call of the yeti? Since we found no footprints or other evidence the next day, because of a fresh fall of snow, we would never know what the strange sound was.

Yetis are usually described as standing at least two meters (6 feet) tall with brown or reddish-brown hair, although some yetis are described as being shorter

102

or having black or even white hair. A huge sloping head sits atop massive shoulders and a barrel chest. The creature does not have much of a neck, witnesses have said. As we shall see, a large number of activities have been ascribed to yetis, including kidnapping, sexual assault, killing yaks and even climbing Mount Everest!

Since the late 1800's, there have been literally hundreds of references to yetis and sightings of the creatures themselves or of their footprints. Legends from the Karakorams across the Himalayas (a vast area spanning northern Burma, Assam, China, Bhutan, Sikkim, Nepal, Tibet, and India) talk about these creatures. Supposedly, they are incredibly strong, and can uproot trees and lift large boulders. They live in caves in the high, inaccessible mountains, being very shy of humans, whom they avoid at all costs. Yetis are generally said to be herbivores, though certain reports make them into omnivores, like bears and humans. In Nepal, Sikkim, Bhutan and Tibet they have been reported to have killed yaks, breaking their necks with their tremendous strength.

Yetis got the name "abominable snowmen" in 1921 when the first British Everest expedition, led by Colonel H. W. Howard-Bury, sighted a number of large man-apes, or "men in fur coats," moving in single file along the ice above the expedition. The expedition found footprints in the snow that were quite large, and distinctly resembled a human footprint.

The Sherpas told Colonel Howard-Bury that the creature was the Metohkangmi or Mehteh-Kangmi, or

103

"man-beast of the snowy mountains." At the Rongbuk monastery near Mount Everest on the Tibetan side, a lama told the British that five Mehteh-Kangmi lived in the upper reaches of the glacier. When the Colonel telegraphed the incident to his aides in Calcutta, the name of the creature was garbled and came out as "Metch Kangmi," which a Calcutta columnist, trying to make sense of the words, deciphered as "wretched snowman," or as he later put it, "abominable snowman."

And, for the modern age, at least, a legend was born.

Early Reports of a Hairy Man-Ape in Asia

Probably the earliest report of what appear to be hairy apemen come from Persian and Greek accounts of Alexander the Great and his invasion of India.

I was able to find online at the Internet Ancient History Sourcebook site (located at: www.fordham.edu/HALSALL/ancient/arrian-bookVIII-India.html) the Greek historian Arrian's *Anabasis Alexandri: Book VIII*, translated by E. Iliff Robson in 1933, which has a curious passage about hairy ape-men in it. The book chronicles the invasion of India by Alexander the Great's troops in 326 BC and *Book VIII* is mainly concerned with the voyage of an Admiral named Nearchus to the Indus River.

In Chapter 23 we learn: "Leaving the outlets of the Arabis they coasted along the territory of the

104

Oreitans, and anchored at Pagala, after a voyage of two hundred stades, near a breaking sea; but they were able all the same to cast anchor. The crews rode out the seas in their vessels, though a few went in search of water, and procured it. Next day they sailed at dawn, and after making four hundred and thirty stades they put in towards evening at Cabana, and moored on a desert shore."

In Chapter 24 we are told of battles with hairy men with sharp claws:

Thence they set sail and progressed with a favoring wind; and after a passage of five hundred stades the anchored by a torrent, which ,was called Tomerus. There was a lagoon at the mouths of the river, and the depressions near the bank were inhabited by natives in stifling cabins. These seeing the convoy sailing up were astounded, and lining along the shore stood ready to repel any who should attempt a landing. They carried thick spears, about six cubits long; these had no iron tip, but the same result was obtained by hardening the point with fire. They were in number about six hundred. Nearchus observed these evidently standing firm and drawn up in order, and ordered the ships to hold back within range, so that their missiles might reach the shore; for the natives' spears, which looked stalwart, were good for close fighting, but had no terrors against a volley. Then Nearchus took the lightest and

105

lightest-armed troops, such as were also the best swimmers, and bade them swim off as soon as the word was given. Their orders were that, as soon as any swimmer found bottom, he should await his mate, and not attack the natives till they had their formation three deep; but then they were to raise their battle cry and charge at the double. On the word, those detailed for this service dived from the ships into the sea, and swam smartly, and took up their formation in orderly manner, and having made a phalanx, charged, raising, for their part, their battle cry to the God of War, and those on shipboard raised the cry along with them; and arrows and missiles from the engines were hurled against the natives. They, astounded at the flash of the armor, and the swiftness of the charge, and attacked by showers of arrows and missiles, half naked as they were, never stopped to resist but gave way. Some were killed in flight; others were captured; but some escaped into the hills. Those captured were hairy, not only their heads but the rest of their bodies; their nails were rather like beasts' claws; they used their nails (according to report) as if they were iron tools; with these they tore asunder their fishes, and even the less solid kinds of wood; everything else they cleft with sharp stones; for iron they did not possess. For clothing they wore skins of animals, some even the thick skins of the larger fishes.

So what of this bizarre account? Were these men ("hairy, not only their heads but the rest of their bodies; their nails were rather like beasts' claws;") some sort of yeti battalion for the Hindu kings of this unidentified region of western India? Was there a time when the wild hairy men of Asia were on friendly terms with the Yogi-Kings of ancient India and actually fought against barbarian invaders? It is a fantastic thought!

A Yeti by Any Other Name would Still Smell Bad

As mentioned earlier, yetis got the name "abominable snowmen" in 1921 when the first British Everest expedition, led by Colonel H. W. Howard-Bury, sighted a number of large man-apes, and was told that the creature was the Metohkangmi (Mehteh-Kangmi) or "man-beast of the snowy mountains."[1, 2, 39]

Yeti: Fact or Fiction,[2] a "Know Nepal" series book gives the derivation of the name "yeti" as coming from the slightly different Tibetan *mehton kangmi* or "man of the high regions." Other similar variations are that the word *yeh* means "snow valley" and *teh* means "snowman or man of the high regions." According to

Kampa Dzong, near Mt. Everest, in a photo taken in 1921.

Nepalese Sherpas the word yeti is derived from *yah*: "rock or cliff" and *teh*: "animal," thereby forming the name *yah-teh* or "cliff-animal." The word "yeti" is essentially a Sherpa word, popularized by the many international climbing expeditions that have gone into the Sherpa areas around Everest, Makalu and Kanchenjunga and heard stories of the elusive, hairy man-apes.

As early as 1820 the British explorer J.B. Fraser mentioned the name *bang* for the hairy wildman of the snows. Bang or bhang is similar to *khang* or *kangmi*, also lending itself to the name of another famous giant ape-creature, King Kong, or dare I say, *King Kangmi* in Tibetan.[2]

Other entries in the long list of names for yetis are *chu-mung*: the spirit of the glaciers; *dredmo* or *dremo*: a person who was born a human but has become a savage wildman; *dzu-teh*: a large, shaggy brown creature that eats cattle; *megur, migu,* or *miegye*: the Sikkimese word for yeti; *nyalmu* or *nyulmo*: a wild, hairy creature about nearly four meters (12 feet) tall that is very powerful and eats animals. Also listed as names for yeti are *mirke, sagpa, rimi, thelma, rakshas, ban-manche, van-manas* and *Mahalangoor,* a Nepalese word for "big monkey." *Rakshas* means "demon," *ban-manche* means "jungle man," *van-manas* means "man of the forests." Another Tibetan name is *mi-de,* or *mig-de,* which means bear-man, the Tibetan word *de* meaning "a large bear."[2]

Kunzang Choden in her book *Bhutanese Tales of the Yeti*, states that the most common names for yeti

109

are *migoi* (strong man) or *gredpo*. She also reports that a smaller version of the yeti called *mechume* or *mirgola* live in the dense bamboo forests at high altitudes. They are bipeds about a meter in height and have long arms. They are usually reported to be brownish-red in color with hairless, human-like faces, and a fringe of hair over the forehead. Most sighting of these creatures are reported by cattle herders who are forced to venture into the depths of the forests in search of missing cattle.[12]

There are many other names for the yeti in Central Asia, such as *almas* in Mongolia and the Altai Himalaya Region. The very fact that these creatures are well known in many different parts of Central Asia (and Southeast Asia) and have so many different names, shows that there must be something real to this creature—they are known locally and so must be given a name. I have to admit, however, that the yeti is very much a boogey-man, and a yeti by any name would smell as bad as any skunk ape in the swamps of the Arkansas or Louisiana.

It should be pointed out here that though the yeti has many names, it is almost universally thought to be very bad luck to ever see one. Even talking about yetis is bad luck. Many in the Himalayas believed that to encounter a yeti is sign that the witness will die soon. Thus, an encounter with a Yeti is to be avoided, and even the whole subject is best not talked about too much. Yet, despite this superstition surrounding the yeti, many tales of yeti encounters have come out of Nepal, Bhutan, Sikkim and Tibet.

110

Tenzing Norgay and Annelies Lohner at Mt. Everest, 1947.

Yeti Footprints Capture Headlines

After it was decided that Mt. Everest was the highest mountain in the world an exciting era of exploration began. Expeditions set out from Darjeeling in British colonial India, the end of the railway in those early days. From here untold numbers of expeditions set out, many of them in secret, and in some cases the expedition had only one member, often an eccentric Englishman, Scot, Canadian or South African. With the often hilarious, confusing and sometimes harrowing reports of Himalayan survival issued from these groups came the first accounts to the west of hairy hominids living in the remote reaches of the Himalaya.

The British reading public eagerly awaited accounts of new discoveries and marvels, and some yeti footprints would make a jolly good story! Howard Bury in his 1922 book *Mount Everest: The Reconnaissance: 1921*, says that they came across strange footprints in the snow in the Makalu and Chamlang area just east of Mt. Everest and west of Kanchenjunga:

> On September 22, leaving Raeburn behind, Mallory, Bullock, Morshead, Wheeler, Wollaston and myself started off to Lakhpa La camp. We left the 20,000-foot camp in 22 degrees of frost at four o'clock in the morning, accompanied by twenty-six coolies, who were divided up into four parties, each of which was

properly roped. It was a beautiful moonlight night, and the mountains showed up nearly as brightly as in the daytime. We rapidly descended the 200 feet from our terrace to the glacier, when we all "roped up." The snow on the glacier was in excellent condition, and as it was frozen hard we made good progress. Dawn overtook us on the broad flat part of the glacier, the first of the sun falling on the summit of Mount Everest, which lay straight in front of us, and changing the colour of the snow gradually from pink to orange, all the time up sharp and clear in the frosty air. We mounted gradually past Kartse, the white conical-shaped peak climbed by Mallory and Bullock a month ago from the Kama Valley. We wended our way without much difficulty through the ice-fall of the glacier, below some superbly fluted snow ridges that rose straight above us. Then followed a long and at times a somewhat steep climb over soft powdery snow to the top of the pass. Even at these heights we came across tracks in the snow. We were able to pick out tracks of hares and foxes, but one that at first looked like a human foot puzzled us considerably. Our coolies at once jumped at the conclusion that this must be the "Wild Man of the snows," to which they gave the name of Metohkangmi, " the abominable snow man," who interested the newspapers so much.

On my return to civilized countries I read

113

with interest delightful accounts of the ways and customs of this wild man whom we were supposed to have met. These tracks, which caused so much comment, were probably caused by a large "loping" grey wolf, which in the soft snow formed double tracks rather like those of a barefooted man. Tibet, however, is not the only country where there exists a "bogey man." In Tibet he takes the form of a hairy man who lives in the snows, and little Tibetan children who are naughty and disobedient are frightened by wonderful fairy tales that are told about him. To escape from him they must run down the hill, as then his long hair falls over his eyes and he is unable to see them. Many other such tales have they with which to strike terror into the hearts of bad boys and girls.

Howard-Bury was popularizing two subjects exciting to the readers of British and other newspapers: that Mount Everest could be climbed by mountaineers with the equipment of the time—and that a mysterious man-ape, a virtual missing link, had been seriously reported from the Himalayas.

Howard-Bury and his group, after discovering these "yeti prints," then continued on to the Chamlang La (Chamlang Pass), coming over the main Himalayan range from Tibet and seeing the forest-covered valleys of the southern Himalayas. Indeed, these deep river valleys which cut through the Himalayas and Hindu

114

Kush into the Tibetan Plateau are heavily forested—to the point of tropical jungle in many cases—which makes high mountain passes subject to frequent snow fall prime sites where anomalous footprints might be found.

Explorers were often amazed as they looked down on the southern side of the Himalayas into Nepal (as well as Bhutan) and saw the lush, warm valleys that were absent on the Tibetan Plateau, and which they were forced to march through because of the blockade on foreigners imposed by Nepal (and Bhutan). Other nations passed such laws and attempted to keep foreigners and Western influence out of their countries, including Japan, Tibet, Oman and a number of other countries.

Walt Unsworth in his authoritative 1989 book, *Everest*, mentions the yeti several times and would seem to be a believer in the Yeti. Says Unsworth on page 66, referring to Howard-Bury's 1921 expedition:

> As the party climbed up the Lhakpa La again on the 22nd [of September] they were astonished to see giant footprints in the snow, which the porters immediately recognized as those of Metohkangmi—the Abominable Snowman or Yeti. Similar tracks had been reported in Sikkim in 1889, and were to be reported and photographed many times in later years.

Despite this distraction it was a very tired

115

party that assembled on the col, and none of them were keen to go on. 'I observed no great sparkle of energy or enthusiasm among my companions,' Mallory wrote later.

Indeed, the sight of any yeti tracks by the party would be likely to dampen spirits rather than lift them since, as I pointed out earlier, it is very back luck to see a yeti or come in any sort of contact with them. Even talk of yetis is considered unlucky.

Unsworth goes on in his book to mention that the 1922 British Everest expedition, with many of the same members as the 1921 reconnaissance, had finally met with head lama of the Rongbuk Monastery near the Tibetan side of Mount Everest:

> The expedition reached the Rongbuk valley on 30 April. The name means 'the valley of steep ravines,' and it is indeed a most desolate place seldom free from the piercing wind coming off the mountain. To the Tibetans it is a holy place; at the entrance to the valley, opposite the village of Chobuk, was a large mani (or prayer) stone beyond which it was forbidden to kill any living creature, and five miles up the valley was the Rongbuk monastery, one of the most sacred places in Lama Buddhism.
>
> The Rongbuk Lama, having completed the year of seclusion which had prevented him from meeting Mallory in 1921, received Bruce warmly. The General was impressed, as were

all who met this remarkable person: 'He was a large, well-made man of about sixty,' wrote Bruce, 'full of dignity, with a most intelligent and wise face and an extraordinarily attractive smile.' On a later visit another member of the team, equally impressed, put it more succinctly: 'Gee! That chap is either the holiest saint or the greatest actor on earth.'

The Lama inquired of Bruce his reasons for wishing to climb Chomolungma (the local name for Everest) and Bruce, astutely grasping the situation, realized that any conventional explanation would be useless. Instead he drew upon the spiritual. They came as pilgrims, he explained, for Chomolungma was the highest mountain in the world, and any man who reached the summit must necessarily be nearer Heaven. The Lama could understand that. He invited Bruce to partake of Tibetan tea, but the General, who hated the stuff, declined on the grounds that he had sworn not to touch butter until his pilgrimage was over. He also promised that no animals would be slaughtered in the valley, a rule which was rigorously enforced — even the animals destined to provide meat for the expedition were butchered beyond the Chobuk mani stone and brought to Base Camp as carcasses.

Bruce also took the opportunity to question the Lama about the yeti, the tracks of which had been seen in 1921, and he was calmly

117

informed that five yetis lived in the upper reaches of the valley. From other monks in the monastery, the expedition learned that the yetis were much feared. They were said to be man-like and covered in long hair. Sometimes they raided villages, carrying off women, killing men and drinking the blood of yaks.[7]

Indeed, Sherpas greatly fear the yeti, and believe that to see one is very unlucky and often means an untimely death. That yetis will occasionally kill yaks by grabbing them by the horns and breaking their

An old print of an orangutan.

necks with their incredible strength is very disturbing to Sherpas, Tibetans and other cattle-yak herders in the Himalayas and Tibetan Plateau. Unsworth has a footnote in his book that contains this curious information:

> At Khumjung monastery they keep a yeti scalp which has been examined scientists and pronounced a fake, but the stories about this monster are so numerous and so consistent in detail that nobody can dismiss them out of hand. Tracks have been seen and photographed on several occasions. Quite recently a herd of yaks was killed in Khumjung and the girl tending them struck dumb and bereft of reason with horror. The people are convinced it was the work of a yeti. Whatever one may think of these stories, the fact remains that the Abominable Snowman is one of the great unsolved mysteries of the present day, possibly the last and greatest of them all. Perhaps it should be left a mystery, so that our grandchildren may still have something to wonder at.

With this remark, Unsworth joins the ranks of knowledgeable mountaineers who think that there is a genuine mystery concerning the yeti, and that it is not a bear or imaginary cryptid. The incident with the young female Sherpani who was struck dumb by fear at the astonishing sight of the yeti took place in July 1974. More on this episode in the next chapter.

Unsworth mentions the yeti one more time with a

reference to the famous Swiss-American mountaineer Norman Dyhrenfurth's participation in the 1958 search for the yeti, on an expedition led by Tom Slick. Unsworth is a scholar on all things Everest, and for him, the abominable snowman is something to seriously consider.

The Rum-Doodle Bar in Kathmandu is the traditional place where mountaineers go after their climbs to have a drink with their friends. The walls are covered with cardboard cutouts of yeti feet signed by the members of various expeditions, and these cardboard yeti feet are the coasters; newspaper stories of the yeti are in glass frames on the walls. While there is plenty of joking about the yeti, it seems to be a subject that is taken seriously by some. Others maintain that the yeti is a creation of western myth-makers and vague legends of a Himalayan boogey man.

Tibetan and Sherpa lamas often speak of the yetis, especially in the Khumbu area of Nepal (in the vicinity of Mount Everest) and the upper Arun Valley. Although Unsworth does not mention it in his account, it is said that during the visit in 1922, the head lama of the Rongbuk Monastery in Tibet offered to show British General C. G. Bruce the valley nearby where the tetis might be seen to frolic. Oddly, Bruce, who was more interested in climbing Mount Everest (at which he failed miserably), declined to take the Lama up on his offer. Later, in 1958, monks at the Rongbuk Monastery claimed that yetis had destroyed a sacred rock monument overlooking the monastery.[11, 39]

120

An early illustration of an orangutan.

The first known photograph of the mysterious footprints that were to make yetis famous were taken by the British mountaineer F.S. Smythe in 1936. Smythe and his team were crossing a 5,029 meter pass in the central Himalayas when he came across "the imprints of a huge foot, apparently a biped." He took a photograph of the footprints and the Sherpas with him declared them to be from a *mirke*, or wildman.

According to Kesar Lall, a well-known Nepalese chronicler of yeti stories, the Sherpas with Smythe made this formal written statement: "We, Wangdi Norbu, Norbu Bhotia and Pasang Urgen, accompanying Mr. Smythe over a pass when we saw tracks which we know to be those of a Mirke or Wildman. We have often seen bear, snow leopard, and other animal tracks, but we swear that these tracks were none of these. We have never seen a Mirke because anyone who sees one dies or is killed, but these are pictures of the tracks which are the same as we have seen in Tibetan monasteries."[1]

The photograph made the British papers and there was much scientific speculation as to the origin of the tracks. According to experts, the curious tracks might have been made by snow leopards, bears, pandas, langurs, wolves, Tibetan outlaws or Hindu ascetics seeking a remote cave to meditate in.

Finally, a panel of zoologists at the Royal Society, headed by Sir Julien Huxley, decided that the footprints shown in the photograph were those of a bear (*Ursus arctes pruinesus*). Further attention was drawn to the footprints in 1937 when RAF wingcom-

The 1951 Shipton footprints.

mander M. Bauman was noted for writing, "While not wishing to draw a red herring across this fresh line of inquiry, may I recount an experience of my own in Garhwal last year? With two Sherpas I was crossing the Bireh Ganga glacier when we came upon tracks made in crisp snow which resembled nothing as much as those of an elephant."[1]

One only wonders why Sherpas and Himalayan explorers would be unable to recognize bear tracks, being quite common, or why elephants would be marching over high passes in the Himalayas? Perhaps coming up with any alternative answer to the one given by the people who actually live among these mysterious creatures is necessary, no matter how ridiculous these "scientific" answers may seem.

123

Throughout the 30s the subject of yetis and abominable snowmen appeared in newspapers around the world. In 1935 it was reported that a yeti was killing sheep at a Himalayan village called Kathagsu. Later, the villagers were said to driven the mysterious creature away.

In 1936 it was reported that footprints had been discovered in the Upper Salween (Nepal) at an altitude of about 4,876 meters by Ronald Kaulback. Said Kaulback, "Five sets of tracks, which looked as though made by a bare-footed man," were discovered in the snow. A more curious (and dubious) 1938 tale was of a British official who was captured and kept confined to a cave by a wildman somewhere in Sikkim.[1]

ᚠ ᚦ ᚠ

The Famous Eric Shipton Encounter

After the war years, attention returned to mountaineering in the Himalayas. Yetis were to hit the headlines in a big way in 1951. In that year the famous photograph taken by British explorer Eric Shipton was published in the London newspapers and magazines. Shipton had discovered and photographed yeti footprints on several occasions. Then, in 1951, near the sacred mountain of Gauri Shankar (a mountain that is forbidden to be climbed by the government of Nepal), his team found a trail of enormous human-looking footprints in fresh powdery snow. They followed the trail until it disappeared in a

124

The oft-seen 1951 photograph of a yeti footprint taken by Eric Shipton.

Eric Shipton standing beside the famous 1951 footprints.

rocky moraine.

As W. H. Murray tells the tale in his 1953 book *The Story of Everest,*[11] Eric Shipton and his companion, Dr. Michael Ward, were descending a snow covered glacier on the south side of Nuptse, a sub-peak of Mount Everest, when they came across a set of yeti tracks. They were at 5,600 meters on the Menlung glacier that had just received a light covering of snow. They discovered odd fecal matter and across the fresh snow were very distinct footprints of not one, but several, huge bipedal animals.

Says Murray, "Sen Tensing recognized them at once. At least two had left spoor. It did not resemble the spoor of any known bear or monkey... Shipton and Ward followed the tracks for nearly two miles down the glacier, finally loosing them on the lateral moraine. Some of the prints were particularly clear and must have been left within the last 24 hours. Pad marks and toe marks could distinctly seen within the footprints, which were 12 inches long, and where the creature had jumped the smaller crevasses, the scribble marks of its nails could be seen on the far side."[11]

The expedition party consisted of leader Eric Shipton, Mike Ward, Bill Murray, Tom Bourdillon, Edmund Hillary, Earle Riddiford, Angtharkay, Pasang Bhotia, Nima, Sen Tensing and six others. Towards the end of the expedition the climbers were making an exploratory travel in the Gauri Sankar groups to the southwest of Everest, when they discovered the prints. Shipton wrote of this incident in his 1985 book

The Six Mountain-Travel Books[90] (Pg. 621):

It was on one of the glaciers of the Menlung basin, at a height of about 19,000 feet, that, late one afternoon, we came across those curious footprints in the snow, the report of which has caused a certain amount of public interest in Britain. We did not follow them further than was convenient, a mile or so, for we were carrying heavy loads at the time, and besides we had reached a particularly interesting stage in the exploration of the basin. I have in the past found many sets of these curious footprints and have tried to follow them, but have always lost them on the moraine or rocks at the side of thc glacier. These particular ones seemed to be very fresh, probably not more than 24 hours old. When Murray and Bourdillon followed us a few days later the tracks had been almost obliterated by melting. Sen Tensing, who had no doubt whatever that the creatures (for there had been at least two) that had made the tracks were "Yetis" or wild men, told me that two years before, he and a number of other

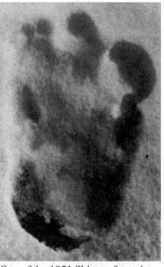

One of the 1951 Shipton footprints.

128

Sherpas had seen one of them at a distance of about 25 yards at Thyangboche. He described it as half man and half beast, standing about five feet six inches, with a tall pointed head, its body covered with reddish brown hair, but with a hairless face. When we reached Katmandu at the end of November, I had him cross-examined in Nepali (I conversed with him in Hindustani). He left no doubt as to his sincerity. Whatever it was that he had seen, he was convinced that it was neither a bear nor a monkey, with both of which animals he was, of course, very familiar.[90]

The publication of the photo in the *London Times*

caused a sensation, and the world was launched into a yeti craze that lasted into the early 1960's. Hollywood made feature films about the Yeti such as *The Abominable Snowman* (1957, with Forrest Tucker and Peter Cushing), and such cartoon heroes as Johnny Quest and Tin Tin had their episodes in search of yeti. Scores of books, fiction as well as non-fiction, appeared on the yeti, culminating with Ivan T. Sanderson's *Abominable Snowmen: Legend Come to Life,* published in 1961.

Other footprints were discovered during this important "yeti decade" by various parties such as the Wyss-Dunant expedition (1953) and Abbe P. Bordet (1954). In 1958 the Nepalese government made the yeti a protected species because of the immense interest taken by the international community in finding a live specimen. The government of Nepal, following its system of charging a "rental fee" for mountains, fixed the fee for a Yeti expedition at 5,000 rupees.

Today Shipton's photo is probably the most well known yeti or sasquatch footprints, freshly preserved in newly fallen snow. They were measured to be 12 inches long and 8 inches wide. What could they be, other than the footprints of an enormous hairy apeman—the abominable snowman? Are they the tracks of a Himalayan bear that had melted and enlarged in afternoon sun as skeptics have suggested? Well, probably not.

We should give Shipton the credit he is due—he was not a hoaxer, or a gullible fool. What he saw was

130

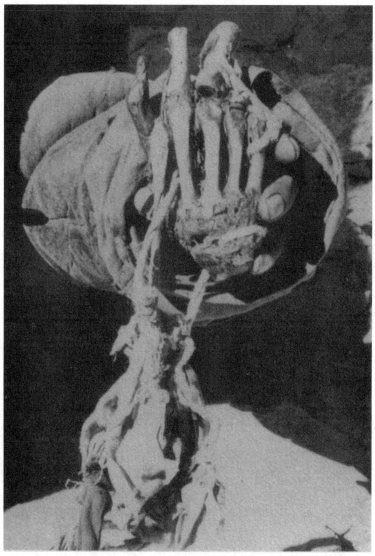

The Pangboche hand in 1958. It is now missing.

unusual and incredible. He wisely took several photos of it while his guides assured him that these were the tracks of a yeti. Why should we doubt them?

Shipton's photographs stirred the British public, and in 1954 the London *Daily Mail* newspaper launched what was probably the largest yeti expedition to ever assault the Himalayas. Called the Daily Mail Snowman Expedition, it was lead by the British climber John Angelo Jackson. This expedition made the first trek from the Mount Everest region in Nepal to Kanchenjunga on the border of Sikkim, at that time an independent country (now it is a state of India).

Jackson's team photographed paintings of yetis at the Thyangboche Monastery and acquired some hair specimens from the yeti scalp kept at the nearby monastery at Pangboche. Later the team tracked and photographed a large number of footprints in the snow that were largely unidentifiable. The flattened nature of the footprints was attributed to erosion and widening from melting and wind.

The hair from the Pangboche scalp was analyzed in Britain for the *Daily Mail* by Frederic Wood-Jones, an ex-

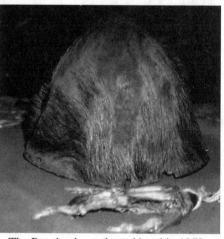

The Pangboche scalp and hand in 1958.

132

pert in human and comparative anatomy, comparing them with hairs from known animals such as bears, mountain sheep and orangutans. The hairs appeared black to dark brown in dim light, and red in sunlight. He concluded that the hairs were quite old and had not been dyed.

Wood-Jones said he was unable to pinpoint what animal the hairs had come from. He was, however, convinced that the hairs were not of a bear or anthropoid ape. He also concluded that the hairs were not from a scalp. He suggested that they might be from the shoulder of an animal, possibly a hoofed one. He contended that some animals do have a ridge of hair extending from the pate to the back, but no animals have a ridge (as in the Pangboche relic) running from the base of the forehead across the pate and ending at the nape of the neck. However, since the yeti is an unknown animal, it may well have such a ridge. In fact, popular depictions of yetis and sasquatch do tend to include such a ridge. Wood-Jones essentially added to the mystery of the yeti by his inconclusive findings and not being able to actually identify the hair samples to any certain degree. Therefore, the existence of the yeti was still very much a possibility.

Tom Slick circa 1958.

133

⁂ —⌇— ⁂

Tom Slick, the Yeti & the CIA

The expedition by the *Daily Mail* caught the attention of a flamboyant Texas oil millionaire named Tom Slick, Jr. who was also influenced by the publication of Belgian cryptozoologist Bernard Heuvelmans' (1916-2001) groundbreaking 1955 book, *On The Track of Unknown Animals*.[32] Slick was born in 1916 and graduated from Philips Exeter Academy in 1934 and Yale University in 1938. Slick's father, Tom Slick, Sr., made millions as the "King of the Wildcatters," and Tom Slick, Jr. had a privileged upbringing that included trips to Europe. On a trip to Scotland with his Yale classmates, Slick and his friends decided to search for the Loch Ness Monster which had gained fame at the time. Though they discovered nothing significant, for Slick it was the beginning of a life-long interest in cryptids.

In 1956, while traveling in and around Nepal, he

The Lethbridge Herald

LETHBRIDGE, ALBERTA,
THURSDAY, AUGUST 2, 1956

Texas Oil Man After "Snowman" With Dogs, 'Copter

KATMANDU, Nepal — (Reuters) —Texas oil man Tom Slick is going after the Abominable Snowman — with bloodhounds and a helicopter.

Slick announced his plans to hunt the elusive monster of the Himalayan snows in a letter to Katmandu's leading hotel proprietor, Boris Lissanovitch.

He said he will start out after the Snowman—known in Nepal as Yeti—next spring. He will scour the Ganesh Himal region north-west of Katmandu near the Tibetan border.

He has yet to apply to the Nepalese government for permission for his expedition.

Although Yeti tracks have been reported frequently by mountaineers, an expedition sponsored by The Daily Mail of London early in 1954 has been the only serious attempt to capture a snowman. None was sighted by the party.

134

interviewed a number of different yeti witnesses, and decided to back a yeti expedition of his own. Slick began his personally financed expeditions to Nepal in 1957. He had met an Irish/Australian big game hunter named Peter Byrne who had also been in the Himalayas in 1956 searching for the yeti. Bryne happened to meet up with Tenzing Norgay, the Sherpa who had first climbed Everest with Edmund Hillary, and over a cup of tea Norgay told Byrne about Slick's interest in the yeti. Byrne contacted Slick, and the two spent several months assembling a compact, commando-like team to find the elusive apeman.

When Slick and Byrne's plans for the 1957 expedition gained international attention, the Nepalese government refused to allow the expedition to continue unless the team found a respectable organization to back them. Eventually, the highly respected San Antonio Zoo from Slick's hometown decided to sponsor the expedition. He may have had another sponsor as well: the American Central Intelligence Agency (CIA).

During the 1959 trek called the Slick-Johnson Snowman Expedition, the team collected what they believed to be "yeti feces." Upon analysis the feces were found to have a parasite which could not be classified. Since parasites are often unique to their host, this was an indication of a previously unknown animal, most probably a yeti.[5]

Also during the 1959 Slick-Johnson Snowman Expedition, Peter Byrne and his brother Bryan discovered tracks at 10,000 feet in the upper Arun

135

Valley region. The Arun Valley is one of the deepest valleys in the world, and is like a deep knife slash cutting through the Himalayas all the way to the Tibetan plateau. The river valley goes for thousands of feet down to an almost tropical climate at the valley floor.

Documents published by Loren Coleman in his book *Tom Slick and the Search for the Yeti*[5] reveal that Slick had actually gone into Tibet, a country generally said to be off-limits to foreigners. This was during the time of the Chinese takeover of Tibet, and a great deal of international intrigue was occurring. There are rumors that Tom Slick was secretly working with the CIA to help get the Dalai Lama out of Tibet and was using his search for the yeti as a cover.

Slick died in a mysterious airplane crash in Montana in 1962. The cause of the crash of his Beechcraft airplane has never been found and Coleman claims that several of Slick's acquaintances claimed that there had been an "internal explosion" in the airplane. The two Johnsons, Slick's partners, also died shortly after Slick of unnatural causes.[5]

Slick had asked Peter Byrne to head the Pacific Northwest Bigfoot Expedition, as it was called, after he read about the discovery of footprints in California. Byrne eventually moved to Oregon, raised millions of dollars for Bigfoot research and was later to go on to write the 1975 book *Bigfoot: Man, Monster or Myth*.[77]

It is interesting to note that Slick was also a friend of the enigmatic Howard Hughes. Around the

Bryan Byrne looks at yeti tracks in the Arun Valley, March 1959.

same time as Slick's odd airplane accident, Howard Hughes also "disappeared," supposedly becoming a recluse on the top floor of a Las Vegas hotel, and later in a wing of a hotel in the Bahamas. Few people saw Howard Hughes during those years, and his friend Tom Slick, Jr. would certainly be unable to look him up, having died in the airplane crash. Did the "murder" of Slick have to do with his connections to Howard Hughes, or did it have something to do with his yeti expeditions and work for the CIA?

Slick, it is said, smuggled a finger of the famous Pangboche yeti hand out of Nepal and into India.

137

In order to get the ancient relic out of India without passing the difficult Indian and British customs in London, he enlisted the help of his friend Jimmy Stewart to smuggle the finger from New Delhi to London. Amusingly, the story goes that Jimmy Stewart (the famous actor) had his wife hide the finger of the yeti in her case of underpants, so that the customs officials would be embarrassed to look too closely.

᠅ —ᴧᴧ— ᠅

The Hillary-World Book Encyclopedia Expedition

This era of yeti hunting ended with the World Book Encyclopedia expedition of 1960 led by Sir Edmund Hillary. Hillary was joined by the famous zoologist Marlin Perkins, who was to become the well known host of the American television program *Mutual of Omaha's Wild Kingdom* which ran from 1963 to 1985. Perkins died the year after the show ended on June 14, 1986.

Hillary and Perkins filmed their journey over the Trashi Lapsa Pass in the Rowaling Himal and this footage was later used in a *Wild Kingdom* episode. They also brought the famous Khumjung Yeti scalp for testing in Europe and North America. This yeti scalp is still at the monastery in Khumjung and is available for viewing on most days for a small donation to the monastery.

The Khumjung scalp was taken to London, Paris and Chicago for testing. Dr. Austin L. Rand, Chief

Marlin Perkins, Edmund Hillary, friends, plus a "Yeti Gun."

Curator, Department of Zoology, and Prof. Philip Hershkovitz, Curator of Mammals at the Field Museum of Natural History (Chicago) suspected that the yeti scalp might belong to a Himalayan bear.

Other tests at the Musée de l'Homme in Paris concluded that the scalp was probably the hide of a serow, a rare Himalayan hoofed goat-like animal with reddish-brown hair. The Belgian zoologist Dr. Bernard Heuvelmans was, however, a dissenting vote

139

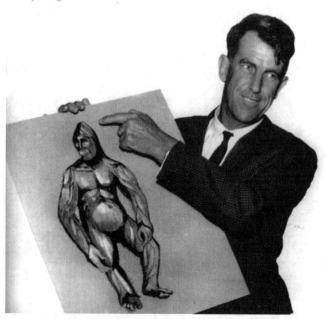

Edmund Hillary with a poster of a yeti.

on the serow decision, concluding the scalp to be from some unknown animal. Hair-testing techniques are much better now and it would be interesting to test these samples again. Hair found at certain wildman sites in China and Nepal have recently been "proven" to have come from some unknown animal species.

Hillary for a short time was strongly associated with yeti hunts, and had seen large footprints, he claimed, while scaling Everest with Tenzing Norgay in 1953. But he was to say that he was officially a skeptic of the abominable snowman in his later days. One wonders what a yeti would be doing that high up in the Himalayas, anyway. The general belief

140

of zoologists who genuinely consider the yeti a possibility is that they do occasionally cross high, icy passes in the Himalayas, but generally live in the thick brush and forests in the steep ravines that occur up to about 18,000 feet in some areas, like the Arun Valley. Still, some of larger yeti may live—and hibernate—in remote caves above the timberline. Certainly this is how the yeti are popularly portrayed in movies, comic books and portraits.

Yetis in Central Nepal

While most yeti sightings in Nepal are in the eastern section, yetis have been frequently sighted in central Nepal, particularly in the Mustang, Dolpo and Annapurna regions. In February of 1958 it was reported in the Kathmandu weekly *Kalpana* that the Rajah of Mustang was the possessor of a yeti skin. Mustang is a remote, semi-autonomous region on the Nepali-Tibetan border, and largely forbidden to foreigners. The Rajah's men were said to have shot a yeti. *King Features* columnist George Dixon joked in his column in 1958 that, "The Rajah can't decide if the hide he sits on is the Abominable Snowman or a brown bear. I hope the same kind of indecision is not motivating President Eisenhower..."[1]

In 1970 it was widely reported in the media that British mountaineer Don Whillans claimed to have witnessed a strange man-like creature while scaling

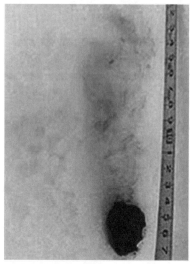

Takahashi's 2008 yeti footprint.

Annapurna I, the tenth highest mountain in the world. Whillans said that while scouting for a campsite, he heard some odd cries which his Sherpa guide attributed to a yeti's call. Later that night, Whillans saw a dark shape moving near his camp. The next day, he observed a few human-like footprints in the snow, and that evening, through his binoculars, viewed an apelike creature walking on two legs for 20 minutes as it apparently searched for food not far from his camp.

Whillans, one of the most famous of British climbers, was a believer in the yeti, I guess we could say. He died from a heart attack in 1985 at the age of 52.

The famous writer Peter Matthiessen wrote in his 1979 best-selling book *The Snow Leopard* that he and naturalist George Schaller witnessed a creature across a valley in the remote Dolpo region that both thought was yeti.

The Japanese, who are avid mountain climbers, have also taken an interest in the yeti, and the most famous of their yeti hunters is a 60-year-old painter from Tokyo named Yoshiteru Takahashi. Takahashi,

142

as part of a Japanese mountaineering team, has scaled the 8,167-meter Dhaulagiri in central Nepal several times since the 1970s. Said Takahashi in a 2003 interview (http://www.camp4.com/moreoffroute.php [article no longer available]):

> I have climbed the Dhaulagiri (White Mountain) massif four times, and every time, I saw footprints of the yeti. In 1971, one of my expedition members saw one of these creatures. It looked like a gorilla and stood only 15 meters away from him, watching him, for about 40 seconds. It was about 150 cm tall and stood on its hind legs, like a man. Its head was covered with long, thick hair and he was certain it was not a bear or a monkey.

Takahashi returned to the area numerous times, and on another expedition to the same region in 1994, he discovered what he describes as a "bolt-hole," a natural cave that stretched back 5 meters into a rock face at 5,000 meters above sea level. The Japanese climber said, "Animals had definitely visited the cave and there were more of the footprints in the snow around the mouth of the cavern." Unfortunately, according to him, his camera failed and he couldn't record his find.

According to the 2003 interview, the expedition to find the yeti in 1994 was prompted by the earlier discoveries of footprints that he describes as being similar to those of a human child and measuring up to

143

20 cm long. He also said he could smell the creatures' musty, animal odor. Says Takahashi:

> The footprints that I saw were similar to the one photographed by British explorers Eric Shipton and Michael Ward in 1951... The ones I found were smaller and thinner, more like a human foot, with an arch between the heel and the toes. There are no animals that leave that sort of track.

Takahashi, with support from a Japanese newspaper, staked out the flanks of Dhaulagiri, for 2 months in 2003, one more of his many adventures in the area. The online Russian newspaper *Pravda* reported on one of Takahashi's expeditions in central Nepal in 2005, saying that, "The researchers saw a Yeti walking at a large distance. They found 13 footprints of the animal, each of them measured 35 centimeters long and 20 centimeters wide. Takahashi said afterwards that he was certain of Yeti's existence."

Takahashi was back in the news again on October 20, 2008 where he gave a news conference and reported that his team had found further footprints of a yeti in the Annapurna region. Photos of the footprints were released to the media, and even made it into the well known political blog called *The Huffington Post* (www.huffingtonpost.com).

Gigantopithecus: The Missing Link

Despite a great deal of skepticism, there is no reason why some giant missing link type creature should not exist as the many reports indicate. After all, giant ape creatures that are very similar to humans are proven to exist. We have the well known examples of the mountain gorillas of central Africa and the very human-like orangutans of Southeast Asia. The giant ape Giganthopithicus is known to anthropologists to have existed within the last 10,000 years. Why could some not have survived to this day? Reports from around the world seem to indicate that they have.

In 1934 a Dutch paleontologist and geologist named Ralph von Koenigswald was on a study trip to Hong Kong when he came across a number of large teeth lying about in the jars of a Chinese chemist's shop. One tooth in particular caught his

145

Myra Shackley's drawing of Giganthopithicus.

The fearsome bite of a gorilla.

attention, the third lower molar that was twice as large as the corresponding tooth in the mouth of an adult male gorilla. The volume of the tooth, compared to the volume of a man's tooth, was five or six times as great.[6]

Dr. von Koenigswald was fascinated by this huge primate molar, bought it and used it to reconstruct a hypothetical primate which would have stood somewhere between eleven and thirteen feet tall. Over the next five years two more of the giant molars were discovered in Chinese chemist shops that called the oddities "dragons' teeth."

From these first teeth Dr. von Koenigswald reconstructed a creature that he called *Gigantopithecus*, a creature which today has over one thousand additional teeth to its credit, discovered through the efforts of the Chinese Academia Sinica around the province of Kwangsi in south China. Dr. von Koenigswald, unfortunately, was imprisoned by the Japanese as an "enemy alien" during their occupation of Indonesia during World War II, thereby cutting his research short.

In 1956 a jawbone belonging to *Gigantopithecus* was discovered in a phosphate cave in Kwangsi province. The Chinese paleontologist Dr. Pei Wen-chung concluded that the jawbone was between 400,000 and 600,000 years old and that the giant creature had fed on a mixed diet of vegetables, grains and meat.[6] The evidence for a giant ape-creature was firmly established—was this the creature known in the Himalayas as the yeti?

The pointed head of a gorilla is similar to that attributed to the yeti.

The British anthropologist Myra Shackley argued that the *almas* and other "wildmen" of Central Asia were the last remains of the ancient Neanderthal that once roamed the prehistoric earth. Shackley was a noted Neanderthal expert in the 1960s and 70s, a lecturer at the University of Leicester in England and the author of the controversial 1983 book *Still Living?*[13]

Shackley maintained that the various reports of Almas in Mongolia and other "wildmen" in Chinese and Central Asian folklore, were probably Neanderthals who had survived their so-called extinction about 30,000 years ago. Shackley felt, however, that the yeti was a descendant of the giant ape *Giganthopithicus* and different from the Neanderthal almas, also called *chuchunaa* by the Mongols and

148

Tibetans.

Shackley felt that *Giganthopithicus* was the explanation for yetis as well as sasquatch and bigfoot. The almas were more akin to Neanderthals and Shackley theorized that there were three or four species of animals that were the cause of the various reports of giant, hairy apemen. Hairy Neanderthal men, still living a primitive existence without fire, language or clothing accounted for certain "wildman" tales around the world, while various man-apes similar to orangutans or *Giganthopithicus* were the cause of the other sightings. No one single answer could therefore be expected for the yeti enigma.

The mystery of the yeti continues to hold its fascination. Sometimes I remember how I lay awake for hours in my sleeping bag on that icy night near Mount Everest years ago. My ears strained to hear past the wind—to hear the sound of footsteps in the snow around my tent. In the distance ice fell from the glacier and crashed into the rocks below. Does the yeti still roam the chilly mountain valleys of the Himalayas? On remote mountain passes in the dead of night there is sometimes heard a sharp, shrill cry— is it the call of the yeti?

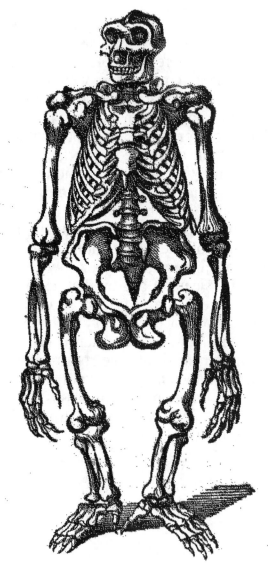

The skeleton of a gorilla.

The land of the yeti, almasty, wildman and orangutan.

Yetis, Sasquatch & Hairy Giants

CHAPTER 5

KANCHENJUNGA DEMONS

As a firm believer in the Snowman,
the least I can do is defend his abominable
existence.
—*Himalayan Explorer Desmond Doig*

༄ —₩— ༄

Kanchenjunga Demons and the Arun Valley

Yetis have very often been sighted in the Kanchenjunga region which spans areas of Sikkim, Nepal and Tibet. Kanchenjunga is the third highest mountain in the world and the Arun River runs just to the west of it. This is an area of high yeti incidence where they are sometimes called "Kanchenjunga Demons."[39, 14]

The Arun River flows from Tibet into a gorge next to Mount Kanchenjunga and then south through the Arun Valley of eastern Nepal. As noted in the last chapter, during the 1959 Slick-Johnson Snowman

Expedition, Bryan and Peter Byrne discovered what they believed to be yeti tracks at 10,000 feet in the upper Arun Valley region. As stated, the Arun Valley is one of the deepest valleys in the world, and is like a deep knife slash into the Tibetan plateau. The river valley goes for thousands of feet down to an almost tropical climate at the valley floor. Overall, it comprises the perfect environment for the sustenance of the yeti.

The Kanchenjunga-Arun Valley area includes all of eastern Nepal, including the Everest and Makalu areas. Also the areas around the heavily trekked tourist towns around Namche Bazaar and Lukla Airport which services many of the trekkers and guides who are going to the Everest Region. Directly to the east of this area is the Rowaling Himal and the forbidden mountain of Gauri Shankar.

Gauri Shankar is an icy mountain peak that is reputed to be the abode of Shankar, the guise of Shiva one of the gods of the all-important Hindu Trinity. For this reason, the Nepali government forbids climbing on Gauri Shankar, it is thought to be a sacred mountain of mystery and magic. Yetis and Hindu holymen called Sadhus are known to be found in the remote mountain forests.

Even today, the Arun Valley region is a remote area rarely visited by foreign explorers. Though heavily populated in the lower areas, and one of the most poor areas of Nepal, its upper reaches contain ideal habitat for yetis: steep forested ravines and valleys with isolated mountain passes and glaciated peaks that are among the highest in the world. Indeed, if one area of the world could be said to contain a large breeding population of yetis, it is the Arun Valley and the Kanchenjunga region. Even in the winter, the lower reaches of the Arun Valley do not freeze, and have a relatively mild climate.

In 1925, Greek photographer, N. A. Tombazi, a member of the British geological expedition in the Kanchenjunga region, described a creature he saw moving across a Himalayan slope at an altitude of around 15,000 feet near the Zemu Glacier. He estimated it was about a thousand feet away and viewed the creature for about a minute.

Later that year, Tombazi wrote a book entitled *Account of a Photographic Expedition to the Southern Glaciers of Kangchenjunga in the Sikkim Himalayas* (London, 1925) and said: "Unquestionably, the figure in outline was exactly like a human being, walking upright and stopping occasionally to uproot or pull at some dwarf rhododendron bushes. It showed up dark against the snow and, as far as I could make out wore no clothes."[4, 9]

But before he could take a photograph, the hairy apeman disappeared. Tombazi left the team to check out the terrain, and discovered in the snow 15 footprints from one and a half to two feet apart, "…similar in shape to those of a man, but only six to seven inches long by four inches wide at the broadest part of the

155

foot. The marks of five distinct toes and the instep were perfectly clear, but the trace of the heel was indistinct… the prints were undoubtedly those of a biped." Later, the local people told Tlombazi the creature he described was a "Kanchenjunga demon."[4, 9]

Today, much of the area now lies within the

An illustration of a yeti attack from a 1950s French magazine.

156

Kanchenjunga National Park. This park is one of the most important in the Indian Himalayas and also embraces the gigantic Zemu glacier which comes off of the east side of the mountain. Sprawled across an area of 850 sq km, is the largest wildlife reserve in Sikkim, a state of India.

Most of this steep, jungle-forest and mountain park has not been explored yet, and it could harbor numerous unknown animals. In order to explore this vast park, it is necessary to obtain a permit and fulfill other formalities, which are required by the government of Sikkim. The park and surrounding area is teaming with wildlife such as the Snow Leopard, Himalayan Black Bear, Tibetan Antelope, Wild Ass, Barking Deer, Musk Deer, Flying Squirrel, Clouded Leopard, Blue Sheep, Himalayan Thar, Tibetan Wolf, Serow, Great Tibetan Sheep, Red Panda and many other animals—including various versions of the yeti, say the locals.

The name Kanchenjunga (the old spelling of the mountain was Kangchenjunga, and sometimes Kanchendzonga) literally means 'the Abode of Gods consisting of Five Treasure Houses.' These five treasure houses signify the five lofty peaks that comprises Mt. Kanchenjunga: Mt. Narshing, Mt. Pandim, Mt. Siniolchu, Mt. Simvo and Mt. Kabru. An aura of mystery hangs over the Kanchenjunga massif, and the lore that surrounds it including the legends of yetis as well as tales of hidden caves that are said to be entrances to the underground world of Shambala or Agartha.[57,58]

157

As early as 1832, the British became aware of some sort of apeman-monster when B.H. Hodson, the British representative in Nepal, reported that somewhere in eastern Nepal his servants had been attacked by a monkey-demon known as the *rakshas*, a Nepali-Sanskrit word for "demon."

Then, in 1914 a British forestry officer stationed in Sikkim named J.R.P. Gent wrote of discovering huge footprints made by some large creature that clearly frightened his local work crew and guides. Though he did not state it, he was probably told that the prints had been made by Kanchenjunga Demons.

One of these "demons" actually saved the life of a British Raj official according to the man's own report. In 1938 Captain d'Auvergue, curator of Calcutta's Victoria Memorial, was traveling alone in the Himalayas when he became injured. He was struggling over a high pass along the Sikkim-Tibetan border when a blizzard struck the pass. He was partially snow-blind from traveling over brightly lit snowfields earlier, and with the blizzard surrounding him, he lost his way and collapsed in the snow. He would have died of exposure during the blizzard, he related, except that a 9-foot (3 meter) yeti saved his life by covering Captain d'Auvergue with his giant body during the worst of the storm. Later d'Auvergue recovered sufficiently and as the storm subsided, he got a sense of his surroundings and was able to make it down from the high pass.

In one version of this story, the giant apeman actually took d'Auvergue some distance to a cave

158

where he was fed scraps of food and nursed back to health over a period of several days. Like many of the older tales of the yeti, this one has gotten a bit confused over time.

Chinese drawing of a yeti.

A Mummified Yeti?

The kind and nurturing version of the Kanchenjunga Demon was soon dispelled, however, when a Norwegian mineral expert named Jan Frostis claimed that he had been was attacked by two yetis while searching for uranium in 1948. Frostis claimed that while hiking alone in the Kanchenjunga area, looking for the valuable element, he accidentally stumbled onto two yetis near what is called Zemu Gap, along the Sikkim-Nepal border. The terrified Frostis fought the two apemen off and made it back to Gangtok where doctors saw that his shoulder was badly mangled and he required extensive stitches and medical treatment to recover from the lesions. This experience of Frostis' was apparently the origin of the popular expression, "yetis ripped my flesh."

In 1955, the bestselling book *The Long Walk* was published, which chronicled the 1942 experiences of Slavomir Rawicz and six companions in escaping from a Russian Siberian WWII concentration camp.

159

The seven men were attempting to get to freedom in India, and over many months walked south through Mongolia, the Gobi Desert and Tibet. Rawicz describes a curious incident where, near the end of their extraordinary trek, they were attempting to cross a pass somewhere near the border of Sikkim and Bhutan (he reckoned) when he and his companions were blocked from approaching the top of the pass by two giant apemen that he estimated as being about eight feet tall. Rawicz claimed that they watched the two yetis from a distance of about 100 yards for nearly two hours. Eventually the abominable snowmen left the area and Rawicz and his group were able to proceed south. They were eventually captured by a troop of Gurkas working for the British Raj and taken to Calcutta. Rawicz says he eventually went to Iraq and rejoined the Polish army.

While Rawicz's story seems to provide more evidence of the reality of the yeti, and it happened in the vicinity of Kanchenjunga, it is now often thought of as a hoax story. Rawicz may have been capitalizing on the fame of the Eric Shipton footprint of 1951. Perhaps his publishers had desired an abominable snowman episode for Rawicz's book in order for it to become the bestseller that it did indeed become. Shipton, Peter Fleming, the Tibetanologist Hugh Richardson and others have doubted the book's accuracy.

Rawicz's book is exciting enough without any embellishment, and still remains a classic among stories of astonishing survival and bizarre epic journeys. Perhaps, the discrediting of the story was a function of the times. As we have seen in the case of Edmund Hillary and others, while it was fashionable to believe in the yeti in the 1950s and 60s, it became unfashionable to believe in them in the late 70s and 80s; former believers and witnesses changed their stories so as not to appear gullible or dimwitted.

In a bizarre twist to the amazing tale of *The Long Walk, Wikipedia* reports that in May of 2009, Witold Ginski, a Polish veteran of WWII living in the UK, made the claim to the press that the story was true but that it was actually his story, and not that of Rawicz. Apparently none of the men mentioned in the story were ever contacted, if they could have been, and the tale seems to be a mixture of fact and fiction.

In the 1950s, other strange yeti stories came from the area. The British anthropologist Myra Shakley relates that in 1958, Tibetan villagers from Tharbaleh, near the Rongbuk Glacier came upon a drowned yeti. They described the creature as being like a small man with a pointed head and covered with reddish-brown fur.[13]

Shakley also mentions that in May of 1957, the Kathmandu *Commoner* carried a story about a yeti head that had been kept for 25 years in the village of Chilunka, about 50 miles northeast of Kathmandu. The head reportedly had been severed from the corpse of a yeti slain by Nepali soldiers, who had hunted down the creature after it had killed many of their comrades. She then makes a curious note about another specimen, relating that Chemed Rigdzin

161

Dorje, a Tibetan lama, spoke of the existence of a complete mummified yeti.[13]

Wow! Not just a hand, foot or scalp, but an entire mummified yeti! Pretty exciting, and, as pointed out earlier, the DNA from mummified parts of genuine yetis could be used to clone a living, but captive yeti—shades of Mighty Joe Young! Somehow scientists would probably not let such an experiment as this pass by if they were given a chance to obtain DNA from a mummified yeti. Perhaps it has happened already.

That some remote monastery somewhere in the vast reaches of Tibet has a mummified yeti does not seem especially strange. If yetis are real, then their interaction with humans in Tibet and elsewhere must have been going on for many thousands of years. There should be dead yetis, mummified yeti parts, yeti paintings, stories and such. And, indeed there are. An entire mummified yeti has so far not surfaced, but a careful search for the possible location, starting with lama Chemed Rigdzin Dorje and where he lived, might ultimately produce the extremely valuable artifact.

The Yeti Lonely Hearts Club

Nepali authors dimonstrate that there is a great deal of lore associated with the yeti, recounting many tales. The yeti is said to sometimes invade monasteries or remote mountain villages. Monks at Thyangboche

Monastery, near Mount Everest, claim that a creature, described as a yeti, came out of the forest and loitered around the wall of the monastery. Monks threw food at it, and it became something of a begging nuisance. Finally, the Head Lama ordered it driven away, so the monks got out their cymbals, gongs and horns, and drove the creature back into the forests.

Yetis, with their great strength and somewhat curious behavior, are believed to be quite dangerous, though they generally avoid humans. Many Sherpas and Tibetans feel that it is extremely bad luck to meet a yeti, and that just to look at one can mean death. Veteran cryptozoologist John Keel reports that, in 1949, newspapers in India carried a story of a Sherpa herdsman named Lakhpa Tensing who was said to have been torn apart by a yeti in the bleak pass of Nangpala near Nanga Parbat. This is one of the highest mountain passes in the world, far beyond the reach of most animals and rarely visited by humans.[54]

One might imagine the life of a yeti to be a lonely one. As might be expected, there are a number of tales of lonely and amorous yetis kidnapping humans to be their mates. Such tales are also told of bigfoot in the Pacific Northwest of the United States and Canada.

One well publicized tale was told in 1968 by an old Buddhist nun named Noma Dima. This story was published in Nepali newspapers of the time and retold in such books as *On the Yeti Trail*.[2] All direct quotes in the following paragraphs are taken from the book.

Noma Dima was from a Sherpa family who lived at a remote monastery named Tang-Burje in

163

the Khumbu Himal near Mount Everest. According to Noma Dima's story, her father had died within a week of her birth and her mother had brought her at a young age to the monastery at Tang-Burje (apparently in the early part of the 20th century).

At 17, she was fetching water from a stream for the monastery when she was abducted by a male yeti. "Just when I got ready to return a fifth time with my load, somebody at my back lifted me up bodily. I felt hard, rough hair grazing my neck and cheeks. As I cast a glance behind, I was dumbfounded at the sight of a ghastly monster. It was a blood-curdling experience. I lost my power to speak or cry aloud. Within moments, I fell unconscious and I can hardly recollect how long I remained in a stupor."

༄ —ᨑᨑᨑ— ༄

I Married a Yeti

The yeti eventually took her to a cave that was hidden by thick bushes. The cave was small and natural with the bones of various animals and a strong stench. The yeti warmed her at night by sleeping beside her and fed her small frogs he had collected plus some wild fruits.

"I barely had an appetite due to nervousness and fear," said Noma, "Nevertheless, I ate a few fruits. Apparently, this cheered my captor. He did not go out. Throughout the day and the following night, he kept pressing me against his hard, hairy chest. By the next dawn, I had become the unwed wife of my

164

abductor, who was a yeti."

In describing the creature, part animal and part man, she is quoted as saying, "The creature was exceptionally tall, taller than any man I have ever seen. He walked on two legs that were shorter in proportion to his huge frame. His feet were not too large and his toes grew far apart. The hands were abnormally long and they touched his knees when he stood erect. His head was unusually small as compared to his huge frame, and rose like a coconut shell from the middle of the forehead (in other words, a pointed scalp). But for his face and palms, hands and feet, his entire body was covered with a long, thick overgrowth of hair. With his sharp and long nails, big teeth set on a sturdy jaw, he could tear animals asunder in no time. While walking, he stood erect on two legs like a human being, but while climbing a steep rock or a snow covered mountain, he used all fours like a monkey. He could climb steep rocks with unimaginable ease and speed. He could leap very high, very wide."

During the winter, the Yeti would turn over huge boulders in the frozen streams and collect frogs. He took Noma on excursions by carrying her piggyback and leaping with ease from rock to rock. Once he spied a bull yak roaming below them on ranges that were relatively free of snow, and had her witness his match of strength with the bull.

"As he stood close to the bull, the creature gave a shrill, yelling cry. Before the bull could get ready, the yeti clutched both his horns. The bull and yeti were engaged in a duel for a few minutes. Whenever

165

the bull tried to raise its head, the yeti forced it down with intense pressure. After a few minutes of trial of strength between the two, the yeti pulled the beast towards a big rock standing behind him. Pulling the bull near its chest, he gave a violent jerk which repulsed it several yards back. Its horns now freed, the bull paused a while and the next moment made a terrible charge at the yeti. For a split second, the creature stood motionless till the bull reached within a yard of his arms. He now swiftly stepped aside with the result that the bull's head was dashed against the rock. The bull was dead in no time. The yeti now asked me to come down. When I reached the bull, I found its head cracked into two pieces. Both of us shared a meal of its brain and left the rest for other creatures."

After about a year she had morning sickness, as she was now pregnant with a half-human, half-yeti child. She ate little and craved fried bread. One day the yeti left and was gone all night. She sat up in the cave all night out of fright. "Next morning I saw two figures in the distant snowscape taking big strides toward the cave. When both came close, I saw two yetis, but the stranger who came was totally different from my captor. The visitor had long breasts loosely dangling over her nape. It was an aged she-yeti. She spent nearly half an hour examining my body before she went back. When my captor returned after seeing off the visitor, he brought along a few bunches of berries. I relished their sour taste."

In the afternoon the yeti bade her to follow him.

"After a three-hour walk, I realized that my village was near at hand. I could recognize it from the colorful banners fluttering on poles around the monastery."

The yeti gestured that he wanted her to return to her village and that he would visit her. Noma found her mother cooking dinner when she entered her home. "She was stunned to see me attired in deerskin. I narrated to her the entire sequence of my bizarre adventures with the grotesque biped of the snowland."

Noma says she gave birth to a boy some six months later. Long hair covered his entire body and though he looked a great deal like a human he had the face of a monkey. Along with his broad chest he had short legs and long arms. "During this entire period," says Noma, "its father repeatedly called on me, exercising utmost caution to escape the notice of villagers. He would sneak in whenever my mother was away. With his strong sense of hearing, he perceived the sound of footsteps of the approaching person and fled before anyone could enter our home."

She warned her yeti "husband" not to come to

World Weekly News headline.

167

the village, but he continued to make the trips. He would bring fruit for Noma and his son but was afraid of fire and lamps.

After some time it became known that her son was part yeti and that Noma had been kidnapped by one of the fearsome creatures. The Head Lama of the monastery, where Noma continued to work, had no objection to her employment and recalled several instances of childbirth from the yeti's union with human females. Also, he was aware of the popular superstition that an untimely end awaited anyone who saw a yeti.

This 1968 retelling of an event many decades before (I will guess that this happened around 1910) underlines that the superstition of "bad luck" being associated with a yeti was a genuine custom in the Himalayas. Apparently, contact with half man-half yetis was also bad luck.

A few years went by and the young yeti-manchild would sometimes have problems with other children. The villagers feared that the presence of the young half-yeti would bring calamity on the village, and indeed, the crops for the last three years had been poor. The father yeti was seen by a Sherpa one night which sent a panic through the high mountain village.

Noma tried to warn the yeti not to return, but nevertheless he returned one night. She told him to leave but he refused to depart before holding his son as he always did. He had already been spotted by the villagers and soon an angry mob, weapons in hand and torches lit, cornered him near Noma's house.

Though he was not afraid of their weapons, the torches frightened him and he sustained heavy injuries as the villagers flung spears and kukri knives at him. In a bid to escape he jumped into a crevasse on the edge of town, falling down a virtual cliff from a great height. The villagers were now reassured that the yeti must have died in such a fall.

Noma believed that her yeti-husband must be dead but he returned to her two weeks later, dropping silently into the room which she shared with the boy. He caressed her face and kissed the sleeping child. He had been cut and burned by the villagers, plus one of his legs was now crippled from his leap into the crevasse.

Noma relates the sad ending to her story: the yeti had wanted to take his son with him but Noma refused to release him to the life of a yeti. The yeti remained sitting for some time and then got up to leave. He kissed her and picked the boy up in his arms. Suddenly he tore the boy into bits, leaving a small heap of flesh and bones.

"Before I could utter a word, he rushed out. I had lost both my son and husband. The following morning brought the news that the charred, dead body of a yeti bearing many marks of burns and stab injuries had been found in the stream below the village."[2]

Yeti Sightings of the 1970s

Yetis hit newspapers around the world in July of 1974 when the Nepalese and Indian newspapers carried stories about a yeti that had attacked and killed some yaks between the in the Khumjung area of Nepal (near Mount Everest and the Arun Valley).

The story was eventually carried in the *International Herald Tribune* on July 23, 1974. The entire report read as follows: "A 19-year old Sherpa woman says she encountered the Abominable Snowman while she was tending a herd of yaks in the Himalayan district of Khumbu. RSS, the Nepalese news agency, said that the woman, whose name was not given, was knocked unconscious by the creature, said to be one and half meters tall and hairy. It then killed three yaks."

The Sherpani's name was actually known: she was Lhakpa Dolma, aged 19, of Khumjung village near Everest, who was tending yaks alone in a remote pasture named Machermo, near Gokyo, when she heard the sound of coughing. Looking around she suddenly saw a huge monkey-like creature.

According to Lhakpa Dolma, the yeti was about one and half meters tall (five feet) and incredibly strong, with a dark complexion, deep-set eyes, a wrinkled forehead and thick, stout fingers and long nails. While the upper part of the body was covered with brown hair, the lower half had a darker tinge. The yeti walked on two feet and on all fours, though it was slower when walking on all fours.

The creature seized her and carried her to a nearby stream where he dumped her in a steep depression

170

A Buddhist lama holds the Pangboche yeti scalp and hand, circa 1960.

along the banks. She was shocked but not hurt.

For the next half hour, she watched in horror as the yeti attacked the yaks, punching them and twisting their horns to break their necks. The yeti killed and ate the brains of three yaks, taking away a portion of one of the yaks. Some of the other yaks were also injured. Other people arrived from Khumjung the next morning and found the dead yaks and stunned girl. The Sherpas put rocks over footprints to preserve them.

The police from Namche Bazaar came to investigate the incident, making it the first yeti story that was officially investigated by the Nepalese government. Inspector Ramji Bahadur Khatri of Namche Bazaar sent officer-detective Chatra Man Rai to investigate the incident. Rai arrived five days after the incident and was shown the footprints surrounded by stones and took photographs and sketches of the prints. The footprints were approximately 31 centimeters long and 10 centimeters wide.

No firm conclusion was reached by the Nepalese authorities although, according to Kesar Lall, it was reported in the *Nepal Conservation Society* newsletter, that "the people involved have no ulterior motive in creating a hoax. In fact, if the Yeti is a living creature the *prima facie* evidence from the incident at Machermo would constitute ample proof of its presence there on July 11, 1974."

On March 27, 1975 *The Rising Nepal* reported that a trekker from Poland had encountered a yeti in February. Polish trekker Janus Tomaszczuk was

172

with two friends on the Everest trail going up to the highest, most remote yak huts and small lodges. His knee had become swollen and his friends had gone on ahead of him to the Everest camp of Lobuche. He tried to make it to the high camp of Lobuche, but his swollen knee was disturbing him so he decided to turn back to the small settlement of Pheriche back down the trail. However, his knee became worse and it was beginning to get dark. A cold wind was blowing and he collapsed onto the trail in exhaustion, climbing into his sleeping bag and sleeping among the boulders along the trail.

At about 7:30 that evening it was quite dark, except for the gleam of the snow high up on the mountains around him. Then, for a few fleeting moments, he thought he saw a man moving swiftly about 50 meters away. Without thinking, he called out, "Hello! Can you help me? I am here."

There was no answer. The creature swiftly walked away, swinging its long arms. It then occurred to Janus that it might be a yeti and he felt a chill down his spine. But he was too exhausted to flee so he lay there in his sleeping bag wondering if he would be attacked later by an abominable snowman.

The morning came and Tomaszczuk returned down the trail to Pheriche where no one knew of any persons passing that way the night before, which confirmed his suspicions. He returned to Kathmandu where his yeti sighting was published in the newspaper and other publications, thereby joining the lengthy history of yeti lore.[1]

173

☙ ——— ❧

The 1986 Yeti Photo

One of the only known photos of a yeti was taken by a man named Anthony B. Wooldridge in 1986 while trekking in the Arun Valley area of eastern Nepal. Wooldridge told newspaper reporters he had photographed a yeti and provided them with a picture that briefly made news around the world.

Wooldridge claimed that in March of 1986, he arrived at a steep snowfield shortly after an avalanche had swept along the field and wiped out the trail in front of him. He then spotted the dark figure of a yeti in the distance. He took the photo across the snowfield. Wooldridge later concluded, after much ridicule that it was "probably a rock."[24]

The September 1986 issue of *BBC Wildlife Magazine* carried the story. Said the magazine:

> When, in early March of this year, Tony Wooldridge first saw fresh animal tracks on the slopes of the snow on either side of him, the thought of a yeti did briefly cross his mind, but only as a funny idea. He was, of course, in the same general part of the western Himalayas where, in 1937, H W Tilman followed a set of large ape-like footprints for more than a mile, and where, in 1976, Peter Boardman and Joe Tasker emerged from their tent on a morning

174

The 1986 photo by Anthony Wooldridge of the "yeti" seen in lower right.

after a night disturbed by unidentifiable low growls to discover that, whatever the thing was that had kept them awake, it had apparently—and this may have been what the growling was about—scoffed 36 Mars bars complete with wrappers before wandering off ahead of a wake of tracks very much like the ones Tilman had found.

Other mountaineers had also had food go missing in this neighborhood, and Wooldridge, who was the first person to have passed through this valley since the autumn snows, was vaguely aware of such stories. Nevertheless, if there is anything that always happens to someone else, it is an encounter with a legendary animal, and after a quick smile at the yeti idea, Wooldridge forgot it. There are lots of interesting sights to be seen in these mountains, and the last thing you need to do up here, especially if you are

175

alone, is to fantasize.

Unlike most Westerners who come to the Himalayas, Wooldridge was not a trekker, a tourist or a climber. He was there as a charity fund-raiser. In ordinary life he is a physicist who does research and development for the CEGB in Manchester [UK], and he has been on walking and climbing trips to the

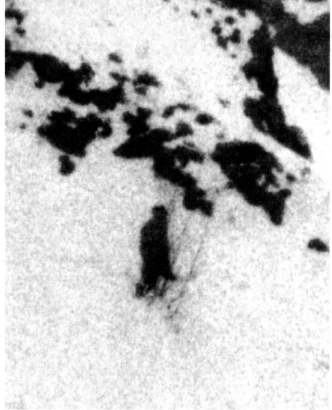

Close-up of the "yeti" in Wooldridge's 1986 photo.

Alps and the Andes, but on this occasion he was on a 200-mile sponsored solo run for an organization called Traidcraft, which promotes trade, intermediate technology and fair pay and conditions in Third World countries, including India. He was staying mainly in the 1,800 m. high town of Joshimath, north-east of Delhi and not far from the Tibetan and Nepalese borders, and was ranging out from there in different directions through the high valleys, over a day or two days or three days. Each day he would set himself a goal and try to run to it in time to run back either to Joshimath or to another, outlying base before nightfall.

It was eleven o'clock on the morning of the fifth day out when he saw the footprints. He had run from Govind Ghat, a village north of Joshimath, to a couple of empty bungalows known as Gangaria and was now trying to reach the closed end of the highest valley he'd gone through so far, about 4,000 metres.

At 3,300 metres he saw the footprints and was struck by their clarity, smiled at the idea of a yeti and then wondered what really might have left them. "I thought it was probably some sort of large langur monkey, because there were a lot of them about, lower down. Between Govind Ghat and Gangaria there were a lot of colonies of them. And I do remember reassuring myself that it didn't look like a big cat... snow leopards are the only thing I had

177

been told were in the area."

… Then, a little farther on—it was about noon by now—he heard a crash and what he describes as a long rumbling. "My first reaction was that's an awful avalanche somewhere. And then I thought, no it can't be because nowhere around could I see any sign of any snow movement. Maybe I was trying to rationalize it to myself. I don't know. I put it down to soldiers in the valley dynamiting for roads." He pressed on up the slope, which seemed suddenly to get much steeper. It was also as the sun was shining on it, getting warmer and making Wooldridge very nervous. And then, sure enough, stretching across his path was the sweep of debris of a freshly fallen avalanche. "I think now, with hindsight, that this was the noise I heard. I went across the next 50 yards or so to get to another spot where the slope evened out so I could get a good view of it and try to work out where it started, what had started it and what the risks were of something else happening.

"The thing that really caught my eye was this great big smooth slide in the snow as if some pretty heavy rock had slid down it." But there was no rock. Where the rock should have been or where signs that the rock had bounced away should have been, there was nothing—except "tracks leading away right from the base of the snow slide across the slope behind

178

a little shrub and beyond it. And right behind the shrub was a shape that couldn't have been a rock."

In an unpublished written account of the incident, Wooldridge describes this shape as "a dark, hairy creature perhaps up to two meters [six feet] in height, standing erect on two legs. It had a squarish head and long powerfully built torso." In talking about it, he also mentions knee-length arms with brown hair on them.

Edward W. Cronin, in his book *The Arun: A natural history of the world's deepest valley*, compiles all of the remarkably consistent recent eyewitness accounts of the yeti into this description: "Its body is stocky, apelike in shape with a distinctly human quality to it, in contrast to that of a bear. It stands five and a half to six feet tall and is covered with short coarse hair, reddish-brown to black in color sometimes with white patches on the chest. The hair is longest on the shoulders. The face is hairless and rather flat. The jaw is robust, the teeth are quite large, though fangs are not present and the mouth is wide. The shape of the head is conical with a pointed crown. The arms are long, reaching almost to the knees. The shoulders are heavy and hunched. There is no tail." (*BBC Wildlife Magazine*, Sept. 1986)

However, Wooldridge was later to retract his statements; even though he apparently believed in the

179

yeti, he decided that what he had photographed was probably a rock, even though he could not find that rock. After returning to the site in 1987, Wooldridge wrote a letter to the British journal *Cryptozoology,*[105] which published excerpts in a 1987 article:

> The bush in the 1986 photos was still there; the Yeti wasn't; the snow was somewhat deeper. Wooldridge and some companions took more pictures of the site:
> "Stereo pairs of photos taken in 1987 have been used to produce a three dimensional map of the terrain near the bush. When this is used to derive an absolute scale for pairs of photos from 1986, it shows that, whatever I photographed in 1986, lies below the snow level in the 1987 photos. The object is leaning slightly uphill, and no movement can be detected when comparing photos taken at different times in 1986. The apparent change in position relative to the bush in some photos taken from different camera positions is caused by parallax. This evidence demonstrates beyond a reasonable doubt that, what was believed to be a stationary, living creature was, in reality, *a rock.*"[105]

So, was this rare still-photo of a yeti actually of a rock? We will probably never know. It seems unlikely that someone would photograph what they thought was an animal and then decide later that it was a rock, but Wooldridge seems to have been a reluctant yeti

180

Stills from the "Snowwalker Video."

witness from the start. The ridicule that is often heaped upon persons who claim to have encountered a yeti or sasquatch is often so intense that it becomes necessary to back down on the original claim and just let the matter be done with. Often, people just keep quiet about unsettling encounters with these frightening beings, which may well be a good idea in some cases.

One of the things we might conclude is that as high tech digital cameras with powerful zoom lenses, as well as small digital video cameras, become more and more common we will probably get more and more photos of elusive crypto-critters like the yeti.

Video footage of a yeti in Nepal was supposedly taken in 1992 by hikers. The trekkers, who are unnamed, but presumably American, were said to be high in the Himalayas of Nepal (but no specific location is given) where they took an amazing video of an apelike creature walking upright along the slopes.

181

This famous clip, now on Youtube.com and watched by thousands of people, has become known as the "Snow Walker Video." The video starts out with a shaky camera trying to focus on a dark object on a steep snow covered mountainside and then, once the camera stabilizes, it briefly depicts an apelike creature walking on two legs making its way through the snow. A few stills from the 51-second-long video are shown here. The entire video can be seen on the Internet at the Youtube site by doing a search for "Snow Walker Video."

There is also a feature film named *The Snow Walker* that was released in 2003. It is a film about a maverick bush pilot who survives a plane crash in the remote Arctic tundra and walks back to civilization. It has nothing to do with the Youtube video of a yeti.

However, most researchers consider the entire Snow Walker matter to be a hoax, and a sophisticated one at that. According to the website encounterswithbigfoot.com, a site largely dedicated to authentic bigfoot accounts, the "Snow Walker Video" was a hoax made for a Paramount UPN television series called *Paranormal Borderland*. The show ran on the UPN network from March 12 to August 6, 1996. According to encounterswithbigfoot.com, the footage was then purchased by the Fox Network for a program called *The World's Greatest Hoaxes*.

According to encounterswithbigfoot.com, the footage was some "of the most elaborate hoax footage ever produced." It does seem suspicious that the provenance of the video is basically unknown. We are only told that was taken in 1992 in Nepal,

182

but the witnesses are not given, nor any specific location within the vast nation of Nepal. The arms of the creature in the video are unusually long and seem very natural. Perhaps the footage was genuine, but acquired from persons who wished to remain anonymous for any number of reasons. The video footage and stills from the video are very intriguing. It seems to me the film must either be a clever hoax, one pulled off by Hollywood, as suggested, or some of the best footage of a yeti ever taken.

The Migoi of Bhutan

Bhutan seems to be an extremely active yeti area as well. The rugged, remote mountain kingdom contains few roads, with many steep jungle-mountain ravines and gorges. It is an ideal habitat for yetis and stories of them abound in the reclusive Buddhist kingdom, an independent country whose foreign affairs are largely conducted by India.

In the remote eastern area of Bhutan is the important town of Trashigang. Fifty miles east of Trashigang is the Sakteng Wildlife Sanctuary, an official sanctuary for the *migoi*, as yetis are known in Bhutan. The drive from Trashigang to Sakteng entails a rough drive over difficult mountainous terrain, where roads are frequently cut off by boulders. Sakteng Wildlife Sanctuary is an unusual one as it was created to preserve the abominable snowman, probably the only

183

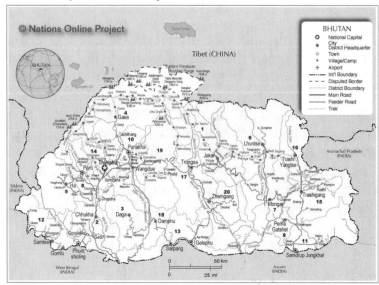

national park in any nation dedicated as a preserve for what many consider a mythical animal. There are many stories and legends about the migoi in the area, and local Bhutanese people insist that there have been many sightings of yetis in this region. At Sakten the migoi is known for its phenomenal strength, magical powers (such as the ability to become invisible) and knowing how to walk backwards to fool any trackers.

The forests of Sakten have not yet been explored fully because foreigners in this region are restricted (as in general in Bhutan) and locals do not venture very far into the jungles. Situated in the easternmost part of the Kingdom, Sakteng Wildlife Sanctuary was declared a protected area in 2003, making it the newest protected area in Bhutan. It sprawls across

650 sq. km., incompassing amazing biodiversity and a variety of intact Himalayan terrestrial ecosystems such as alpine meadows, temperate forests and warm broadleaf forests. Isolated nomadic tribes live in this sanctuary such as the Brokpas. These indigenous tribal people are often reticent and unwilling to interact with outsiders. Bhutan is appropriately called "the hermit kingdom."

The isolation of the Sakteng region causes it to be teeming with rare animals such as Snow Leopards, Red Pandas, Himalayan Black Bear, Barking Deer and Himalayan Red Foxes. The Bhutanese government is slowly allowing more and more tourists into the area, many with the goal of encountering and photographing a yeti.

Kunzang Choden chronicles a number of Bhutanese yeti-migoi tales in her enjoyable book *Bhutanese Tales of the Yeti*.[12] Choden emphasizes the strong belief in these cryptids espoused the Bhutanese people, and several types are recognized. The smaller *mirgola* or *mechume* live in the dense forests of larch, spruce, bamboo and rhododendron and are about a meter (three feet) in height. Says Choden, "On occasions they have been known to grin menacingly and make strange noises; they are said to indulge in mimicry. This aspect of their character has given rise to many tales and legends. It is generally agreed that encountering them is a bad omen, which leads to misfortune and even death in some cases."[12]

Choden mentions that the migoi or *migyur*, the larger of the yetis of Bhutan, are so much a part of the

185

culture and history of Bhutan that some ancient pre-Buddhist Bon rituals call for the use of the "blood of a migoi that has been killed by a sharp weapon."[12]

Some of the stories in her book are similar to ones told in Nepal, though many of the tales are quite unique to Bhutan. Says Choden of the migoi:

> The migoi is known by all accounts to be a very large biped; sometimes as big as "one-and-a-half yaks" or occasionally even as "big as two yaks!" It is covered in hair that ranges in color from reddish-brown to gray-black. Its limbs are ape-like and its face is generally hairless. The female has breasts that sag. They are usually encountered alone or as couples but rarely in groups. We are told that they communicate with each other by whistling and they exude an exceedingly foul odor... It is said to have a hollow back, and as children we were often threatened that if we were naughty we would be carried off in the hollow of the migoi's back. In some parts of Bhutan it is believed that the migoi has a special charm called a *dipshing*, which it conceals under its right arm, and it is this charm that endows the creature with the power to become invisible or visible at will. When we were very young we used to be completely fascinated by the concept of *dipshing* and spent hours on end imagining all the wonderful adventures that we could have if had access to such a charm. This

186

naturally heightened our enchantment with the migoi, the possessor of the *dipshing*.

...Unlike other wild creatures the migoi is apparently not afraid of fire, in fact it is often attracted to it and approaches it seeking warmth. From the stories we hear we know that the migoi live in caves and make nests to keep themselves and their young warm. They are believed to be herbivores, although they are known to kill both humans and animals when provoked or perhaps out of fear and extreme hunger. Apparently the migoi manifests a peculiar eating habit in that it grasps its food in its hands and eats only what protrudes on either side of its fists; the food in its fist is then discarded. People say that there is a wild shallot that the yeti is particularly fond of eating. One can tell that a migoi has been in the vicinity when one finds fistfuls of cast away shallots that have been eaten from both ends.

Chinese drawing of a wildman.

The migoi seem to be extremely curious about human being and perhaps it is this curiosity that often

Three Bhutanese postage stamps showing migoi or yeti (male).

makes them vulnerable to human tricks and treachery, sometimes costing them their lives.

Choden tells 21 tales of the migoi in her book, and each has its own curious twist or surprising ending. Many seem to be old tales meant to teach about the habits of the yeti, while others seem to be stories of genuine encounters with a yeti. One familiar tale that also illustrates the copycat tendencies of yetis is of a young Bhutanese girl in a remote area of northern Bhutan who is searching for her younger brother who has not returned to their remote yak pastures at a place called Goelak. She is forced to spend the night in a cave in which a yeti happens to live.

When the yeti returns to the cave, she realizes her predicament, and while speaking in a friendly manner to the yet, she starts a fire in the cave. With the yeti watching her from the other side of the fire, she boils water in a pot and then makes the popular tsampa barley dough by mixing flour in the boiling water and allowing it to cook. Then she fills a ball of dough with yak butter and eats it. She then gives it to the yeti, who imitates her. They eat several of the buttery dough balls and then the girl takes the yak butter and rubs it on her arms and legs. The yeti does the same,

Three more Bhutanese postage stamps showing migoi or yeti (female).

soaking his hairy body in the melted butter. Finally, she carefully holds a stick with glowing embers from the fire over her arms to warm them, and the yeti imitates this as well. Unfortunately for the yeti, his buttered arms, legs and stomach catch fire and the poor yeti bursts into flames. The last view that she has of the yeti is as a flaming apeman running in panic into the thick forest at the bottom of the hill.

A similar story of yeti imitation and trickery is told in Nepal concerning the use of the large knives called kukris. When a remote village was losing yaks and other food to a group of yetis that were continually raiding the village at night, the people concocted a plan. Since yetis will imitate humans they decided to have a big party in the late afternoon and drink lots of the local barley beer known as chang. After drinking copious amount the chang, with the yetis watching them secretly from the bushes, the villagers all picked up their kukris and pretended to hack and chop at each other. They then dropped their kukris on the ground and left the large cauldron of chang outside while they retired to their huts and locked the doors and windows. Sure enough, in the morning the villagers discovered a number of dead yetis in the center of the village—they had gotten drunk on the chang and then picked up the kukris and hacked each

189

other to death in imitation of the villagers.

The Bhutanese believe that the yeti is unable to bend its body and stoop beneath a low door. In a popular tale, two yak herders were searching for some lost yaks when they suddenly came across a migoi sleeping near a shallow ravine. They watched in fascination for a few moments and then quietly tried to get beyond the creature. Unfortunately for them, it woke up and chased them down the mountain. But the men were able to stoop beneath a massive tree that had fallen and blocked the only path in the steep area. When the yeti came to the fallen tree, he hit his head on the trunk, and was unable to pass because he could not bend over. Finally the migoi turned to go back to its territory. As the yak herders glanced back one last time, the migoi had suddenly vanished, using it *dipshing* talisman to become invisible.

Choden says, "In most traditional Bhutanese houses, the thresholds are raised and the horizontal upper portion of the frame of the door is very low. Anyone entering through a doorway must bend the head and lift the leg quite high in order to cross over to the other side. These are deliberate architectural designs to keep out spirits who, we believe, can neither bend their heads nor raise their legs to enter a house."[12]

In another tale, this one of a sleeping yeti in the eastern Sakteng area, a yak herder named Brongtsa, while looking for a missing yak in a thicket, came across the yeti, which he at first thought was his missing yak. As the yeti stood up, Brongtsa instinctively shot the yeti with an arrow. Brongtsa realized that he had made

190

a big mistake in shooting the yeti, as there were many taboos against it, but he decided that in order to survive he had better finish the yeti off as best he could. He shot the yeti with a second arrow and the creature dragged itself in agony to a precipice and disappeared.

Choden's entertaining book includes several tales of women being kidnapped by yetis and becoming lovers of the hairy apemen. Also featured in several of the tales is the element of a fight between a yeti and a tiger. In such a titanic struggle of powerful animals, the yeti is the winner.

One thing seems for sure as far as yetis in Bhutan are concerned: there is a strong oral tradition of the existence of these elusive creatures and the people genuinely believe in them. Whether they are real or not, the Bhutanese government has issued a number of stamps featuring the yeti, and like the Nepalese government, continues to promote the existence of the yeti as part of its fledgling tourist program. To keep overly excited foreigners from harming any of the migoi that they might come across while visiting the country, the government has proclaimed them a protected species. Hopefully, with tourists shooting cameras instead of guns, we will get some good photos of the Bhutanese migoi soon for our scrapbooks.

DNA Evidence of a Yeti

In October of 1998 an American climber and skier named Craig Calonica claimed that while part of an

191

expedition to Mt. Everest he saw two yetis (one tends to imagine such a pair as husband and wife) while descending Everest on the northern, Tibetan-Chinese side. Calonica said that the two creatures walked upright and had thick, black shiny fur. Calonica is world-class mountain skier who has skied down some of the most remote and difficult mountain slopes in the world, reached only after weeks of trekking and climbing. He has skied down Everest and other nearby peaks on expeditions in 1981/82, 1996, 1997 and 1998. It was on October 21, 1998 after skiing down the Chinese side of Mt. Everest that he told Reuters news agency that he had seen the two yetis. They were walking on two legs just like humans. Their arms were longer than human arms and they had very big heads.

Said Calonica, "My point was that I saw something and what I saw was not human, that was not a gorilla, not a bear, not a goat, and it was not a deer." He draws the conclusion that it was in fact two yetis. Calonica said that his Nepali cook also saw the yetis as they passed.

Reports like this from seasoned mountaineers should not be dismissed lightly. After all, who would see yetis in the remote areas of the Himalayas but the climbers, guides and cooks that actually visit these inaccessible areas? What is needed to prove the existence of these legendary creatures is photographic evidence and DNA evidence in the form of hair or flesh.

In fact, in the spring of 2001, some very

192

An old photo of an Englishman and some circus giants in India.

Above: An Albrect Durer 1499 paint-
ing of two wildmen or woodwoses. *Top
Right*: A Prussian coat of arms containing
two wildmen. *Right*: "Big Gust" was only
seven and a half feet tall, but was still a
popular giant in his day.

"BIG GUST" 7 FT. 6 IN. TALL.

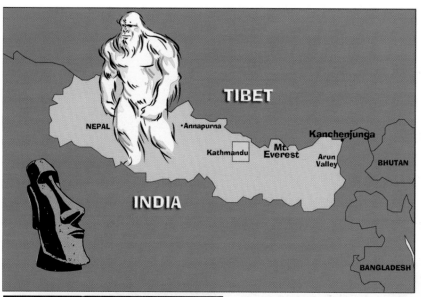

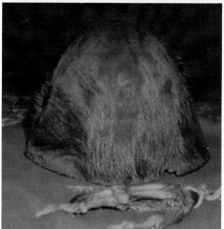

Above: A 1960 photo of the yeti scalp and hand formerly kept at the monastery in Pangboche, Nepal, now missing. *Above Right*: The yeti is pictured as a mystical creature on this trance music CD. *Below Right*: The yeti or migoi is featured on this postage stamp from Bhutan.

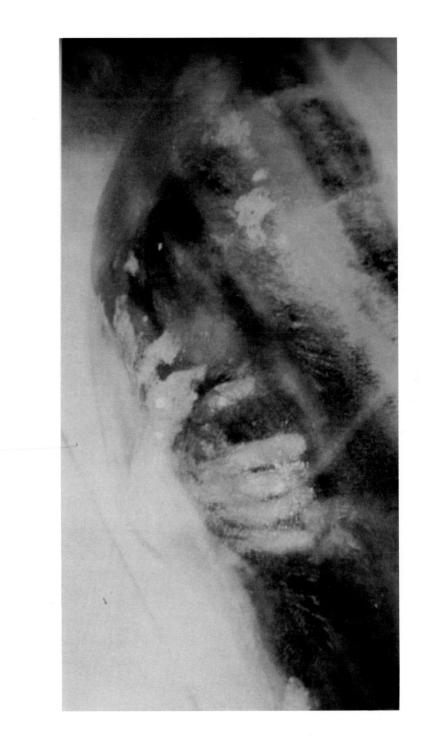

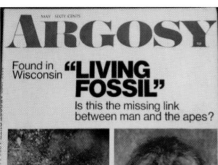

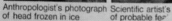
Anthropologist's photograph Scientific artist's r
of head frozen in ice   of probable fea

Left: The cover of the May, 1969 edition of *Argosy* featuring the face of the Minnesota Iceman. *Opposite page*: The Minnesota Iceman in his block of ice. *Above*: A sign on the trail showing the way to the monastery with the yeti scalp. *Below*: The yeti scalp at the monastery in Khumjung can be seen today for a small donation.

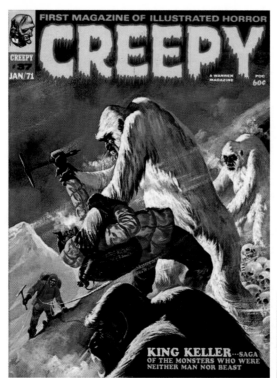

Top: The yeti depicted as savage apemen on the cover of the January, 1971 issue of *Creepy* magazine. *Above*: Two frames from the 1992 Snow Walker video supposedly taken by two American trekkers in Nepal, but thought to be a hoax. *Left*: A postage stamp from Bhutan depicting the famous story of a Bhutanese archer killing a yeti.

Above and Left: Still photos from the 2009 Polish yeti video footage showing a dark, hairy apeman moving about the rocks. *Below*: Closeup of the oldest known bigfoot photo, taken in the 1940s in the Pacific Northwest. Courtesy of Joe Roberts.

Top: Roger Patterson holds up footprint casts, circa 1968. *Right*: A 1997 photo of a Florida skunk ape. *Below*: A 2000 photo taken in a backyard in Sarasota County, FL.

The cover of the February, 1968 issue of *Argosy* with Patterson's photos.

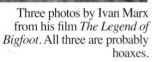

Three photos by Ivan Marx from his film *The Legend of Bigfoot*. All three are probably hoaxes.

Top: One of the photos allegedly taken of bigfoot in November of 1995 by a forest patrol officer from Tacoma, WA. The officer preferred to remain anonymous and presented the photos to Cliff Crook of Bigfoot Central in Bothell, WA. *Left*: One of the photos of bigfoot taken by Ivan Marx, probably a hoax. *Below*: An automatic camera took the so-called Brents-Cam photo, circa 2001.

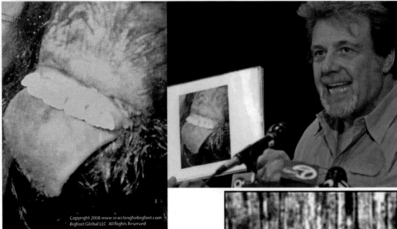

Top: The curious photo allegedly taken of sasquatch in April 2005 by a hidden camera at Moyie Springs in Idaho, near the Canadian border. The circled spot is a piece of bark spit in the air as the creature was apparently eating bark off a tree. *Above Right and Left*: Tom Biscardi of Searching for Bigfoot, Inc. showing a photo of the mouth of a bigfoot at a press conference in August 2008. *Right*: Alleged photo of a Florida skunk ape from the Internet. Date and photographer unknown.

Top Left: Alleged photo of a Florida skunk ape taken on July 8, 2000 by David Shealy in the Big Cypress Swamp. *Top Right and Above*: No information is known about this curious photo that appeared on the Internet that seems to show some sort of ape crouching near a road with an ATV and rider in front. *Left Middle*: A 1997 photo taken by a fire fighter in the Florida Everglades of what he believed was a skunk ape. *Bottom Left*: Alleged photo of a skunk ape from the Internet. Date and photographer unknown.

Opposite and Bottom Right: The interesting photos taken by an anonymous backpacker from Vancouver, WA on Silver Star Mountain in Pifford Pinchot National Forest on Nov. 17, 2005. At first he thought it was a rock, but then it stood up and walked away. *Top*: A photo of a Texas bigfoot given to Donna Shelton at the Kountry Kubbard Restaurant in Lamar, Texas in the summer of 2009.

Top and Left: Two photos of a bigfoot taken near the Hoffstadt Bluffs close to Mount St. Helens on May 9, 2002 and sent to the Bigfoot Researcher Organization (BFRO).

Above: A motion-sensing camera north of Remer, Minnesota took this photograph on Oct. 24, 2009 according to the owner, Tim Kedrowski of Remer. *Left:* On top is the "Backyard Bigfoot" photo taken in Kentucky in 2009. The bottom photo is an enlargement and enhancement of the original photo.

interesting DNA evidence was developed. According to a *Discovery News* article published April 6, 2001, a team working on a documentary for Britain's Channel 4 found a long black hair in the bark of a cedar tree while on location in Bhutan in March. The team was guided by Sonam Dhendup, the King of Bhutan's official yeti hunter for the past 12 years, who took them into a forest where locals claimed to have discovered a piece of a mysterious skin that they thought belonged to a yeti.

British scientists went to work on the samples brought back by the team, comparing extracted DNA to samples from other animals known to be found in Bhutan. The DNA from the long black strand of hair proved impossible to identify. Bryan Sykes, Professor of Human Genetics at the Oxford Institute of Molecular Medicine, one of the world's leading experts on DNA analysis, and the first to extract genetic material from ancient bones said, "We found some DNA in it, but we don't know what it is. It's not a human, not a bear nor anything else we have so far been able to identify. It's a mystery and I never thought this would end in a mystery. We have never encountered DNA that we couldn't recognise before."

Discovery News reported that in the side of the cedar tree, an evolutionary biologist from the University of Oxford named Rob McCall, found scratch marks resembling those made by claws. McCall said he saw odd footprints nearby that were only a couple of hours old. He said that they showed

193

a short print with a narrow heel and toe pads.

In the Channel 4 documentary, one yeti eyewitness—a former royal guard called Druk Sherrik—described his encounter with the migyur, or yeti: "It was huge. It must have been nine feet tall. The arms were enormous and hairy. The face was red with a nose like a chimpanzee."

Unfortunately, exciting evidence like this is quickly ignored and forgotten. Here is what appears to be the strong evidence for the yeti that has been hoped for—the "smoking gun": the hair of an unidentifiable animal found in a place packed with many tales of the yeti!

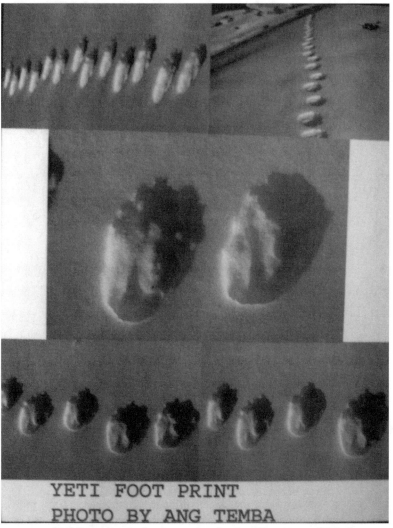

Yeti footprints in the snow taken by Ang Tempa near Makalu.

Artist's drawing of early Mongol yeti reports.

CHAPTER 6

THE YETI IN TIBET, MONGOLIA AND RUSSIA

Whatever you can do, or dream you can do, begin it.
Boldness has genius, power, and magic in it.
Begin it now.
—*William Hutchinson Murray* (1913-1996)
The Scottish Himalayan Expedition

꽃 —ᴠᴠᴠ— 꽃

The yeti is known throughout the Tibetan plateau
and into the Trans-Himalaya regions of the Kun Lun
Mountains and Altai Himalaya. In Mongolia he is
known by the name "wildman" or "wild people" —
almas (singular) or in other dialects, *almasty* or
almasti. The most common name in Tibet for the
yeti is *dremo*. In eastern Tibet, near Bhutan, they are
called *nydag shidag*, and are thought to be guardians

of certain areas.[12]

Apes do not live in the high plateau mountain regions of Tibet, Mongolia, Russia and Central Asia, so the yetis of this region have usually been associated with wildmen, rather than with some sort of giant ape, as in Nepal, Bhutan and Southeast Asia. Almases are usually described as human-like with their bodies covered with reddish-brown hair. They are said to be between five and six and a half feet tall, with anthropomorphic facial features including a pronounced browridge, flat nose, and a weak chin. In many ways they are identical to the yeti.

The main source for incidents concerning almases is British anthropologist Myra Shackley's 1983 book *Still Living?* Shackley chronicled a number of fascinating incidents and had good access to the many Russian sources on the almas. Shackley speculated that these creatures might be the remnants of Neanderthals who had survived over the past 20,000 years, hence the title: *Still Living?*[13]

༃ —w— ༃

In Search of the Almas

According to Shackley, the first report of the almas is the astonishing tale of Hans Schiltenberger who, in the 15th century, was captured by the Turks and sent to the court of Tamerlane, who placed him in the retinue of a Mongol prince named Egidi. After returning to Europe in 1427, Schiltenberger wrote about his experience. In his 1430 book, he described

198

獲圖

Chinese drawing of a wildman.

猩
猩
圖

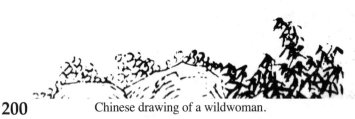

200   Chinese drawing of a wildwoman.

creatures that came from some mountains, apparently the Tien Shan range in Mongolia:

> The inhabitants say that beyond the mountains is the beginning of a wasteland which lies at the edge of the earth. No one can survive there because the desert is populated by so many snakes and tigers. In the mountains themselves live wild people, who have nothing in common with other human beings. A pelt covers the entire body of these creatures. Only the hands and face are free of hair. They run around in the hills like animals and eat foliage and grass and whatever else they can find. The lord of the territory made Egidi a present of a couple of forest people, a man and a woman. They had been caught in the wilderness, together with three untamed horses the size of asses and all sorts of other animals which are not found in German lands and which I cannot therefore put a name to.[13]

Shackley found Schiltenberger's account especially credible for two reasons: "First, Schiltenberger reports that he saw the creatures with his own eyes. Secondly, he refers to Przewalski horses, which were only rediscovered by Nicholai Przewalski in 1881... Przewalski himself saw 'wildmen' in Mongolia in 1871."

The American Tibetologist W. Rockhill wrote of his 1886 journey into Tibet in his book *The Land of the*

Lamas.[75] In it he refers to Przewalski's 1871 account of seeing wildmen in the remote area where he also discovered the famous primitive horse. Przewalski called the wildmen *kung guressu*, or "man beast." Rockhill also heard of stories of these primitive men from the lamas. Says Rockhill of one story told to him by a lama:

Several times, he said, his party had met hairy savages, with long, tangled locks falling around them like cloaks, naked, speechless beings, hardly human... This story of hairy savages I had often heard from Tibetans, while at Peking.[75]

Later Rockhill says that a Mongolian reported to him that he had seen a certain area that had "innumerable herds of wild yak, wild asses, antelopes and geresun bamburshe. This expression means literally 'wild men.'" Rockhill muses that the wildmen might actually be bears, and notes that such legends were common in the Middle Ages, and that they derived from the worship of bears. However, at the end of his book he recounts a story of "men in a primitive state of savagery" who are very hairy, wear primitive garments made of skin and probably live in caves.[75, 64]

The famous mountaineer Reinhold Messner also concluded that the yeti was actually the Himalayan Black Bear in his 1998 book *My Quest for the Yeti.*[91] Messner said he had been fascinated by the yeti

202

Mongolian drawing of a wildman.

since 1986, when he encountered a dark figure in the Himalayas one night and discovered a strange footprint the next day. He said that he had been searching for the elusive animal since that time, even asking the Dalai Lama about the yeti. He concluded at the end, however, that the yeti is not some apeman at all, but a Himalayan bear, or Tibetan bear—the *chemo*—which sometimes walks on two feet, as do all bears.

Messner does recount an interesting tale, which he calls "unbelievable," that his Balti porter told him in the Karakoram Mountains, bordering western Tibet and Kashmir, of a girl who was abducted by a *dremo* or yeti:

> A long time ago, a dremo abducted a girl in Hushe and carried her off to a cave, where he held her captive and fed her. Her brothers looked for her but couldn't find her. Years later, the family's dog found the cave and the girl. When the dog brought the girl's necklace back to the village, her family immediately recognized it. The brothers followed the dog to the cave, where they found their sister and wanted to take her back to the village. Six or seven years had passed since her abduction, and she now had two yeti babies and didn't want to go back to the village. But the brothers forced her to come with them and carried her babies in a basket. When they crossed the glacial torrent near the village, they stopped

204

in the middle of the bridge and dropped the children into the water. The woman became frantic, sobbed, wanted to return to her cave, but they wouldn't let her go. A few days later a dremo appeared, obviously looking for her. The village hunted him down and shot him. The woman died shortly thereafter.[91]

The opinion that the yeti, almas, or Tibetan dremo is actually the chemo-bear of the mountains is sharred by Australian anthropologist Peter Bishop who spends portions of several chapters discussing the yeti and its affect on the early myth making of Tibet in his book *The Sacred Myth of Shangri-La*.[64] Bishop, like Rheinhold Messner, has traveled extensively in Tibet and the Himalayas, but feels that stories of the abominable snowman are just too fantastic to be true, and that the occasional footprint or encounter can be explained by the bears.

Shackley notes a drawing of an almas is found in a 19th-century Mongol compendium of medicines derived from various plants and animals. The text with the

Mongolian drawing of a wildman.

205

illustration is translated as saying, "The wildman lives in the mountains, his origins close to that of the bear, his body resembles that of man, and he has enormous strength. His meat may be eaten to treat mental diseases and his gall cures jaundice."[13]

With Mongolia becoming a client state of the Soviet Union after the Bolshevik Revolution and the death of Bogd Khan, reports of the almasty began reaching Russia. In 1937, Dordji Meiren, a member of the Mongolian Academy of Sciences, saw the skin of an almas in a monastery in the Gobi desert. The lamas were using it as a carpet in some of their rituals. Shackley says, "The hairs on the skin were reddish and curly... The features [of the face] were hairless, the face had eyebrows, and the head still had long disordered hair. Fingers and toes were in a good state of preservation and the nails were similar to human nails."[13]

Shackley was to become friends with the Russian zoologist/cryptozoologist Dmitri Bayanov of the Darwin Museum in Moscow. He wrote the best-known Russian book on yetis and the almas. Bayanov related that in 1963, Ivan Ivlov, a Russian pediatrician, was traveling through the Altai Himalaya in the southern part of Mongolia. Ivlov saw several humanlike creatures standing on a mountain slope. They appeared to be a family group, composed of a male, female and child. Ivlov observed the creatures through his binoculars from a distance of half a mile until they moved out of his field of vision. His Mongolian driver also saw them and said they were

206

common in that area.[13]

After his encounter with the almas family, Ivlov interviewed many Mongolian children, believing they would be more candid than adults. The children provided many additional reports about the almas. For example, one child told Ivlov that while he and some other children were swimming in a stream, he saw a male almas carry a child almas across it.

A significant report came in 1980, when a worker at an experimental agricultural station, operated by the Mongolian Academy of Sciences at Bulgan, encountered the dead body of a wildman. The man said, "I approached and saw a hairy corpse of a robust humanlike creature dried and half-buried by sand. I had never seen such a humanlike being before covered by camel-colour brownish-yellow short hairs and I recoiled, although in my native land in Sinkiang I had seen many dead men killed in battle.

Drawing of a sleeping almas from the early 1900s Russian zoologist Khakhlov.

207

…The dead thing was not a bear or ape and at the same time it was not a man like Mongol or Kazakh or Chinese and Russian. The hairs of its head were longer than on its body."[13]

The Almas of the Pamirs

The Pamir Mountains are a range at the northwestern end of the Himalayan masiff where the Kunlun Mountains of northern Tibet smash into the area just above Pakistan and the Karakoram Mountains. This remote region is where the borders of Tajikistan, China, Kashmir and Afghanistan meet, and this area has been the scene of many almas sightings. In 1925, Mikhail Stephanovitch Topilski, a major general in the Soviet army, led his unit in an assault on an anti-Soviet guerilla force hiding in a cave in the Pamirs. One of the surviving guerillas said that while in the cave he and his comrades were attacked by several apelike creatures. Topilski ordered the rubble of the cave searched, and the body of one such creature was found. Topilski reported:

> At first glance I thought the body was that of an ape. It was covered with hair all over. But I knew there were no apes in the Pamirs. Also, the body itself looked very much like that of a man. We tried pulling the hair, to see if it was just a hide used for disguise, but found that it was the creature's own natural hair. We turned

208

A scene from the 1957 film *The Abominable Snowman* with the body of a yeti.

bare of hair and had callous growths on them. The whole foot including the sole was quite hairless and was covered by hard brown skin. The hair got thinner near the hand, and the palms had none at all but only callous skin.

The colour of the face was dark, and the creature had neither beard nor moustache. The temples were bald and the back of the head was covered by thick, matted hair. The dead creature lay with its eyes open and its teeth bared. The eyes were dark and the teeth were large and even and shaped like human teeth. The forehead was slanting and the eyebrows

209

were very powerful. The protruding jawbones made the face resemble the Mongol type of face. The nose was flat, with a deeply sunk bridge. The ears were hairless and looked a little more pointed than a human being's with a longer lobe. The lower jaw was very massive. The creature had a very powerful chest and well developed muscles... The arms were of normal length, the hands were slightly wider and the feet much wider and shorter than a man's.[13]

In 1957, Alexander Georgievitch Pronin, a hydrologist at the Geographical Research Institute of Leningrad University, participated in an expedition to the Pamirs, for the purpose of mapping glaciers. On August 2, 1957, while his team was investigating the Fedchenko glacier, Pronin hiked into the valley of the Balyandkiik River.

According to Shackley, around midday, he noticed a figure standing on a rocky cliff about 500 yards above him. At first he was surprised, since this area was known to be uninhabited, but then he became frightened as he saw that the creature was not human. It resembled a man but was unusually stooped over. Pronin watched the stocky figure move across the snow, keeping its feet wide apart, and noted that its forearms were longer than a human's plus its body was covered with reddish grey hair. He claimed that he saw the creature again three days later, walking upright. Since this incident, there have

210

been numerous wildman sightings in the Pamirs, and members of various Soviet scientific expeditions have photographed and taken casts of footprints.[13]

Today, Tajikistan is an independent country, having declared independence from the Soviet Union in 1991. The country is still little visited, but is promoted as a beautiful, scenic mountain destination with opportunities for mountaineering, rock climbing, hiking, horse and camel riding—and presumably, yeti and almas hunting. In Tajikistan, the yeti or almas is known as the *golub-yavan* and the *ksy-gyik* in nearby Kazakhstan to the north. South of the Pamirs in Afghanistan and Pakistan they are known as *barmanu*.

In 1992 a yeti-almas expedition into the Pamirs was led by the Russian-French cryptozoologist Dr. Marie-Jeanne Kofman (or Koffmann) and the French cryptozoologist Sylvain Pallix. Kofman and Pallix collected hair samples and droppings, and took photographs and casts of footprints. Kofman described the almas as a large hairy creature weighing as much as 500 pounds that could run at a speed of 40 miles per hour.

World Weekly News headline.

Reports of the Almas from the Caucasus Mountains

Dr. Marie-Jeanne Kofman was also involved in researching the almas or almasty in the Causcasus Mountains west of the Caspian Sea in Armenia and southern Russia and Georgia. She issued a 1984 report in Russian entitled in English, "Brief Ecological Description of the Caucasus Relic Hominoid (Almasti) Based on Oral Reports by Local Inhabitants and on Field Investigations," translated from Russian into English by Dmitri Bayanov. It said in part:

> The following example from my field observations will help illuminate the Almasti's alimentary ways: A section of a corn field where an Almasti "girl," sighted in the vicinity by the locals a short time before, must have been searching for sweet cobs, opening the wrapping leaves and taking a bite here and there, apparently to test the sweetness of the corn, without even tearing some of them off; this allowed us to obtain the creature's tooth line contours of the upper and lower mandibles; left-overs of a rat, having some characteristic peculiarities: the rat had been disemboweled very neatly and expertly, with the tail bitten off; fresh feces consisting almost exclusively of cherry stones, over 160 in all (cherries were not ripe at the time), and "tails," plus

212

some seeds of different plants; a collection of almost fresh but unripe vegetables and fruits lying on a bedding of dry grass inside a low grotto rather difficult of access: the collection contained: eight potatoes, three apples, two small pumpkins, a half-nibbled corncob, a half-eaten sunflower center, some dog rose berries, plus four round pellets of horse dung (it is believed the Almasti eats horse dung because of its salt content). Among animal foods of the Almasti what strikes one as unusual is the placenta of domestic animals and, therefore, possibly of wild animals as well. The Almasti's taste for it is so well-known that old herders, being in retirement and not quite realizing how different the conditions of keeping herds are at present, advised me to visit herds of horses and flocks of sheep in the spring to catch the Almasti searching for placenta. "You ask what the Almasti eats? He eats placenta, he eats dead horses, dead animals" (Report No. 19 K). "Sheep were giving birth then, and the Almasti was taking their placenta. Once, when I came nearer, he grabbed the placenta and, grumbling, went away behind the stones" (Report No. 111 K).[106]

Shackley gives the fascinating tale of an almas captured in the Caucasus region in the 19th century, sometime around 1850. According to testimony from villagers of Tkhina, on the Mokvi River, a female

213

Khwit, part almas, 1954.

almasti was captured in the forests of Mt. Zaadan and held prisoner. For three years the female was kept imprisoned in a shed, but then she became domesticated and was allowed to live in a house. The villagers called her Zana.

According to Shackley, her skin was a greyish-black colour, covered with reddish hair, longer on her head than elsewhere. The female creature was capable of inarticulate cries but never developed a language. She had a "large face with big cheek bones, muzzle-like prognathous jaw and large eyebrows, big white teeth and a fierce expression."[13]

Eventually Zana, through sexual relations with a villager, had children. One of her children was a man named Khwit, who was very hairy and known to be someone who got into many fights. He died in 1954 and at least one photo of him has been published. Some of Zana's grandchildren, including Khwit's children, were seen by Boris Porshnev in 1964. In Shackley's account of Porshnev's investigations, he noted: "The grandchildren, Chalikoua and Taia, had darkish skin of rather negroid appearance, with very prominent chewing muscles and extra strong jaws." Porshnev also interviewed villagers who, as children, had been present at Zana's funeral in the 1880s.[13]

214

According to Ivan T. Sanderson in his book, *Abominable Snowmen: Legend Come to Life*, in the Caucasus region, the almas is sometimes called *Biaban-guli*. Sanderson claims that in 1899, a Russian zoologist named K. A. Satunin, spotted a female Biaban-guli in the Talysh hills of the southern Caucasus. He stated that the creature had "fully human movements."[9]

Sanderson then asserts that in 1941, V. S. Karapetyan, a lieutenant colonel of the medical service of the Soviet army, performed a direct physical examination of a living wildman captured in the Dagestan autonomous republic, just north of the Caucasus Mountains.

According to Sanderson, Karapetyan said:

I entered a shed with two members of the local authorities. When I asked why I had to examine the man in a cold shed and not in a warm room, I was told that the prisoner could not be kept in a warm room. He had sweated in the house so profusely that they had had to keep him in the shed. I can still see the creature as it stood before me, a male, naked and barefooted. And it was doubtlessly a man, because its entire shape was human. The chest, back, and shoulders, however, were covered with shaggy hair of a dark brown color. This fur of his was much like that of a bear, and 2 to 3 centimeters [1 inch] long. The fur was thinner and softer below the chest. His wrists

215

were crude and sparsely covered with hair. The palms of his hands and soles of his feet were free of hair. But the hair on his head reached to his shoulders partly covering his forehead. The hair on his head, moreover, felt very rough to the hand. He had no beard or moustache, though his face was completely covered with a light growth of hair. The hair around his mouth was also short and sparse. The man stood absolutely straight with his arms hanging, and his height was above the average—about 180 cm [almost 5 feet 11 inches]. He stood before me like a giant, his mighty chest thrust forward. His fingers were thick, strong and exceptionally large. On the whole, he was considerably bigger than any of the local inhabitants. His eyes told me nothing. They were dull and empty—the eyes of an animal. And he seemed to me like an animal and nothing more.[9]

Significantly, says Sanderson, the creature had lice of a kind different from those that infect humans. Sadly, the captured wildman of Dagestan was shot by his Soviet military captors as they retreated before the advancing German army, according to published accounts. Perhaps the Russians felt he could have become a secret weapon for the Nazis—or even used in their infamous genetic experiments. This scenario sounds like some B-movie plot of the 40s and 50s—but, hey, sometimes truth is stranger than fiction.

216

Shortly afterward, in the 1950s, Shackley reports that a man named Y. I. Merezhinski, senior lecturer in the department of ethnography and anthropology at Kiev University, was doing research in Azerbaijan (in the northern part of the Caucasus region) when he began hearing stories of a wildman. The local people told Merezhinski of an almas-like wildman called the *kaptar* that lived in a remote mountain forest. An expert hunter named Khadzi Magoma told Merezhinski that he would take him to a stream where the kaptar sometimes bathed at night. In exchange, the hunter asked Merezhinski to take a flash photo of the creature for him with his camera.

Russian yeti, Dec. 1941.

Merezhinski agreed to do this for the hunter and they went to the stream, near which several albino *kaptars* were said to live.

From a hiding spot, Merezhinski saw one at a distance of only a few yards. Says Shackley, "It was damp, lean and covered from head to foot with white hair. Unfortunately the reality of the creature was too much for Merezhinski, who instead of photographing

217

it shot at it with his revolver but missed in his excitement. The old hunter, furious at the deception, refused to repeat the experiment."[13]

Nearly all of these reports are from professional scientists who often directly observed a wildman. As an anthropologist, Merezhinski was well qualified to evaluate what he saw and there is no reason to doubt his story or observations. It is difficult to conclude that these stories are cases of mistaken identity or mere fantasties.

Compounding the problems of authenticating these reports is the fact that Dagestan and Georgia are very underdeveloped and have been going through a protracted war with Islamic separatist groups. Russia is only now becoming a modern country, but the ubiquitous presence of cell phones with super high-tech cameras in them may bring us more photos of these wildmen than we have been used to seeing in the past.

᛭ ⸻ ᛭

A Yeti Family Terrifies Campers in the Ukraine

The Ukrainian newspaper *Situation* reported on August 21, 2005 that a group of 12 campers (seven adults and five children), were hiking on the Demedzhi Plateau in Crimea, between North Demedzhi Mountain and Stol-Gora (Table Top) Mountain, when they encountered a family, or tribe, of yeti, called *kapustin* in Ukrainian and Russian. Kapustin in Russian refers to a hairy, man-beast commonly

218

seen in the Crimea region and the Caucasus.
Said the newspaper:

> "On that Sunday, Ivan S., 21, and his group
> of 12 tourists were spending their second
> day camped on the plateau. The kids went to
> sleep early, while the adults stayed up a while.
> The night was very bright with a full moon,"
> reported Crimean ufologist Anton A. Anfalov.
> "Ivan's assistant, Sasha, and several of the
> men left the campsite to use the bathroom and
> when they returned, they looked terrified and
> trembled with fear, It was then everyone heard
> a frightful growl near the camp."

Ivan, Sasha and the others grabbed their camping
axes and knives and faced the creatures, which
looked like naked, hairy men, nearly eight feet tall.
Said the newspaper article:

> "There were three creatures," Sasha said.
> "And they were about 6 meters (20 feet) away
> from us. The hairy humanoids were 2 to 2.5
> meters in height (about 6 feet, 6 inches to 8
> feet tall). Their true height was hard to estimate
> because they were all crouched down and
> balancing themselves on their fists, like large
> apes. All three were growling at us. Their faces
> were very hairy, almost without wrinkles, and
> their eyes were not shiny at all. Their heads
> were set or positioned very low, as if they had

219

no necks. On their backs they had something like humps on their spine."

The witnesses say they were unable to determine if the creatures were male or female.

"The creatures were very aggressive. Everyone was scared and the beasts' growls awoke the children who became hysterical," Sasha said.

The standoff lasted for about 45 minutes. Finally the creatures turned and bounded away with strange ape-like bouncing leaps.

The campers spent a sleepless night around their fire. In the morning Ivan and the others searched the ground around their camp, but due to a dense layer of fallen leaves the creatures didn't leave any distinct prints.

The Demedzhi Plateau's Stol-Gora Mountain sounds like a good spot to do a little yeti hunting, if this story is true. Perhaps some Ukrainian television station is sponsoring a cryptozological expedition as I write this. I think that we will be hearing more about the Crimean kapustin in the future.

$$\text{з} —w— \text{з}$$

The Sheregesh Russian Yeti

The Russians have capitalized on the yeti at the relatively new ski resort called Sheregesh at the northern foot of the Altai Himalaya. Known

220

for the best snow in Russia, Sheregesh is now the snowboarding capital of Siberia. Recent reports of almas in the area have the Russians hoping that Sheregesh will become a famous tourist spot because of the "Sheregesh Snowman." Sheregesh is a former remote miners' settlement near Novokuznetsk (home of the Kuzbass mines). About twenty years ago the ski resort was built at the nearby Zelenaya mountain. With the growing popularity of skiing and snowboarding in Russia, the town transformed gradually. It now is rapidly expanding with new cafes and hotels catering for more and more tourists each year. The resort itself is developing quickly with new lifts being built every new season.

The Russian news agency Russia-ic (Russia-ic.com/news) released this brief story with a photo of a yeti statue on May 14, 2009:

> The sculpture of Yeti made of cedar wood fixed near the entry to Sheregesh, a Kuzbass settlement and popular ski resort. The appearance of this monument comes from persistent rumors about Yeti met thereabouts and dozen hunters' applications sent to regional administration. Naturally, the beholders met him near the Azass caves. As its known, all the self-respecting Abominable Snowmen prefer caves for living. The expedition organized by local officers has really detected some trails supposing to belong

221

to this creature. Nevertheless the wooden Yeti stands beside the entry into Sheregesh with snowboard in his hands. The artist says that it is a comic detail not to frighten people but most likely Yeti calls the habitants and guests of settlement for a healthy lifestyle.

Presumably, local media will continue to get reports of yetis in the region. With wealthy Russians and foreign snowboarders, all with the latest cell phone cameras, flocking to Sheregesh perhaps we will see a sudden flurry of new photos on the Russian Internet.

༗ —៸៸៸— ༗

The Search Goes on for Yetis and Almas

In fact, not only is there a new, well equipped army of yeti hunters out there with cell phone cameras and video cameras, but the mega-company Google has become part of the quest. The Russian newspaper *Pravda* reported on April 6, 2009, that Russian scientists were using Google maps in their efforts to find yeti habitats. They are apparently referring to the same cave, known as Azass or Azassky.

The article, entitled "Russian scientists use Google maps to find yeti," said:

> The authorities of the Russian town of Kemerovo arranged a special expedition to find the yeti habitat which was discovered by

Google maps.

Recently there have been more than 20 claims from the local hunters who said they had seen strange creatures in the forests. These creatures resembled yeti. After the claims from the local hunters Kemerovo authorities decided to create the team of scientists for yeti searches.

The expedition turned out to be successful. Scientists managed to find 'fresh' yeti footprints in the Azassky cave.

Scientists found two identical yeti footprints. One of them was left on the rock and it dates back 5,000 years ago, and the other footprint which was left not long ago was found at the bottom of the cave.

"They are absolutely identical. Five thousand years ago yetis settled down in this cave and now their descendants are still living here. The conditions in the cave are suitable for yeti. The cave defends them from rains, snow and wind. There is also a lake in the middle of the cave where yetis can find clean water," say the scientists.

Unfortunately, the scientists did not manage to see yetis that time. They say their snowmobiles were too noisy and yetis had to hide somewhere in the forests. However, the scientists say they managed to reach their main goal—they got the proof that yetis are living there. A new expedition to the site will be arranged this summer.

Moscow explorers discovered a wigwam of a creature unknown to science in the snow-covered forest.

Members of the Kosmopoisk association have returned from an expedition to Russia's Kirov Region where they searched for a Bigfoot that allegedly lived in that region. Kosmopoisk leader Vadim Chernobrov says the expedition has discovered a den occupied by a mysterious giant and an underground passage dug obviously not by a human.

The article goes on to give the story of a Russian forest warden named Ivan Konovalov. Konovalov, the article says, has been working as a warden for 30 years in the Kirov Region and at first he did not plan to stay in that area for any extended time. However warden Konovalov had an important meeting in November 1985 and changed his mind.

Says the *Pravda* article:

Ivan Konovalov tells about that meeting: "It was snowing on the day when I was walking along the fir wood and suddenly heard snap of twigs. I turned around and saw an awesome creature covered with dark hair that was much taller than me. It smelt strongly. The beast leant against a pine tree and started bending it down to the ground.

The tree was rather thick, but it cracked

224

under the creature's burden. Then the creature started breaking the tree against the knee. Its hands were as thick and long as its legs. Quite of a sudden, the creature felt something and turned its "face" to me. I saw two black eyes and the impression at the bottom of the eyes deeply impressed me. I still remember the look of the eyes. Then the creature flung the tree and quickly left. But I stood thunderstruck and could not move a finger."

After that awesome meeting the forest warden was anticipating another meeting with the Bigfoot. However, the man did not doubt that it was a snowman. Ivan Konovalov thinks the creature unknown to science has some mysterious capabilities resembling hypnosis.

It was only twice that he managed to come across the creature face to face. Another time Ivan Konovalov met with a she-yeti and a baby. They noticed the forest warden and ran deep into the forest emitting sounds resembling dog's barking.

This unusual story is reminiscent of Bhutanese tales of yetis having the power of invisibility and other magical attributes. This is also a scene in the 1957 movie *The Abominable Snowman* with Forrest Tucker and Peter Cushing. At the end of the film, Tucker, who is playing an American big game hunter very similar to Tom Slick, comes face to face with the yeti. Tucker is dumbstruck, and the eyes of the yeti

225

are hypnotic and engaging, just as Ivan Konovalov described. Large snakes are also said to have a mesmerizing effect on their prey, who are paralyzed with hypnotic fear as they look the snake in the eye, moments before it strikes.

༐ —ᴧᴧᴧ— ༐

Polish Yeti Makes the Headlines

A very recent report came from the former Russian satellite state of Poland where the sighting of a European yeti hit newspapers and Youtube on August 28, 2009. The *Austrian Times* online edition (austriantimes.at) reported that a Polish man took video footage of a hairy apeman in the Tatra Mountains (known as "the Polish Alps") on southern Poland's border with Slovakia,

Said the article:

> Yeti experts are heading to Poland after a local man filmed a "monstrous, hairy creature" while on holiday in the Tatra Mountains.
>
> There have been rumours of a Polish Yeti in the area for centuries but this is the first time one of the strange creatures has been captured on film.
>
> Piotr Kowalski, 27, from Warsaw was on a walking holiday in the Tatra mountains in Poland when he saw a mountain goat on one of the slopes. As he started filming, his attention

was suddenly grabbed by the Yeti creature emerging from behind some rocks.

"I saw this huge ape-like form hiding behind the rocks. When I saw it, it was like being struck by a thunderbolt," he told the daily *Superexpress*.

"Coming from Warsaw, I never really believed the local stories of a wild mountain ape-man roaming the slopes. But, now I do."

The film has been handed over for examination to the Nautilus Foundation, which deals with unexplained phenomena.

"The film clearly shows 'something' that moves on two legs and is bigger than a normal man," says Foundation President Robert Bernatowicz.

"But because the camera shakes so much it is difficult to say what it is exactly. We need to

A still from the 2009 Polish yeti video.

227

go to the site and see what traces, if any, were left."

One can view the video on Youtube by doing a search such as "Polish yeti video." The video is surprising clear, and is clearly of something unusual. I have watched it several times with great interest, and to me it appears to be genuine. Literature on the Tatra Mountains says that besides species common also in other areas of Poland (such as deer, roe, fox and badger), the Tatras boast rare animals like lynx, brown bear, eagle, heath-cock, alpine chamois and now—yetis.

Another curious "European Yeti" is the so-called Yeti de Bourganeuf. This was the supposed body of an almas or almasty that was displayed briefly at a fair in Bourganeuf, France in March of 1997. Photos of the creature taken at the fair labeled it an almasty and inferred that it had come from the Caucasus Mountains or Central Asia. It was said to be 2.63 meters tall (8 feet, 7 inches) and was kept on ice in a freezer. A French researcher named Christian Le Noel said that it was claimed that the creature came from Tibet via China to eastern Germany where it had also been on display. It has vanished and except for the few photos, little else is know about the Yeti de Bourganeuf.

And so, enough Europeans in the 1950s started going to remote corners of the Himalayas to find evidence of yetis, almases, dremos and abominable snowmen, it turns out that these creatures are more

228

easily photographed in remote mountain corners of Eastern Europe! Poland has sent many mountaineering expeditions into the Himalayas, some in search of the yeti, but they would be more likely to see one in their own country, it seems. The search for yetis, sasquatch and hairy giants seemingly takes us around the world, from jungle islands like Borneo and Sumatra to the mountains of Russia, Armenia and Poland. Next stop: North America, where the tradition of bigfoot runs deep across the country—from the grasslands of Ohio to the dense forests of the Pacific Northwest.

All: The Yeti de Bourganeuf: A body displayed briefly at a fair in Bourganeuf, France in March of 1997. Thought to be an almasty from the Caucasus Mountains or Central Asia, it may have been an authentic body. It has vanished.

PART THREE:

SASQUATCH

CHAPTER 7

BIGFOOT AND
THE GRASSMAN

Behold, Esau my brother is a hairy man,
And I am a smooth man.
—*Genesis 27:11*

᳙ —₩— ᳙

Though most of my cryptozoological adventures
have been searching for evidence of the yeti on various
treks in Nepal starting in 1976, my early introduction
to the subject was in Durango, Colorado in 1967. I
was in junior high school at the time and a lecture was
given one evening by the famous California bigfoot
hunter Roger Patterson. This was a year or so before
he was to make his now-famous 16mm film footage
of a female sasquatch walking briefly across a field
in northern California. He was promoting his new
book, *Do Abominable Snowmen of America Really
Exist?*[16]

I enjoyed his slides and lecture. He presented

233

a slide of the sasquatch photo printed in the *San Francisco Chronicle* on December 7, 1965, and various other evidence that America did indeed have its own abominable snowman. Patterson even played a reel-to-reel tape recording that featured the rather frightening call of a bigfoot late at night in some remote mountain campground. It was a bit sensational, but it stuck in the memory, to say the least. I bought a copy of Patterson's book, only $1.95 back in 1967, and my search for sasquatch and abominable snowmen had begun.

Over the years I bought other cryptozoology books, including Bernard Heuvelman's classic *On the Track of Unknown Animals*[32] and went on the occasional investigative trip in search of cryptids. I was surprised at how common bigfoot was across the United States. They say that coyotes are in every state in the USA (except Hawaii)—was it possible that bigfoot was also in every state? As we shall see, reports of hairy giant apemen originally came from the Midwest and Eastern portions of the country.

$$\gamma\!\!\!\!\gamma \longrightarrow \gamma\!\!\!\!\gamma$$

Earliest Reports of Hairy Apemen in the Eastern USA

One of the earliest bigfoot-grassman newspaper stories was reported in the *Boston Daily Times* on April 1, 1839. The article was sent to *Cryptomundo* by Scott McClean, who wondered if it was just a coincidence that the bizarre story was published on April Fool's Day. Still, the story has a ring of

234

authenticity to it. The story is of a lumber steamship that goes up the Mississippi to Prairie Du Chien in Wisconsin and then continue north to what is now known as the Minnesota River, but what was called the Saint Peters River back then. While spending time at this northerly timber camp the lumbermen encounter—and capture a bigfoot. The article was entitled, "When Will Wonders Cease?"

Said the article:

> Robert Lincoln, Esq., Agent of the New York Western Lumber Company, has just returned from the Saint Peters river, near the head of steamship navigation, on the upper Mississippi, bringing with him a living American Ourang Outang, or Wild Man of the Woods, with two small cubs, supposed to be about three months old. Mr. Lincoln informs us that he went out to the north-west as Agent of the New York Lumber Company, in July last, with a view to establish extensive saw-mills, on the pine lands near the Falls of Saint Anthony; and he has given us a detail of the operations of the company, and the circumstances which lead to the capture of the extraordinary creatures mentioned above.
>
> Those who are acquainted with the leading features of the Valley of the Mississippi, are aware that there is little or no pine timber throughout the States of Illinois and Missouri, or in the extensive territories of Wisconsin and

Iowa. The inhabitants of that region are obliged to use oak and walnut for common building purposes, and the labor of working such materials is very great. The greatest portion of the pine timber that finds its way into the upper part of the Valley, is floated down the Ohio, and from thence carried up the Mississippi and Illinois rivers by steamboats. The most ordinary kind of pine timber is worth $60 per thousand, in any part of Illinois or the territories; in New England the same quality sells for about half that sum. There are some very extensive and immensely valuable pine lands near the Falls of Saint Anthony, on the Upper Mississippi; but until recently they have been in the possession of the Sac and Fox Indians. In the summer of 1838, a treaty was ratified with these Indians, by which they ceded the whole of their pine lands to the United States. The ceremonies of this treaty were performed at Fort Snelling, about the first of July last. Capt. Marryatt, the famous English novelist, was then on the Upper Mississippi, and was present to witness the war dances on this occasion, which, it is said, were conducted with unusual splendor. He also spent several days among the Indians, and by the assistance of the American officers at Fort Snelling, obtained a large collection of ornaments and curiosities.

Some shrewd men at Albany and New York who knew what the treaty referred to, was about to be ratified, and who were aware, also, of the value of the timber, formed a company, with a substantial capital, and engaged a large number of enterprising mechanics and laborers to go out and establish saw-mills for cutting timber on the Saint Peters. They rightly supposed that the land would not "come into market," as the phrase is, for several years, as it is worth but little except for timber. Those who wish to obtain land for cultivation, go into the more fertile parts of the territories. Companies may therefore "claim" land, establish mills, and cut off the timber where ever they can find it, without fee or license. The timber may then be floated down the Mississippi in rafts, for a mere trifle, and sold at the highest prices any where on the river.

The New York Company sent out their expedition in July last. The workmen and laborers with the principal part of the machinery went by way of New Orleans, and at that city they chartered a steamboat and proceeded up the Mississippi. The whole business was under the direction of Mr. Lincoln. They had on board all the necessary tools and saws, together with the apparatus for a grist mill, oxen, horses, cows, a good stock of provisions, arms, ammunition, &c. &c. They passed directly up the river, only stopping to take in wood and water, until they reached Prairie Du Chien, at the mouth of the Wisconsin. Here they put their animals on

237

shore, and remained two days.

On the third day they reembarked and finally reached the Saint Peters in safety. Their enterprise proved highly successful. They found the timber of the first quality, and the facilities for building mills much greater than they anticipated. The work went on very prosperously, and in a few months Mr. Lincoln had the satisfaction of launching his rafts on the headwaters of the Mississippi! They continued to prosecute their labors vigorously, until winter set in, when a part of the workmen started for Saint Louis, and a part of them remained to superintend the cutting of timber.

During the winter, Mr. Lincoln and several of the workmen made frequent excursions in pursuit of game, which was very abundant, and their camp was one continued scene of festivity. The Indians brought in large quantities of furs, which Mr. Lincoln purchased for a mere trifle, and lined his cabins with them throughout, which rendered his rude huts very warm and comfortable. The whole party were as hearty as bucks, and appeared to enjoy themselves exceedingly.

About the 15th of January, two of the carpenters who had been out in pursuit of a gang of wolves that had proved very troublesome, came into the camp and reported that they had seen a huge monster in the forest, on a branch of the Mississippi, having the form of a man, but much taller and stouter, covered with long hair, and of a frightful aspect. They stated that when first seen, he was standing on a large log, looking directly at them and the moment they raised their muskets, he darted into the thicket and disappeared. They saw him again in about half an hour, apparently watching them, and when they turned towards him he again disappeared. Mr. Lincoln was at first disposed to think lightly of this matter, believing that the men might have been mistaken about the size and height of the object, or supposing it might have been a trick of the Indians to frighten them.

He was informed, however, by some of the natives, that such a being had often been seen on the St. Peters, and near the Falls of the Mississippi, and they proposed to guide a party of the workmen to a bluff where it was thought he might be found. The men were all ready for an adventure, and arming themselves with rifles and hunting-knives, they started for the bluff under the direction of Mr. Lincoln and the Indian guides. On the way they were joined by several of the natives, and the whole party numbered twenty-three.

The arrived at the bluff late on the afternoon of the 21st of January, and encamped in a cave or grotto, at the foot of the hill. Early the next morning, two of the Indians were sent out to reconnoiter, and in about an hour

239

returned, and said they had seen the wild man, on the other side of the hill. The whole party immediately prepared for the pursuit. Mr. Lincoln gave positive orders to the men, not to fire upon him unless it should be necessary in self-defense, as he wished, if possible, to take him alive. The Indians stated that although a very powerful creature, he was believed to be perfectly harmless, as he always fled at the approach of men. While Mr. Lincoln was giving his men their instructions, the wild man appeared in sight. He ordered them to remain perfectly quiet, and taking out his pocket-glass surveyed him minutely. He appeared to be about eight or nine feet high, very athletic, and more like a beast standing erect than a man. After satisfying himself with regard to the character of the creature, Mr. Lincoln ordered his men to advance. The Indians had provided themselves with ropes, prepared to catch wild horses, with which they hoped to ensnare and bind the creature, without maiming him.

The instant the company moved towards the wild man, he sprung forward with a loud and frightful yell, which made the forest ring; the Indians followed close upon him, and Mr. Lincoln and his men brought up the rear. The pursuit was continued for nearly an hour, now gaining upon the object of their chase, and now almost losing sight of him. The trees, however, were quite open, and free from underbrush,

240

which enabled them to make their way very rapidly. Whenever they came very near him, he started forward again with a yell, and appeared to increase his speed. He finally darted into a thicket, and although they followed close and made much search, they were unable to find him.

They then began to retrace their steps towards the place of encampment, and when within about a mile of the cavern, the wild man crossed their path, within twenty rods of the main body of the party. They immediately gave chase again, and accidentally drove the creature from the forest into an open field or prairie.

The monster appeared to be much frightened at his situation, and leaped forward, howling hideously. At length he suddenly stopped and turned upon his pursuers. Mr. Lincoln was then in the advance. Fearing that he might attack them, or return to the woods and escape, he fired upon him and lodged a charge of buck-shot in the calf of his leg. He fell immediately, and the Indians sprang forward and threw their ropes over his head, arms and legs, and with much effort succeeded in binding him fast. He struggled, however, most desperately, gnashed his teeth, and howled in a frightful manner. They then formed a sort of litter of branches and limbs of trees, and placing him upon it, carried him to the encampment.

A watch was then placed over him, and every effort made that could be devised to keep him quiet, but he continued to howl most piteously all night. Towards morning two cubs, about three-feet high, and very similar to the large monster, came into the camp, and were taken without resistance. As soon as the monster saw them he became very furious, gnashed his teeth, and howled, and thrashed about, until he burst several of the cords, and came very near effecting his escape. But he was bound anew, and after that was kept most carefully watched and guarded. The next day he was placed on the litter and carried down to the mills on the Saint Peters.

For two or three days, Mr. Lincoln says, he refused to eat or drink, or take any kind of food, but continued to howl at intervals for an hour at a time. At length, however, he began to eat, but from that time his howls ceased, and he has remained stupid and sullen ever since. The cubs took food very readily, and became quite active and playful. Mr. Lincoln is a native of Boston, and some of the workmen engaged at his mills are from this city. He arrived here [in Boston] Saturday afternoon in the brig *St. Charles*, Stewart, master, from New Orleans, with the wild man and the cubs, and they were all removed from the vessel that evening. By invitation of Mr. Lincoln, who is an old acquaintance, we went down to his rooms to

242

examine this monster. He is a horrid looking creature, and reminds us very strongly of the fabled satyrs, as we have pictured them to our own mind. He is about eight feet three inches high, when standing erect, and his frame is of giant proportions in every part. His legs are not straight, but like those of the dog and other four-footed animals, and his whole body is covered with a hide very much like that of a cow. His arms are very large and long, and ill-proportioned.

It does not appear from his manner that he has ever walked upon "all fours." The fingers and toes are mere bunches, armed with stout claws. His head is covered with thick, coarse, black hair, like the mane of a horse. The appearance of his countenance, if such it may be called, is very disgusting nay, almost horrible.

It is covered with a thinner and lighter coat of hair than the rest of the body; there is no appearance of eye-brows or nose; the mouth is very large and wide, and similar to that of a baboon. His eyes are quite dull and heavy, and there is no indication of cunning or activity about them. Mr. Lincoln says he is beyond dispute carnivorous, as he universally rejects bread and vegetables, and eats flesh with great avidity. He thinks he is of the ourang outang species: but from what little we have seen, we are inclined to consider him a wild animal,

243

somewhat resembling a man. He is, to say the least, one of the most extraordinary creatures that has ever been brought before the public, from any part of the earth, or the waters under the earth, and we believe will prove a difficult puzzle to the scientific. He lies down like a brute, and does not appear to possess more instinct than common domestic animals. He is now quite tame and quiet, and is only confined by a stout chain attached to his legs.

This is the first creature of the kind, we believe, ever found on this continent. It was to be expected, however, that in penetrating the remote recesses of the new world, monsters would be found, and great natural curiosities brought to light; and it has been a matter of surprise to many that so little of the marvelous has ever been discovered. But we cannot tell what the wilds of the far Northwest, the shores of Lake Superior, the regions of the Rocky Mountains, and the vast territory of the Oregon, may yet bring forth.

It is Mr. Lincoln's intention to submit these animals to the inspection of the scientific for a few days, in order to ascertain what they are, and after that to dispose of them to some persons for exhibition. Mr. Lincoln himself will return to the Saint Peters in the course of two or three weeks.

P. S. Mr. Lincoln informs us that he will exhibit the Wild Man and his cubs, gratuitously,

244

this forenoon, in the rear of No. 9 Elm Street. We presume our citizens will not be slow to take advantage of this offer.

This astonishing story was to foreshadow hundreds, if not thousands, of similar stories to be printed in newspapers in the US and Canada for the next 180 years. Like other captured apemen, we will probably never know what happened to this poor creature. What we do know is that this is not the last story of its—these creatures were to be spotted throughout the Ohio and Mississippi River valleys. Locally, they would come to known as "the grassman."

⁂

Early Reports from Ohio and the Midwest

Another early grassman incident was reported in the *Minnesota Weekly Record* on Saturday, January 23, 1869. The title of the story was "A Gorilla in Ohio." The first gorilla was captured in Liberia in 1847. Said the article:

> Gallipolis [Ohio] is excited over a wild man, who is reported to haunt the woods near that city. He goes naked, is covered with hair, is gigantic in height, and "his eyes start from their sockets." A carriage, containing a man and daughter, was attacked by him a few days ago. He is said to have bounded at the father, catching him in a grip like that of a vice,

hurling him to the earth, falling on him and endeavoring to bite and to scratch like a wild animal. The struggle was long and fearful, rolling and wallowing in the deep mud, [half] suffocated, sometimes beneath his adversary, whose burning and maniac eyes glared into his own with murderous and savage intensity. Just as he was about to become exhausted from his exertions, his daughter, taking courage at the imminent danger of her parent, snatched up a rock and hurling it at the head of her father's would be murderer, was fortunate enough to put an end to the struggle by striking him somewhere about the ear. The creature was not stunned, but feeling unequal to further exertion, slowly got up and retired into the neighboring copse that skirted the road.[44]

Christopher Murphy, Joedy Cook and George Clappison record a number of interesting incidents in the Midwest in their book *Bigfoot Encounters in Ohio: Quest for the Grassman*.[66] They report that on May 26, 1897 near Rome, Ohio in the very south of the state, Charles Lukins and Bob Forner claimed that they encountered a wildman while cutting timber out of town. After struggling with the "gorilla-like creature" they were able to drive it into retreat among the cliffs. They called the creature a "terror" and said it was about six feet tall. This report came from the *Cleveland Plain Dealer*, May 27, 1897.

The authors also chronicle several other events

in the 1800s, such as farmers around Logan, Ohio reporting in May of 1897 that a strange animal had appeared in the vicinity and numerous sheep had disappeared. Several old pioneers who heard the beast crying at night thought it was a panther. They hunted for the strange animal but failed to kill or capture it.[66]

In the 1940s, the authors report that a family driving through Hanging Rock in Lawrence County saw a reddish-brown ape-like creature standing on Hanging Rock Hill looking down at the highway.[66] The rest of the book is packed with grassman encounters from the latter half of the 20th century, and even some accounts from the new millennium.

Newspapers in Ohio have chronicled more grassman accounts than one might imagine, such as this one that ran in Dayton's *Ohio Daily News* on June 24, 1980 with the headline, "'Bigfoot' Sightings Scare Socks Off Pair":

Bellefontaine, Ohio—Does Logan County have a "Big Foot" stalking its wooded hills between West Mansfield and the Union County line? Sheriff's deputies are investigating a sighting by an off-duty Russell's Point police officer who said he saw a "seven-feet-tall, hairy animal" in his barn yard Sunday night and a similar report from Union County last Tuesday. Ray Quay, a Russell's Point police officer who owns a small farm on Twp. Road 132 near West Mansfield, said he was

247

"surprised and dumbfounded" about what he saw Sunday night.

"I was unloading eight pigs I had bought about 11 p.m. I shut off the light in the barn and went around the corner to see what my two dogs were raising Cain about. They never bark when I'm around. I stepped around the corner of the barn and saw this hairy animal. I thought it was a man so I hollered at him. It took off and I've got some weeds out back I haven't mowed and they are waist high or higher and the creature went through them with no problem," Quay said.

Four deputies searched the area but found nothing. Deputies said that last Tuesday Patrick Poling, who lives on County Rd. 142 in Union County east of West Mansfield, was cultivating a field when he said he spotted a creature walking out of some woods and stride along a road near where the farmer was working.

Poling said he walked over to try to get a better look at the creature, but it ran back into the woods. Poling's description was similar to that of the creature Quay said he saw. Poling said the creature walked up-right all the time. The Lima [bigfoot] research team, a non-profit organization, took measurements and a cast of three claw marks found on the Union County farm. The claw prints are about 40 inches apart. The claw mark has four toes and measures 16 inches by 4 inches, deputies said.

The grassman has shown up along rivers, sleeping on roads (such as the one seen by Donna Riegler of Marysville, Ohio on June 24, 1980—a hairy creature that hobbled away after she put the car in reverse) and in cornfields in rural areas. He even showed up on the Jack Nicklaus-designed golf course near Dublin, Ohio several times in 1973.

Nicklaus designed the Muirfield Village Golf Club in 1966, and it was apparently named after him for some years. In October of 1973 two security guards, plus other witnesses, said they saw an eight-foot "hairy monster" near the course. Later they saw the creature actually on the golf course. The spokesman for the Franklin County Sheriff's Department said that the monster was spotted three times by the guards around the facility. A footprint about 12 inches long and seven inches wide was discovered alongside a creek, and the supervisor of the security firm for the course doubled the number of guards on duty.[66]

The Indiana Grassman of the Thickets

The grassman is not confined to Ohio by any means. As one would expect, he has been seen in Indiana, Kentucky, Illinois and in nearly every other state in the US. On May 1, 1980, newspapers in Indiana carried the strange story of a young couple, Tom and Connie Courter, who, with a six-week-old baby in the back seat, had a grassman encounter in rural Ohio County, Indiana.

The Courters had left their mother's house and were driving back up Henschen Road between the towns of Aurora and Rising Sun to their trailer. Once home, Tom got out of the car first so that he could get the diaper bag out of the back seat. As he turned back around, he heard a strong noise which sounded like an "UGH." As he looked up, he saw a large hairy animal about "18 inches" away.

Tom said in an interview that the creature was about 12 feet tall, black and hairy, with large red eyes. He further stated that its head was shaped like a human's and that its arms were hanging to the ground. Tom quickly jumped into his car and spun his tires, as the creature took a swing at him. Tom said that the creature hit his car. Both Tom and Connie were obviously very scared and they went directly back to their mother's house.

On the next night, they stayed at their mother's house until 11:45 before heading home. This time, Tom was prepared with his 16-shot .22. They had been parked in front of their trailer for a while when they saw the same animal standing next to a tree on the other side of the road. Tom fired one shot at the creature, but missed. He fired several more shots. He said that the animal seemed to dive to the ground and then vanish.

The Courters filed a police report, but the Ohio County Sheriff's department were very skeptical, and said they could find no evidence of the creature. (This incident was reported by the Bigfoot Research

Organization)

The next year the Vincennes, Indiana newspaper *The Valley Advance* (Vol. 18, No. 6, October 6, 1981) that several people had encountered a hairy apeman in the White River area of southwest Indiana.

Said the article with the headline, "White River Encounters: Area Residents See 'Something Big and Hairy'":

Jack Lankford is an avid fisherman and hunter who says he never left a fire unattended until the night of Aug. 22. That's the night he saw a "creature" while fishing in the White River bottom land about six miles south of Highway 50. Roger and Barbara Crabtree say they live in fear of a "hairy creature" they have seen twice near their Decker Chapel home in southern Knox County close to the White River.

Terry and Mary Harper haven't seen anything, but something attacked their house at 2002 South 15th Street, Vincennes. The unknown assailant ripped and apparently chewed on aluminum siding and tore away part of the metal trim around the backdoor of the house. It left behind teeth marks, blood and tufts of white hair about two inches long.

So far the incidents are unrelated. No evidence of a creature has been found in the areas where the sightings took place. However, Lankford says what he saw was no bear, and the

251

Crabtrees know that people may not believe, but their fear is "very real."

Lankford anticipated a "good bit of fishing" last Aug. 22 when he went to his favorite spot on the lower part of what is called Beaver Dam in eastern Knox County. The fisherman had built a campfire a few yards from the bank and was using a lantern to watch his lines.

The Washington, Ind., resident had been there a couple of hours when he started having an "eerie feeling" that someone was watching. About 20 minutes later Lankford looked up and saw two eyes, each about one-inch in diameter, glowing red from the lantern and nearby campfire glow and staring at him from about 50 yards away.

Lankford could see a hairy body sticking about four feet out of the water, but the light was too dim to reveal the face, he said. Lankford said the creature looked like a well-built, big-boned man with "extra" long forearms and covered with brown, matted hair. It apparently was standing in about four feet of water. "It just stared at me and me at it. It was trying to figure out if I was looking at what I was seeing," he said.

The "booger," as Lankford's grandmother called it, appeared to study Lankford, tilting its head from side to side and making no noise, he said. After a short time, the creature turned away, reached to grab a tree limb, and pulled itself from the water.

As it walked away Lankford noticed that the arms extended to around the knees and that it had to weigh "well over 200 pounds."

"It made a loud squeal or high-pitch shriek when it left, something like a young pig would make when you try to hold on to it."

Lankford heard the sound again while he was hurriedly packing his fishing gear. He says he has heard the noise in that area three or four times since early spring, but didn't think much of it.

Since seeing the creature, Lankford has not heard the noise. He said he would like to meet it again.

"The last time I didn't think to follow it because it didn't show any sign of wanting to harm me. I'm one person who respects other persons and beings, and I would like to see the creature captured unharmed and studied," Lankford commented.

Lankford told only his family immediately after seeing the creature. He decided to report the incident to the Daviess County Sheriff's Department after reading a newspaper article about the attack on the Harper house.

"I've talked to people who live in the area, and they said if it is someone trying to pull a hoax they are taking a big risk of getting shot. The sheriff's deputy told me the same thing," Lankford noted.

Terry and Mary Harper, their children and neighbors did not hear anything out of the ordinary between midnight and 6:30 a.m. on Aug. 26, but during that time about four or five feet of siding some three feet high was ripped and chewed, along with metal trim around the backdoor. One piece shows what looks like a claw mark.

"We had the house fans on all night and they can be noisy. We really didn't hear anything," she said.

Terry Harper was leaving for work when he saw the damaged siding. The damage amounted to about $500, Harper said, and included blood, large teeth marks and white hair. Blood was also found near the back light about six to seven feet above the ground, Mrs. Harper said.

The dog refused to come out of its house and had its paws over its eyes and whined when it was checked.

Officials from the Knox County Sheriff's Department have told the Harpers that tests on the blood reveal that it is not human, and that a wolf or some other wild animal may have done the damage. Investigating officers told Mrs. Harper that hair taken from the scene has been lost.

"We don't know what to be frightened of, and I can't say that it is a 'bigfoot' or not," Mrs. Harper said.

Harold Allison, an area naturalist and writer of a weekly nature column in *The Valley Advance,* studied pictures of the damage and believes no animal native to the area could have caused the damage.

"The only animal I can think of from my experience capable of that kind of damage would be a wolverine. But there are no wolverines within 500 miles of this part of Indiana," Allison commented.

The incident has kept the Harpers busy on the telephone, talking with newspaper, television and radio reporters about the "house attack." Mrs. Harper has been interviewed by radio stations from as far as Boston, Chicago, Dallas and Los Angeles. The incident received a brief mention on the ABC-TV World News program.

Through a United Press International news story, an investigator from S.I.T.U. Research Services, a private company in Little Silver, N.J., has contacted the Harpers and currently is looking into the incident.

"The investigator thinks it's a bigfoot, but he can't be sure because we didn't have any blood stains left to send him. He said if we could get him a blood sample, he could tell us exactly what it was," Mrs. Harper related. S.I.T.U., which reportedly specializes in unexplained phenomena investigations, sent the family a report of a 1977 attack in New Jersey.

255

The New Jersey incident involved a creature like the one described by Lankford, but with a human face covered by a beard and mustache. Wood panels on a barn were ripped up and chewed at about the same height as the Harpers' house.

The most recent sighting of what one area newspaper has called the "Knox-ness monster," occurred Sept. 26 at about 2:30 a.m., along the Decker Chapel Road, west of Highway 41.

Crabtree was returning with his family from Princeton and was less than two miles from home when he saw "something big" walking in the road.

As Crabtree came closer he noticed fur, long arms and a "skipping walk like an ape." The headlights appeared to startle it, Crabtree recalls, and the creature swung its arm at the car. Crabtree swerved off and back onto the road to miss the creature and stopped to watch as it continued its walk down the road.

Crabtree's wife, Barbara, who was awakened by the quick turn, persuaded her husband not to follow and to call the Knox County Sheriff's Department. Mrs. Crabtree said she had seen it the day before in a cornfield near the family's backyard, a "dirty, white-haired creature" not more than 50 feet away.

Mrs. Crabtree grabbed her two pre-school daughters and backed to the front porch, she said. The creature "took a couple of steps" toward her but stepped back when the family dog started barking and ran toward it.

She got her daughters and nine-year-old son, who was throwing rocks at it, into the house and locked all doors and windows. She tried to call the sheriff but was unable to get through because of a busy party telephone line, she said.

In her view the creature was about seven to eight feet tall and weighed around 500 pounds. It was covered with "fuzzy" dirty white hair except for its head, which was brown hair.

"It had a pinkish face and big, glassy eyes. The thing had an awful, sour smell, something like dead meat that had set out for three or four days," she said.

The creature also made a growling noise, which the family has heard at least two times since the second sighting, Crabtree said.

The sheriff's deputies have been unable to find any evidence of the creature and consider the case closed, officer Jim Wilson said.

"The department is treating it as an unconfirmed sighting because the Crabtrees were the only ones to report it," Wilson explained.

The family is now looking for another house and has purchased a shotgun.

"I don't care what anyone thinks. I saw what I saw and no one has to believe me," Roger began. "When nightfall comes around here, my family is plenty scared. I don't even go out after dark."

Well, something going bump in the night in southern Indiana was definitely scaring the Crabtrees. It probably wasn't a bear, as is often postulated as a solution to such events. This grassman also had white or gray hair, which has been described on various hairy giants, including yetis and certain desert bigfoot. Are these the grandfathers of these ultra shy apemen? As they get older does their hair turn from reddish-brown to white? As with humans, this would seem to be the case.

Grassman seen near Knoxville, IN.

Kentucky Grasswoman

Kentucky is another state with its share of grassman accounts. According to the Bigfoot Research Organization (Bfro.net) there were several cases in 1980, including the reporting of a tall, white haired ape-like creature on October 7 near the town of Mayslick in Mason County.

According to the BFRO report, the witness, known as "C.F.," was watching television with his family when they heard a loud noise on the front

258

porch. C.F. said that he heard his son's pet rooster squawking so he peered out the front door, where he saw a white, hairy creature with pink eyes. He said that the creature must have weighed about 400 pounds and was about seven feet tall. It was holding the rooster by the neck and then threw it against the side of the house. The white haired grassman then proceeded around the back of the house to a vacant lot. C.F. says he grabbed his .22 pistol and followed the apeman. He fired at the creature twice, as it ran out of sight. BFRO says that there was a small article concerning the incident in the *Cincinnati Enquirer*.

The same white haired grassman (or could it have been a different one?) was seen the next month, November 5, 1980, also in Mason County, Kentucky. According to the BFRO report, which was taken from a police report and information given by a reporter named Doug McGill from the local radio station WFTM, an Alabama truck driver identified as "N.C." said that he was hauling steel west on U.S. Route 68 when he saw a figure on the opposite side of the highway. He slowed his vehicle and turned on his high beams thinking that it was a hitchhiker.

When he approached the figure, he was shocked to see a six-to-seven foot tall "ape-like" creature with white hair. After his encounter, he contacted some locals on C.B. channel 22 to see if there was a circus or zoo in the area. He thought that possibly an ape had escaped. When police were called to investigate, they took N.C.'s statement and filed a report. He stated to police that he had never been to this area before and

259

knew nothing about alleged bigfoot reports in the area.

World Weekly News headline.

The white haired bigfoot that was seen at this time seems quite kingly as he stands by the highway watching the cars and trucks go by. "What's it all about?" he may wonder as he stares at the big rigs with their lights and honking horns. These are the real monsters that we have to worry about, I suppose.

※ —₩— ※

Skunk Apes of the Southern Swamps

Down south in "skunk ape territory," the grassman is a lot smellier and nastier than the regal white-maned grassmen of the Ohio River Valley. The skunk apes and their kin live down south in Florida, Alabama, Mississippi, Louisiana and Arkansas. You smell 'em first, and, if yer lucky, you won't see 'em.

One incident reported in the *Sentinel Star* of Orlando, Florida (October 5, 1977) pretty much spells it out. Entitled "Lurking Bigfoot Trick or Threat?," the article said:

Halloween is still three weeks away but strange creatures are already being seen around Central Florida this week.

A 22-year-old hitchhiker reported sighting

the legendary Bigfoot, saying the beast was tall, dark and stinky. It lurked in the darkness in a lightly forested area off U.S. 441 half a mile south of Belleview, he said.

"I've got some information about Bigfoot," the tremulous voice on the telephone said. "I think I just saw it."

Monday morning a security guard for an Apopka nursery told police a 10-foot-tall hairy animal with a chestfull of reddish-gray fur and small ears attacked him, ripping off the terrified guard's shirt.

Donnie Hall, 27, said he fired several gunshots at the creature in vain. The Bigfoot sighter—a Belleview welder who didn't want his name known—said the beast was brown and black. "I'm six feet tall and it was bigger than me. It smelled horrible, like garbage."

Neither of the two creature sightings was substantiated.

A Florida Game and Fresh Water Commission agent who examined tracks at John's Nursery in Apopka said they all appeared to be man-made.

Marion County Sheriff Don Moreland chuckled about the Bigfoot report. "I've been in law enforcement for 20 years here and I don't remember any reports of monsters. Flying saucers, yes, but I don't recall any monsters."

The year 1977 was a good year for skunk apes

261

skulking about in the night in Florida. On November 15 of that year the *Evening Telegram* (Superior, Wisconsin) and other newspapers reported the United Press International (UPI) report from that day entitled "Creature Sighted." The article said:

> A 67-year-old Baptist minister who says he hasn't had a drink in 40 years tells how he stood eyeball-to-eyeball for 30 seconds with a great, hairy creature in the Ocala National Forest.
>
> The Rev. S. L. Whatley, pastor of the Fort McCoy Baptist Church, said he spotted the thing out of the corner of his eye while he was cutting wood with a chain saw three weeks ago.
>
> Whatley recalled Monday, "It was standing upright, in the middle of some palmetto bushes, and that sapsucker was at least 7 1/2, maybe 8 feet tall.
>
> The minister said the creature "had dark, lighter-than-black hair on its head and chest, not much on its arms, and none on its face. It had kind of a flat face, a flat nose, its eyes were sunk in its sockets."
>
> Whatley said he quickly went back to his truck to get an ax because "me and that creature was going to mix it up," but by the time he returned from the truck the creature had disappeared.
>
> He hastened to add that he hasn't had a drink in 40 years.

Another skunk ape story from Altoona, Florida was sent out by UPI on July 2, 1980 and picked up by the Houston *Chronicle* and other newspapers. Said the *Chronicle* story headlined, "Police Think Mystery Footprints are Fakes":

> Most investigators figure it's a hoax, but there is enough doubt in their minds to order casts made of the size 18 foot-like prints found in a remote area of the Ocala National Forest.
>
> "I think it's a hoax," said Doug Sewell, chief investigator for the Lake County Sheriff's department. "There was no indication that something big enough to make those prints went back through the woods."
>
> Less sure, however, is Lake County Sgt. Dee Kirby, called out to make casts of the half dozen 17-inch-by-6 1/2-inch footprints found near a bulldozer in the vicinity of Camp Ocala, a federal job training site.
>
> He said the prints showed a definite arching of the instep. five distinct toes and even some wrinkling along the instep. "The prints had a full four feet of distance

A 1997 photo of a Florida skunk ape.

263

between each of one," he said, speculating that if they were real the creature that made them must be 10-to-12 feet tall and weigh close to 1,000 pounds.

The prints were discovered by a private contractor doing roadwork for the U.S. Forestry Service. Forestry officials also made casts of the prints, but doubted if they would investigate further.

Informal speculation centered on whether the creature was the infamous "skunk ape"—Florida's own version of Bigfoot and the abominable snowman—reportedly last sighted in the Everglades.

They are just as big, hairy and smelly in Alabama as they are in Florida. Chad Arment, in his book *The Historical Bigfoot*,[44] reproduced the strange story from Anniston, Alabama that ran on April 15, 1938 about an apeman being sought in a swamp in the Choccolocco valley. Reported in the *Oshkosh Northwestern* and other newspapers (taken from the UPI press release) was entitled "Hairy Wild Man Sought in Swamp." Said the newspaper story:

A wild man who runs on all fours, chases dogs and frightens farmers is being sought in a dense swamp in the Choccolocco valley.

Sheriff W. P. cotton led a posse in search of the strange beast which, farmers insisted, was accompanied by a woman and a child—both as

264

savage in appearance and actions as the man.

Rex Biddle, a farmer, told Sheriff Cotton that the man approached his home walking on all fours in the manner of an ape.

"He was about five feet tall, and had hair all over his body," Biddle said. "He was unclothed. Despite his beastlike appearance, his nose and other features indicated he was human."

Biddle said he reached for his gun but didn't shoot because "I didn't know whether that would be legal."

Roy Storey, another farmer, said the creature followed him for a time and then "dropped to all fours and chased my pet dog into the swamp."

Residents of the district petitioned the sheriff to "catch this thing or we are moving out."[44]

The Alabama skunk ape surfaced again in 2004 when a story cropped up out of the town of Clanton on July 8. The local television station NBC13 of Birmingham and Tuscaloosa ran a feature on the nightly news and then posted this story on its web site under the title "Bigfoot Legend Thrives in Chilton County: Man-Like Creature Lives in Peach Grove, According to Legend":

Whether you're a believer or not, the legend of Bigfoot is alive and well in Chilton County.

265

For decades people there have been talking about the strange creature that apparently has an affinity for the local peach crop.

In the 1960s, some strange footprints were found in a Chilton County peach grove. Now the original investigator reminisces about the time he spent tracking Bigfoot.

"In our opinion it was definitely not a fake. It was a real track," said James Earl Johnson, the former Chilton County investigator, whose case sparked a legend back in the 1960s.

"We checked the peach orchard, and there was a trail leading out of the peach orchard, and it was tracks—strange looking tracks, similar to a human but bigger and wider," said Johnson.

With nothing but a print to go on, picking a name for the elusive creature wasn't very hard. Since then, Bigfoot sightings have been reported across the country, and sketches of the creature vary depending on where the sighting occurred. The name varies as well. In Alabama, the creature is known as Bigfoot, while in northern areas, it's known as a Sasquatch.

"Supposedly, the legend is that a hairy man-like creature that walks on two legs at some point inhabited the bottomland swamp regions in Chilton County in Clanton, Alabama," said Bryan Wyatt, a Bigfoot researcher.

"I know one thing: [Bigfoot] likes Chilton County peaches," said Johnson.

Things are just as bad and swampy in Mississippi. Arment reproduces a fascinating story from 1868 about a giant wild apeman that made the news that year. Seen near Meadville, Franklin County, Alabama where men with hunting dogs:

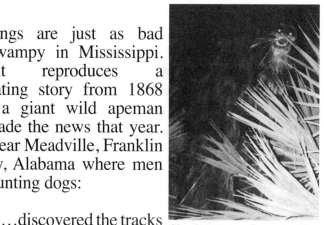

Skunk ape near Sarasota, FL.

...discovered the tracks of the game in some miry places, which appeared similar to the track of a human foot; and they observed, also, that the toes of one foot turned backward. On coming up with the dogs, who were now baying, they beheld a frightful looking creature, of about the average height of man, but with far greater muscular development, standing menacingly a few yards in front of the dogs. It had long, coarse hair flowing from its head and reaching near its knees; its entire body, also, seemed to be covered with hair of two or three inches' length, which was of a dark brown color. From its upper jaw projected two very large tusks, several inches long. ...it fled toward the Mississippi River, and was not overtaken again until within a few yards of the bank. When the party came up with the dogs the second time, the monster was standing erect before them, none of them having yet dared to clinch with it. But when the dogs were urged by their masters, they endeavored to seize it, when it reached forward and grabbed one them them, and taking it in its hands, pressed it against its trunk, which pierced it through and killed it instantly. Becoming alarmed at this display of strength, the hunters fired several shots at the creature, which caused it to leap into the river... after sinking and rising several times, it swam to the Louisiana shore and disappeared.[44]

Arment says that this story came from the *Daily Herald* of Dubuque, Iowa for June 27, 1868, so we see that stories of skunk apes go back well over a hundred years. One thing we might conclude from this account of the grassman—he is a good swimmer! Indeed, the other common southern term for the grassman is swamp ape, and these semi-aquatic apemen basically live in swamps and remote river valleys that contain dense forests.

The Mississippi swamp apes surfaced in 1977 after a

Skunk ape photo from the Internet. Unknown date.

hundred years of keeping out of the news when the Associated Press picked up on a story that occurred near Natchez on the Mississippi River on January 20. Said the *Arkansas Gazette* and other newspapers on that day under the headline, "'Hairy Creature' is Being Sought":

> The police are investigating reports of a "huge, hairy creature" that reportedly was sighted by several Natchez residents.
>
> Those who reported the sighting to police Monday night said the "almost human" creature growled at a dog and fled when a patrol car approached.
>
> The police said they found large footprints, broken tree limbs and other evidence that something was in the area.
>
> Three occupants of one house said they looked out and saw "a huge, hairy creature, well over six feet tall, and dark, barefoot and naked." They said the creature walked with a limp.

This grassman was seen in the area of the mighty Mississippi River. That these creatures could be able to swim even very wide rivers is not surprising. In the American Midwest, at least, it is easy to conclude that the grassman is equally at home in the water as he is on land.

Boggy Creek and the Fouke Monster

The most famous of all the skunk and swamp apes of southern lore is the Boggy Creek Monster. Made famous by the 1972 feature film *The Legend of Boggy Creek*, the Boggy Creek Monster, known originally as the Fouke Monster, is one of the skunk ape version of the Amityville Horror.

The story of the Fouke Monster and Boggy Creek made local and international news in 1971 when in May of that year, the Ford family of the Jonesville area had a frightening experience with a large, hairy apeman critter. The *Arkansas Democrat* (May 3, 1971) reported that the creature pushed its "claw" through the family's screen door while Mrs. Ford was sleeping on the couch. Mrs. Ford's husband, Bobby, and his brother Douglas, pursued the creature into the woods. The local sheriff arrived and took casts of some unusual footprints. An hour later, the creature was back at the Ford's residence. When it was shot at, the hairy apeman disappeared from view again. On May 2, Bobby was outside when he was grabbed and pulled to the ground. After a brief struggle, he escaped his assailant. He was treated at a Texarkana hospital for scratches and shock. Another search found more footprints around the Fords' property.

Later in the month, the *Arkansas Democrat* (May 25, 1971) reported that on the 23rd, several motorists reported seeing a six-to-seven foot creature running across Highway 71 near the town of Fouke. John Green, in his 1978 book *Sasquatch: The Apes*

Among Us, says that a 14–year-old named James Lynn Crabtree witnessed a seven-to-eight foot, reddish haired animal in 1965 near Fouke. Crabtree claims to have shot the creature three times in the face, but with no effect. Said the May 3, 1971 *Arkansas Democrat* newspaper article about the Ford family encounter (headlined "Hairy 'monster' hunted in Fouke sector"):

The Legend of Boggy Creek

Miller County Sheriff's Department officers said early today a search of the area where a mysterious creature was spotted near Fouke early Sunday failed to reveal a clue.

"Members of my department searched the area but didn't find a thing. I don't know what it could have been," Sheriff Leslie Greer said. Bobby Ford, 25, of Rt. 1, Box 220, Texarkana, Ark, who lives approximately 10 miles south of Texarkana on U.S. Highway 71, said the unidentified creature attacked him at his home shortly before midnight Saturday.

Ford was treated at St. Michael Hospital for minor scratches and mild shock and released.

"After the thing grabbed me and I broke free, I was moving so fast I didn't stop to open

271

the door. I just ran through it," Ford said.

The "creature" was described by Ford as being about seven feet tall and about three feet wide across the chest. "At first I thought it was a bear but it runs upright and moves real fast," he said.

Ford, his brother Don, and Charles Taylor saw the creature several times shortly after midnight and shot at it seven times with a shotgun.

"It first started Wednesday when our wives heard something walking around on the porch. Then Friday night about midnight the thing tried to break into the house again.

"Last night it tried to get in again," Don Ford said.

Elizabeth Ford said she was sleeping in the front room of the frame house when, "I saw the curtain moving on the front window and a hand sticking through the window. At first I thought it was a bear's paw but it didn't look like that. It had heavy hair all over it and it had claws. I could see its eyes. They looked like coals of fire ...real red," she said. "It didn't make any noise. Except you could hear it breathing."

Ford said they spotted the creature in back of the house with the aid of a flashlight. "We shot several times at it then and then called Ernest Walraven, constable of Fouke. He brought us another shotgun and a stronger light. We waited on the porch and then saw the thing closer to the house. We shot again and thought we saw it fall. Bobby, Charles and myself started walking to where we saw it fall," he said.

About that time, according to Don Ford, they heard the women in the house screaming and Bobby went back.

"I was walking the rungs of a ladder to get up on the porch when the thing grabbed me. I felt a hairy arm come over my shoulder and the next thing I knew we were on the ground. The only thing I could think about was to get out of there. The thing was breathing real hard and his eyes were about the size of a half dollar and real red.

"I finally broke away and ran around the house and through the front door. I don't know where he went," Bobby Ford said.

"We heard Bobby shouting and by the time we got there everything was over. We didn't see a thing," Don Ford said.

Everyone at the house said they saw the creature moving in the fields close to the house. All said it cold move fast.

Walraven said he was called to the scene about 12:35 a.m. (Sunday, May 2) and searched the area without finding anything. "I looked through the surrounding fields and woods for about an hour. Then, I gave them my shotgun and light. A short time later they called back and told me they had shot at it again. I went back and stayed until 5 a.m."

"Walraven said several years ago resident of the Jonesville Community near Fouke reported seeing a "hairy monster" in the area.

"Several persons saw the thing and shot at it, some from close range. They said nothing seemed to stop it. They described it as being about seven feet tall and looking just like a naked man covered with brown hair," Walraven said.

All that remained Sunday morning at the Ford house was several strange tracks—that appeared to be left by something with three toes—and several scratch marks on the front porch that appeared to have been made by something with three claws.

Several pieces of tin nailed around the bottom of the house had been ripped away and another window had been damaged by the creature, according to Ford.

"We plan to stay here tonight and see if we can get the thing if it returns," Don Ford said.

"I'm not staying here anymore unless they kill that thing," Patricia Ford said.

As for Bobby Ford, he said, "I've had it here. I'm going back to Ashdown."

That same year Fouke was invaded by tourists, bigfoot hunters and the movie crew for the low-budget movie *The Legend of Boggy Creek* to be released the next year.

An article in the *Arkansas Democrat* on October 25, 1981 by local resident Lou Farish mentioned that in 1977 a farmer in nearby Miller County checked his pigpen and discovered the remnants of a small-scale attack on his pigs. Several of them had been ripped open and one carcass was found outside and away from the pen where it had been seemingly dragged and abandoned.

Farish also says in the article that during 1978, several areas of Arkansas were experiencing strange phenomena again. In March of 1978, footprints were discovered by Joe Cook of Appleton. Cook and his brother had been prospecting about 45 miles north of Russellville when they discovered the large footprints. They measured 17 inches in length and seven inches in width. Cook also made mention of several caves in the area. (*Daily Courier*, Russllville, Arkansas, March 12, 1978)

Farish says that on June 26, 1978, 10-year-old Mike Lofton of Crossett, Arkansas, proved his courage by shooting at a 7-foot "something" outside his home. The incident began as Mike was feeding his puppy when it began to tremble. He then saw this thing coming out of the woods. Young Lofton ran into the house and retrieved his father's .22 caliber rifle. He said he fired on the creature and

275

it fled into the woods. (Farish's reference: *The News Observer*, Crossett, Arkansas, July 12, 1978)

The BFRO website (Bfro.net) mentions that there have been other Arkansas sightings including some from the 1930s when moonshining (illegal alchohol distilling) was a big business. BFRO says that the group had the opportunity of talking with Don Pelfrey of Covington, Kentucky in 1982. Pelfrey said he had spent several summers at the home of his relative's in Arkansas. He said his aunt and uncle live about 50 miles east of Hope near the Ozark Mountains and Black Lake. Fouke Creek (the "Boggy Creek"), which runs behind the house, was the center of activity over many years said Pelfrey.

His relatives (who wished to remain anonymous) had seen the creature on several occasions. They described the "monster" as a "gorilla type," except that it looked more human than animal. Its arms are longer than a man's and its face is covered with hair. The apeman allegedly leaves 17-inch footprints.

According to Mr. Pelfrey, one can see the dermal ridges on the prints. The ball of the foot is more flat than a human's and there is no indication of an arch.

BFRO says that Pelfrey told them, "It is about 800 pounds and appears

A scene from *The Legend of Boggy Creek.*

276

to be about 10 feet tall. It sounds like a bear with a screeching voice" he added. He also told them that it leaves a bad stink like that of a skunk. In addition, he said that several animals of the property had been found in a mutilated state, such as chickens, a calf and dogs with large lacerations. He told them of an incident that occurred on his aunt's farm in July of 1977:

My Aunt Martha had two prize hogs that she always hand fed until they were a couple of hundred pounds. Late one night, we heard such a calamity, that we ran to the back porch and turned the light on. When we checked the pen, both hogs were missing. There was no sign of blood or anything else. While looking around the house, we found a huge path through the weeds leading into the swamp. We discovered the remains of the hogs about 500 yards away. There appeared to be large bites and scratches and the vital organs were torn out. It appeared that the hogs were killed for sport rather than food. The neighbors had two dobermans killed. Every bone in their bodies seemed broken. They were mutilated so rapidly, that by the time they got dressed and outside, the dogs were dead. I believe this creature has become more aggressive due to more people venturing into the swamps.

Pelfrey also to the BFRO investigators that the

local authorities will not talk to anyone about the creature. In fact, Pelfrey claimed, they will chase you out of the county. (Brfro.net)

$\stackrel{\circ}{\gamma}$ —$\sim$— $\stackrel{\circ}{\gamma}$

I Know a Skunk Ape When I Smell One
The Fouke Monster surfaced again in 2005 when the *El Dorado News-Times* (May 31, 2005) ran a story on the monster and the most recent reports of its activities. Said the article:

> In Arkansas, when we hear talk of Bigfoot, we think of Fouke, and its highly-publicized trademark "monster."
> So prevalent are sightings and stories about Miller County's Fouke monster, it was featured in its own low-budget movie, "The Legend of Boggy Creek" (and the two ensuing sequels). Though they are known by a variety of other names, these mysterious creatures have been casually dubbed "Bigfoot," because of the abnormally large footprints found near some eye-witness sightings.
> Considering that only two counties separate Miller and Union County, it may not come as a surprise that Union County has had its own share of Bigfoot sightings— the most recent being May 7, 2005.
> According to the Bigfoot Field Researchers

278

Organization (www.bfro.net) and the Gulf Coast Bigfoot Researchers Organization (www.gcbro.com) websites, Union County has had at least six submitted Bigfoot encounters. Most occurred in woodlands and bottoms along the route of U.S. 167, but several have been reported near heavily wooded timberlands along the Ouachita River north of Smackover and to the east of El Dorado near Strong.

In a report (No. 11632) posted on the BFRO website, investigators were sent to El Dorado May 9th to interview the "young man" who reported the latest encounter—and to search the site on Victor Dumas Road where the sighting allegedly occurred.

In his written submission, the unnamed man told investigators that he and a friend were parked at the end of the dead-end road, sitting on the tailgate of his truck, which was facing the woods. Happening around 8 p.m., there was just enough sunlight remaining in the day to clearly see, the witness reported. Approaching the passenger side door of his truck to retrieve his cell phone, the man said, he glanced up to see on the left side of the road a fur-covered creature about 15 yards away. "With great speed, it ran across the narrow road, and paused when it got to the other side," he stated in his account. The man said the dark, hairy creature was stocky, hunched over and walked on two feet. Standing only about

279

5 feet tall, the creature ran with "great speed," according to this account. The other witness, who had remained seated on the tailgate, did not see the creature, but she claims to have heard the loud noise that was made as it darted off into the woods. A strong, foul odor, said to be reminiscent of a skunk or decaying animal, is often noticed even before a sighting occurs, according to information from the websites. There was no odor associated with the Victor Dumas Road sighting, according to the report. In his initial submission, the man made reference to the unusually short stature of the hairy being and posed the question, "Do you think this may be a young sasquatch?"

"Sasquatch is just one of the many names of Native American derivation used to refer to bigfoot. The investigators' comments indicated they believed the man was "sincere."

It was also noted that the young man returned to the site with friends the next day looking for any signs to verify his experience. There was no related evidence found the day of the investigation.

Looking through the databases, Arkansas has 53 documented sightings. Miller County has the most on the BFRO database, followed by Saline County. Baxter County and Union County are tied. One of the more interesting accounts recorded in Union County occurred the summer of 1975. Two boys, aged 15 and

11, were riding on a motorcycle trail in the woods around Bayou D'Loutre just off Sunset Road (before the U.S. 82 bypass was built). The two boys had ventured deep into the woods, against their parents' wishes. They had just crossed a medium-sized creek when the oldest boy looked westward, into the sun. "I saw an 8-foot black figure staring at us behind a pine tree trunk, and then jumping behind it as though it was playing hide-and-go-seek," he wrote.

The creature was described as very thin for its stature. Its hair hung close to the body. Both boys decided it was time to leave. They jumped on their bikes and high-tailed it back the direction they had come. "I never looked behind me again, because I was near panic," the man wrote. After crossing the creek, the older boy, who was riding behind the smaller boy, started hearing the pounding of feet behind him. He claimed he could feel the vibration from the pounding of the last several steps through his handle-bars. The two peddled ever faster, as one of them saw a movement of black to his left. The two friends completed the rest of the shaky journey home without speaking.

This man also claims to have met a man from Rogers, whose best friend saw a Bigfoot in the swamps near Parkers Chapel in the late 1980s. The man recalled how the two boys had smelled horrible odors in those same piney

281

woods and saw unusually large and peculiar piles of excrement that he couldn't link to any other animal.

In the summer of 1973, an 11-year-old boy had an encounter in Union County with something he believed to be a sasquatch. Camping with his family in the Ouachita River bottoms, near Eagle Lake, the boy volunteered to stay behind to gather firewood, while everyone else was out catching fish for dinner. The GCBRO website account claims that something started making gibberish noises, that he said sounded like a Tibetan woman auctioneer. It was loud and fast, reverberating through the bottoms like it was a large gymnasium. It happened three times, he said. The boy, now a grown man, said he has heard panther screams, coyotes, hoot owls, wolves, alligators and bears, but he, to this day, has never heard anything like that sound again.

Perusing various related websites, one can see thousands of documented sightings from areas across the nation. Most are investigated. A large map shows specks of color dotting states across the nation—indicating places where bigfoot encounters have happened. Audio tracks of odd howls and moans attributed to bigfoot can be accessed on one of the sites, which also includes an audio recording of an authentic 911 call from Washington state, in which a panicked homeowner requests law enforcement after he comes face to face with a creature in his own backyard.

Union County is far from alone in its mysterious encounters. Investigations have been launched by reports from Columbia, Ouachita and Drew counties in South Arkansas, North Louisiana, Oklahoma, Mississippi and Texas. In one GCBRO report, a Columbia County hunter shared encounters, second hand information from the past 20 years and claimed to have retrieved dark tufts of hair lodged high among broken tree limbs. In 1992, a Ouachita County woman cleaning a family cemetery, saw a tall, dark, hair-covered figure watching her from the wood line. "I stared—petrified— at the figure long enough to run through the possibilities of what it might be," she wrote in her entry. After staring at the figure "for what seemed like and eternity," the woman turned her back and accepted her fate. "None came," she wrote. "I turned back to face the thing, and it was gone. I made a hasty retreat back to my car." The woman told investigators that her mother was raised in those woods, and never heard of any such encounters.

In the late 1950s, on a hot mid-August day, three siblings saw what they recognized as a bigfoot swimming in the pond behind their rural Drew County home. The 10-year-old brother ran back to the house to get a gun. He returned in time to fire a shot at the creature, who could stay under water for long periods of time and swim at a pretty good clip. They believed the bullet hit the target, but men, who came and searched the pond and the surrounding area after the incident could find nothing.

And so the smelly skunk apes of the swamps continue to terrorize the backwoods communities and trailer parks of the south. As the grizzled skunk ape hunter in *Boggy Creek III* said to a reporter: "Yep, they're big—and hairy too."

But, like most wildmen and hairy giants, they don't bathe much. Folks smell them coming from quite a distance. The local dogs go wild. Teenage girls run to their rooms screaming. It is all like some B-movie gone horribly wrong. Trailer parks are known to attract tornados, rednecks, methamphetamine labs, and, apparently, the grassman, smelly as he is.

CHAPTER 8

SASQUATCH RULES THE FOREST

Science must begin with myths,
and with the criticism of myths.
—*Sir Karl Popper*

When we remember that we are all mad,
the mysteries disappear and life stands explained.
—*Mark Twain*

⚓ —⁓— ⚓

While the grassman of the Ohio and Mississippi River Valleys and the skunk apes of the southern swamps were often seen as only slightly larger than humans, the bigfoot on the western coast of the United States and Canada would appear to be much larger. The bigfoot of the vast forests of the Pacific Northwest are said to reach 12 feet (nearly 4 meters) in height. Typically they are said to be eight or nine feet tall, and perhaps because of the high rainfall in that area, they do not smell quite as much as their cousins back east.

Native Americans have told stories of bigfoot for generations, in which he is given different names, including sasquatch.

One of the earliest known sightings occurred in Jasper, Alberta, in 1811 when a British fur trader and explorer named David Thompson encountered giant footprints in the Athabasca River area. Said Thompson in his diary published by the *Oregon Historical Quarterly*, Number 15 (March-June 1914):

> I now recur to what I have already noticed in the early part of last winter, when proceeding up the Athabasca River ...we came to the track of a large animal, which measured fourteen inches in length by eight inches in breadth by a tape line. As the snow was about six inches in depth the track was well defined, and we could see it for a full hundred yards from us, this animal was proceeding from north to south. We did not attempt to follow it, we had not time for it, and the Hunters, eager as they are to follow and shoot every animal, made no attempt to follow this beast, for what could the balls of our fowling guns do against such an animal? Reports from old times had made the head branches of this River, and the Mountains in the vicinity the abode of one, or more, very

large animals, to which I never appeared to give credence; for these reports appeared to arise from that fondness for the marvelous so common to mankind: but the sight of the track of that large a beast staggered me, and I often thought of it, yet never could bring myself to believe such an animal existed, but thought it might be the track of some Monster Bear.

More stories were to come out of Canada in the 1800s, including the amazing story of Jacko, first told by Ivan T. Sanderson in his book *Abominable Snowmen: Legend Come to Life*.[9] Jacko was said to be a smallish apelike creature captured near Yale, British Columbia in June 1884. Jacko allegedly had been found injured on a railway line near Yale, having fallen off of a cliff. He was "of the gorilla-type" though standing only four feet seven inches tall and weighing 127 pounds. He was covered in long glossy hair about an inch long.

Jacko was exhibited, supposedly, in the local jail, and stories to this effect did appear in local newspapers, such as the *Mainland Guardian* of New Westminster on July 9, 1884. However, cryptozoologists John Green, Loren Coleman and others think that this event may have been more of a newspaper hoax, as were common at the time, than a genuine tale of a young sasquatch who was held in the hoosegow of a remote frontier town.

Still, one wonders about the great detail in the Jacko story, too long to be told here, but one that includes many names of railway men and information about his "keeper," a man named George Tilbury. John Green felt that the newspapers had been somehow duped into printing the stories. In one of the later newspaper stories, 200 people came to the local jail to view Jacko but only saw a half naked human who was in the jail on some petty charge. A rumor exists that Jacko had been earlier placed on a train going back east where he was to end up in a circus show. Jacko, if he ever existed, vanished without a trace.

Still, there are plenty of tales of sasquatch from the north woods, and while there are certainly hoaxes as well we will probably find that where there is smoke, there is fire. And in fact, the forest fire started by the sasquatch may be a big one—a blaze that may take some time to put out!

$$\approx \!\!\!-\!\!\!\sim\!\!\!-\!\!\! \approx$$

Teddy Roosevelt and Bigfoot

One of the earliest known bigfoot stories was told by the future American President Teddy Roosevelt in his early hunting book, *The Wilderness Hunter,* published in 1893. In one chapter, Roosevelt shares a bigfoot tale involving a German fur trapper he calls "Bauman," who was trapping with a friend near the Salmon River in the Bitterroot Mountains along the Idaho and Montana border sometime in the 1880s.

This is the story that Roosevelt told in his book:

I have heard but few ghost stories while

living on the frontier, and a few were of a perfectly commonplace and conventional type.

But I once listened to a goblin story which rather impressed me. It was told by a grizzled, weather-beaten old mountain hunter, named Bauman who was born and had passed all his life on the frontier. He must have believed what he said, for he could hardly repress a shudder at certain points of the tale; but he was of German ancestry, and in childhood had doubtless been saturated with all kinds of ghost and goblin lore, so that fearsome superstitions were latent in his mind; besides, he knew well the stories told by the Indian medicine men in their winter camps, of the snow-walkers, and the specters, and the formless evil beings that haunt the forest depths, and dog and waylay the lonely wanderer who after nightfall passes through the regions where they lurk; and it may be that when overcome by the horror of the fate that befell his friend, and when oppressed by the awful dread of the unknown, he grew to attribute, both at the time and still more in remembrance, weird and elfin traits to what was merely some abnormally wicked and cunning wild beast; but whether this was so or not, no man can say.

When the event occurred Bauman was still a young man, and was trapping with a partner among the mountains dividing the forks of

289

the Salmon from the head of Wisdom River. Not having had much luck, he and his partner determined to go up into a particularly wild and lonely pass through which ran a small stream said to contain many beaver. The pass has an evil reputation because the year before a solitary hunter who had wandered into it was there slain, seemingly by a wild beast, the half-eaten remains being afterwards found by some mining prospectors who had passed his camp only the night before.

The memory of this event, however, weighed very lightly with the two trappers, who were as adventurous and hardy as others of their kind. They took their two lean mountain ponies to the foot of the pass, where they left them in an open beaver meadow, the rocky timber-clad ground being from thence onwards impracticable for horses. They then struck out on foot through the vast, gloomy forest, and in about four hours reached a little open glade where they concluded to camp, as signs of game were plenty.

There was still an hour or two of daylight left, and after building a brush lean-to and throwing down and opening their packs, they started up stream. The country was very dense and hard to travel through, as there was much down timber, although here and there the somber woodland was broken by small glades of mountain grass.

290

At dusk they again reached camp. The glade in which it was pitched was not many yards wide, the tall, close-set pines and firs rising round it like a wall. On one side was a little stream, beyond which rose the steep mountain-slopes, covered with the unbroken growth of the evergreen forest.

They were surprised to find that during their short absence something, apparently a bear, had visited their camp, and had rummaged about among their things, scattering the contents of their packs, and in sheer wantonness destroying their lean-to. The footprints of the beast were quite plain, but at first they paid no particular heed to them, busying themselves with rebuilding the lean-to, laying out their beds and stores, and lighting the fire.

While Bauman was making ready supper, it being already dark, his companion began to examine the tracks more closely, and soon took a brand from the fire to follow them up, where the intruder had walked along a game trail after leaving the camp. When the brand flickered out, he returned and took another, repeating his inspection of the footprints very closely. Coming back to the fire, he stood by it a minute or two, peering out into the darkness and suddenly remarked, "Bauman, that bear has been walking on two legs." Bauman laughed at this, but his partner insisted that he was right, and upon again examining the

291

tracks with a torch, they certainly did seem to be made by but two paws, or feet. However, it was too dark to make sure. After discussing whether the footprints could possibly be those of a human being, and coming to the conclusion that they could not be, the two men rolled up in their blankets and went to sleep under the lean-to.

At midnight Bauman was awakened by some noise and sat up in his blankets. As he did so his nostrils were struck by a strong, wild-beast odor, and he caught the loom of a great body in the darkness at the mouth of the lean-to. Grasping his rifle, he fired at the vague, threatening shadow, but must have missed, for immediately afterwards he heard the smashing of the underwood as the thing, whatever it was, rushed off into the impenetrable blackness of the forest and the night.

After this the two men slept but little, sitting up by the rekindled fire, but they heard nothing more.

In the morning they started out to look at the few traps they had set the previous evening and to put out new ones. By an unspoken agreement they kept together all day, and returned to camp towards evening.

On nearing it they saw, hardly to their astonishment, that the lean-to had been again torn down.

The visitor of the preceding day had

292

returned, and in wanton malice had tossed about their camp kit and bedding, and destroyed the shanty. The ground was marked up by its tracks, and on leaving the camp it had gone along the soft earth by the brook, where the footprints were as plain as if on snow, and, after a careful scrutiny of the trail, it certainly did seem as if, whatever the thing was, it had walked off on but two legs.

The men, thoroughly uneasy, gathered a great heap of dead logs, and kept up a roaring fire throughout the night, one or the other sitting on guard for most of the time. About midnight the thing came down through the forest opposite, across the brook, and stayed there on the hillside for nearly an hour. They could hear the branches crackle as it moved about, and several times it uttered a harsh, grating, long-drawn moan, a peculiarly sinister sound. Yet it did not venture near the fire.

In the morning the two trappers, after discussing the strange events of the last thirty-six hours, decided that they would shoulder their packs and leave the valley that afternoon. They were the more ready to do this because in spite of seeing a good deal of game sign they had caught very little fur. However, it was necessary first to go along the line of their traps and gather them, and this they started out to do.

All the morning they kept together, picking

up trap after trap, each one empty. On first leaving camp they had the disagreeable sensation of being followed. In the dense spruce thickets they occasionally heard a branch snap after they had passed; and now and then there were slight rustling noises among the small pines to one side of them.

At noon they were back within a couple of miles of camp. In the high, bright sunlight their fears seemed absurd to the two armed men, accustomed as they were, through the long years of lonely wandering in the wilderness to face every kind of danger from man, brute, or element. There were still three beaver traps to collect from a little pond in a wide ravine nearby. Bauman volunteered to gather these and bring them in, while his companion went ahead to camp and made ready the packs.

On reaching the pond, Bauman found three beaver in the traps, one of which had been pulled loose and carried into the beaver house. He took several hours securing and preparing the beaver, and when he started homewards he marked with some uneasiness how low the sun was getting. As he hurried towards camp, under the tall trees, the silence and desolation of the forest weighed on him. His feet made no sound on the pine needles, and the slanting sunrays, striking through among the straight trunks, made a gray twilight in which objects at a distance glimmered indistinctly. There was

294

nothing to break the ghostly stillness which, when there is no breeze, always broods over these somber primeval forests.

At last he came to the edge of the little glade where the camp lay, and shouted as he approached it, but got no answer. The campfire had gone out, though the thin blue smoke was still curling upwards. Near it lay the packs, wrapped and arranged.

At first Bauman could see nobody; nor did he receive an answer to his call. Stepping forward he again shouted, and as he did so his eye fell on the body of his friend, stretched beside the trunk of a great fallen spruce. Rushing towards it the horrified trapper found that the body was still warm, but that the neck was broken, while there were four great fang marks in the throat.

The footprints of the unknown beast-creature, printed deep in the soft soil, told the whole story.

The unfortunate man, having finished his packing, sat down on the spruce log with his face to the fire, and his back to the dense woods, to wait for his companion. While thus waiting, his monstrous assailant, which must have been lurking nearby in the woods, waiting for a chance to catch one of the adventurers unprepared, came silently up from behind, walking with long, noiseless steps, and seemingly still on two legs. Evidently unheard,

295

it reached the man, and broke his neck by wrenching his head back with its forepaws, while it buried its teeth in his throat. It had not eaten the body, but apparently had romped and gambolled round it in uncouth, ferocious glee, occasionally rolling over and over it; and had then fled back into the soundless depths of the woods.

Bauman, utterly unnerved, and believing that the creature with which he had to deal was something either half human or half devil, some great goblin-beast, abandoned everything but his rifle and struck off at speed down the pass, not halting until he reached the beaver meadows where the hobbled ponies were still grazing. Mounting, he rode onwards through the night, until far beyond the reach of pursuit.

Teddy Roosevelt, one of America's most popular presidents, was known for his adventurous outdoor spirit and honesty. Roosevelt has no doubt that Bauman's story is true and it is one of the few stories I know of that has a sasquatch killing a human being. It would seem that the reality of bigfoot and the

Teddy Roosevelt in 1885.

296

early stories pertaining to the wild apeman would be given a great deal of credibility if President Teddy Roosevelt was a believer in the elusive and dangerous creature.

⁻ᵼ̈ —⁄⁄⁄— ᵼ̈⁻

Sasquatch Around Mt. St. Helens

The year 1924 became a big year for sasquatch encounters. In that year, a Canadian named Albert Ostman claimed he was kidnapped by a sasquatch family, and an American named Fred Beck claimed that he and some friends fought off a small army of sasquatch in a place called Ape Canyon near Mt. St. Helens in Washington state.

Ostman had kept his experience to himself until 1957 when bigfoot reports were making the news in the Pacific Northwest and he decided to tell his story. He claimed that he had been doing construction work in 1924 and needed to take a break, so he decided to look for gold around the head of Toba Inlet in British Columbia. Something kept disturbing his camp late at night and so one night he decided to stay completely dressed inside his sleeping bag, and keep his rifle handy. He fell asleep, however, and late in the night he felt something picking him up. He still had his rifle with him, which he clutched while he was carried for an hour up a steep hill.

After more ups and downs, he was deposited on the ground, while it was still dark. He claimed that

297

as it got light he could see four bigfoot creatures, two large and two much smaller. This bigfoot family apparently had a young son and daughter, and Ostman speculated that they might have brought him as a suitor to the young female sasquatch.

The young male was about seven feet tall, Ostman said, and probably weighed about 300 pounds. They slept beneath an overhanging rock on dry moss, using moss-filled "blankets" and went out in the daytime to gather grass, shoots, nuts and roots to eat. He never saw them eat any meat.

He eventually made his escape after offering some

Ape Canyon near Mount St. Helens in Oregon.

Fred Beck, who fought the sasquatch at Ape Canyon, seen here in 1965.

snuff to the large father sasquatch on occasion. One time, after a few small pinches, the big sasquatch grabbed the whole box of snuff and gulped it down. Soon the sasquatch started to become sick and rushed off to get some water. Ostman then grabbed his belongings and ran out of the valley, firing some shots from his rifle as he left to frighten the rest of the family. He was not followed and eventually made his way back to civilization.

Down near Kelso, Washington in July of 1924, Fred Beck and four other gold miners were in a remote log cabin in an area to the east side of Mt. St.

299

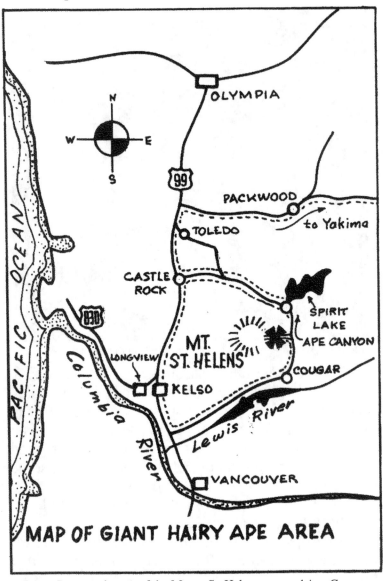

Roger Patterson's map of the Mount St. Helens area and Ape Canyon.

Helens, later to become known as Ape Canyon. They said that they encountered a group of four gorilla-men on the mountainside during the daytime, and fired on them with a revolver to halt an attack at that time. One of the huge creatures was believed slain, and the body rolled over a cliff into a deep ravine. The attack resumed after dark. A man named Smith reported to the Cowlitz County Sheriff that the hairy giant apemen pelted their cabin all night with rocks, and danced and screamed until daylight.

The men described the mountain "devils" as being at least seven feet tall and covered with long, black hair. Their arms were long and trailed, the men told the Portland *Oregonian*, which published an article about the encounter.

Bigfoot hunter Roger Patterson interviewed Fred Beck in 1966 and included the story in his book *Do Abominable Snowmen of North America Really Exist?*[16] Beck told Patterson about shooting one of the sasquatch:

> So we seen him running down this ridge then, and then he took a couple more shots at him. Marion, when he first shot I rushed over there, it was hard going, he said: "Don't run, don't run, Fred, don't run," he said, "he won't go far," he said, "I put three shots through that fool's head, he won't go far."
>
> So we got up the ridge and looked down there he was goin', just jumpin', looked like it'd be twelve, fourteen feet a jump, runnin'. The

301

Roger Patterson's drawing of the attack at Ape Canyon.

old man took a couple more shots at him and the old man said, "My God, I don't understand it, I don't understand it, how that fella can get away with them slugs in his head," he says, "I hit him with the other two shots, too."

Regarding that night in the sturdy cabin of pine logs, Beck told Patterson:

When we seen 'em, you know, why we heard that noise—pounding and whistling, at night they come in there and we had a pile of shakes piled up there, big shakes. Our cabin was built out of logs. We didn't have rafters on it, we had good-sized pine logs, you know, for rafters, two-inch shakes, pine shakes. We had them rafters close apart, they was about a foot apart, 'cause he said he wanted to make a roof what'd hold the snow. We made one to hold the snow. Them buggers attacked us, knocked the chinking out on my dad's, on my father-in-law's chest, and had an ax there, he grabbed the ax.

And the old man grabbed the ax and the logs and then he shot on it, right along the ax handle, and he let go of it. And then the fun started! Well, I wanta tell you, pretty near all night long they were on that house, trying to get in, you know. We kept a shootin'. Get up on the house we'd shoot up through the ceiling at them. My God, they made a noise. Sounded

303

like a bunch of horses were running around there. Next day, we'd find tracks, anywhere there was any sand on the rocks, we found tracks of them.[16, 67]

The *Oregon Journal* reported in 1962, in a story entitled "Monster Sightings rekindle interest in Mt. St. Helens Hairy Giant Saga," that three persons driving along a remote mountain road east of the Cascade wilderness area had said that they saw a 10-foot, white, hairy figure moving rapidly along the roadside. The white-haired sasquatch was caught in the headlights as their car passed, but they were too frightened to turn around to investigate. They apparently reported their sighting to the police.

The *Oregon Journal* also said that a Portland woman and her husband fishing on the Lewis River south of Mt. St. Helens saw a huge beige figure, "bigger than any human," along the bank of the river. As they watched the tall creature, it "moved into a thicket with a lumbering gait."

The article also mentioned that the Clallam Indian tribe of Washington State had traditions of hairy giants on Mt. St. Helens. These hairy giants are called the Selahtik, a tribe of "renegade marauder-like people, who lived like animals in the caves and lava tunnels in the high Cascades."[76]

During the 1950s, as more roads were made into the remote forests of the Pacific Northwest, things started to heat up as far as claims of sasquatch encounters. On August 26, 1957 William Roe

304

San Francisco Chronicle
THE VOICE OF THE WEST

FINAL HOME EDITION ★   MONDAY, DECEMBER 6, 1965   10 C

The Mountain Giants

A comparison of a man and the "man-animal," compiled from reports based
on the numerous eyewitness sightings of the strange mountain creatures.

This illustration appeared in the *San Francisco Chronicle* in 1965.

provided a sworn statement about his encounter
with a female sasquatch. Roe, who had worked as a
hunter, trapper, and a road worker, was doing a jop in
British Columbia during October of 1955. One day
he hiked five miles up Mica Mountain to explore a
deserted mine.

305

This photograph was sent to the *San Francisco Chronicle* and published in 1965.

As he was stepping out of a clearing, he saw what he thought was a grizzly bear. When the animal stood up, he realized this was no grizzly bear! The animal, a female sasquatch, was six feet tall, three feet wide, and weighed approximately 300 pounds. Her arms reached almost to her knees, and when she walked she put the heel of her foot down first.

Roe was hiding in some brush and was able to observe the creature from a distance of some 20 feet. He said that he watched, fascinated, as she used her white, even teeth to eat leaves from a nearby bush. Her head was "higher at the back than at the front"; her nose was flat. Only the area around her mouth was bare—the rest of her body was covered in hair, none of which was longer than an inch. The ears looked very much like a human's. The eyes were small and dark, similar to a bear's.

At this point, the animal caught Roe's scent and walked back the way she had come, looking over her shoulder as she went. As she disappeared into the bush, Roe heard her make a sound he described as "a kind of a whinny."

Roe said he wanted to find out whether the animal was a vegetarian or whether she consumed meat as well. He searched for and found feces in several places. Upon examination, no hair or insect shells were found. Roe concluded this animal lived solely on vegetation. Most researchers agree however, that these animals probably eat a variety of foods, including fish, fowl, frogs and even deer, plus all kinds of berries, pine cones, wild onions and everything

307

else edible, much like bears.[76]

⚝ —ᴧᴧᴧ— ⚝

Roger Patterson and the Bluff Creek Movie Film

As I said in the last chapter, as a youngster I had met Roger Patterson in 1967. It was a year or so later that Patterson was to film the most controversial of all sasquatch photos and movie footage.

Patterson was a former rodeo rider who took an interest in bigfoot after reading Ivan T. Sanderson's book *Abominable Snowmen: Legend Come to Life*. Patterson was born in Wall, South Dakota (famous for Wall Drug and its billboards across the state) on February 14, 1926 and died on January 15, 1972. Starting around 1958, Patterson and his friend, Bob Gimlin, began going into Washington state to do follow-up reports on sasquatch sightings and explore remote areas of wilderness where the apemen were reported to live.

During late August and early September of 1967, Patterson and Gimlin were exploring the Mt. St. Helens area. While they were away, friends in Willow Creek, California, phoned Patterson's home to report footprints found in the Bluff Creek area. The tracks, which were said to be of three different sizes, had been found on new logging roads being built in the Bluff Creek region. This same area was the scene of considerable bigfoot activity nine years earlier. It was here in 1958 that Jerry Crew found large human-like footprints. Newspaper stories of this event coined

308

the term "Bigfoot" which has now become the most popular name for this apeman.

When he returned home to Yakima, Washington and got the news, Patterson contacted Gimlin and the two men made plans to investigate Bluff Creek. They wished to find and film fresh footprints as evidence of the creature's existence in and around Willow Creek, a frontier town that sits near the Oregon border, right in the center of the Klamath and Six Rivers National Forests. Patterson wanted to make a documentary,

Roger Patterson holds up two footprint casts circa 1968.

and rented a Kodak 16mm hand-held movie camera and purchased two 100-foot rolls of color movie film for the expedition. Patterson and Gimlin traveled to the Bluff Creek area in a truck, taking with them three horses.

Patterson and Gimlin set up camp near Bluff Creek and set out on horseback to explore the area. Patterson used 76-feet of the first film roll gathering footage of the scenery to be used as a backdrop, plus took shots of both himself and Gimlin.

Not much happened for the first seven days, Patterson claimed, then in the early afternoon of October 20, 1967 Patterson and Gimlin spotted a female sasquatch down on the creek's gravel sandbar. Patterson's horse reared in alarm at the sight of the creature, bringing both horse and rider to the ground, with Patterson pinned beneath the animal.

Since Patterson was an experienced horseman, he quickly disengaged himself and grabbed his camera. While running toward the creature, he took 24 feet of color film footage. During this time, bigfoot quickly but calmly walked away across the sandbar into the woods.

During all this, Gimlin watched Patterson and sasquatch, his rifle in hand,

Roger Patterson's photo of the back of the female bigfoot as it walked away.

in case his friend was attacked by the creature. The two had previously agreed that under no circumstances would they shoot a sasquatch unless in self-protection. The female sasquatch was estimated to be seven feet three inches in height and weigh 700 pounds; she left footprints 14½ inches long by six inches wide.

Patterson and Gimlin decided not to pursue the sasquatch into the woods for fear of a possible confrontation with the creature and perhaps others of its kind.

The film gained instant fame. The very clear, daylight footage has been subjected to many attempts both to debunk and authenticate it. Some qualified scientists have judged the film a hoax featuring a man in a gorilla suit, while other scientists contend the film depicts an animal unknown to science, claiming it would be virtually impossible for a human to replicate the subject's gait and muscle movement. Indeed, if it is a hoax, it is very good one.

Both men continually dismissed allegations that they had hoaxed the footage by filming a man wearing a fake sasquatch suit. Patterson swore on his deathbed that the footage was authentic and he had encountered and filmed a large bipedal animal unknown to science. Gimlin avoided appearing in public and discussing the subject until about the year 2000, when he began to make appearances at bigfoot conferences and give some interviews.

The documentary featuring the Bluff Creek footage of the female sasquatch was eventually released as a film entitled *Sasquatch, the Legend of*

312

Bigfoot. Though there was little scientific interest in the film or the Bluff Creek footage, Patterson was still able to capitalize on it. Beyond the documentary, the film generated a fair amount of publicity. Patterson appeared on several popular television shows such as the Merv Griffin and Joey Bishop talk shows.

Today, still photos from the film are the most familiar of all sasquatch pictures. Entire books, skeptical and otherwise, have been written about this event. Hopefully, more film footage of sasquatch will emerge. Though, unfortunately, some of it will probably be deliberate hoaxing, part of the fun will be sifting through the video footage as it comes to us — fast and furious.

The Legend of Bigfoot Film Hoax

In 1975 an oddball documentary with a title similar to Patterson's was released: *The Legend of Bigfoot* by the famous hunter and trapper Ivan Marx. *The Legend of Bigfoot* is a unique film by all standards. It is, allegedly, the true story of Ivan Marx, a professional tracker, who becomes obsessed by bigfoot and sets out to film, capture and/or kill a bigfoot.

The film starts with a shot of Marx in his signature red flannel shirt, introducing himself and his topic. Apparently shot in a combination of 16 mm and 35 mm film, the documentary is like an extended episode of the 1960's television show *Wild Kingdom,* or some Lion's Club presentation on big game

313

The oldest known bigfoot photo. Taken in the 1940s in the Pacific Northwest. Courtesy of Joe Roberts.

hunting—except the quarry this time is the elusive bigfoot. But, for Ivan Marx, bigfoot is not so elusive. With his amazing tracking ability, Marx is able to find bigfoot just about everywhere he goes!

In fact, as the movie goes on, it is astonishing how Marx is able to find—and film—bigfoot from the Arctic Circle to the American Southwest. The bizarre mix of seemingly real bigfoot footage with Marx's authentic backwoodsman style (and the gnawing sense that it just isn't quite real), makes the film a genuine curiosity that is quite amusing. If the various shots of bigfoot in this movie were genuine, then Marx would be the most prolific photographer of bigfoot ever to live—or conversely, the biggest hoaxer of bigfoot who ever lived. Indeed, the latter is more probable. But is everything hoaxed in the film? Definitely not. Was Marx a believer in bigfoot? Well, it would seem that he did believe in bigfoot, but hoaxed film footage of the beast anyway. Either way, the saga of Ivan Marx is a fascinating story.

Marx tells us at the beginning of the film that he

314

is a professional tracker who, working occasionally for the government, "removed" rogue animals from areas where they were presumably killing livestock and such. Marx first heard of bigfoot in Kodiak, Alaska where ranchers claimed it was killing their cows. Interested by the stories he heard, Marx began a quest to track down the mysterious beast and bring back proof of its existence.

Marx first travels to the Petrified Forest of Arizona where 700 year-old petroglyphs reveal mysterious man-like creatures with mighty big hands. Marx then finds footprints 18 inches long in 52-inch strides that could only have been made by a critter in excess of 500 pounds. The hair samples he finds nearby were tested and "couldn't be matched with any known animal."

To his credit, Marx uncovers hoaxes in Jackson Hole, Wyoming, and then digs in caves beneath the redwoods in northern California, and stalks the coast of Oregon. Then Marx gets involved with the famous "Bossburg Cripple" bigfoot tracks in Washington State and is able to film the "crippled bigfoot"—the first of the many shots of bigfoot in the movie.

Marx seems to have be-gun his Bigfoot hoaxing ca-reer with this shot of a limp-ing bigfoot, complete with testicles hanging noticeably between the legs. He com-plains that the "experts" weren't convinced, so he'll

Ivan Marx.

315

have to go and get more bigfoot footage. Well, since the movie has only just started, this seems like a good idea. But, just how much bigfoot film footage can one man shoot in a few months? Apparently, quite a lot.

At this point in the film, Marx treats us to some of his more normal wildlife footage, capturing a cougar ("I thought it was a bigfoot at first, but it just turned out to be a cougar") plus other dead or dying animals that have been trapped or hit by cars… but Marx is after something more important, as he keeps telling us!

He heads up to the Yukon in his VW bug where lumberjacks show him some rock cairns that could only have been made by bigfoot because they are in an inaccessible area. After this there is a segment about the gold rush and Marx muses how the influx of gold miners must have had quite an impact on the local bigfoot population, but concludes that bigfoot must hide himself to survive.

Farther north, Marx expounds upon a theory that a local has told him that the reason no one has found any bigfoot remains is because the creatures carry their dead thousands of miles north to bury them in crevasses that open up in glaciers in the summer. He is told by the local Eskimos that bigfoot breeds in the mating grounds of the Alaskan moose. We are treated here to scenes of Glacier Bay and a glacier falling into the ocean, followed by Marx's obligatory moose mating shots and an extended interlude of the Northern Lights.

316

It's time for some more (faked?) bigfoot shots, though. Marx sets up some walkie-talkies on the tundra and waits. Then things get kind of kooky. We're shown footage of something in the early light of dawn that Marx says is the glowing eyes of a Bigfoot. It's odd footage, that's for sure, though it seems like a puppet with flashlights for eyes more than anything else. Marx later confesses that it must have been swamp gas. One begins to guess that Ivan Marx is a heavy drinker, among other things.

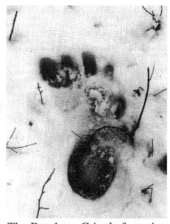

The Bossburg Cripple footprint.

Winter is coming up in the Arctic, so Marx knows he has to find Bigfoot fast. He charters a plane and finds a young Bigfoot standing on a sandbar in a river and gets crystal clear, daylight shots of the dark biped. After footage of some hunters shooting caribou, Marx beds down in Beaver Swamp where he finds more of the giant hairy critters. This time there are two of them splashing around in the water and getting some of that famous stink off of themselves.

With that, the film winds up as best it can, and Marx seems satisfied at last with the evidence for bigfoot that he has presented. Thank God he never shot one of the beasts, though the film has plenty of animal gore and death in it. What is particularly captivating about the movie is that Marx seems so genuine in his

317

demeanor and in his earnestness to capture bigfoot, yet the hoax is so blatantly apparent. It's like Marlin Perkins in the aforementioned *Wild Kingdom* drinking a bottle of Yukon Jack and filming a sasquatch around practically every corner of the woods he stumbles upon.

As the movie ended (for the third time) I sat in my living room slack-

One of Ivan Marx's photos of bigfoot.

jawed and speechless, with the remote control resting motionless in my hand. I had frozen the film a number of times, and had laughed myself silly at Marx's gleeful propensity for splicing stock animal carnage footage (no doubt his own) in with his faked bigfoot shots.

But who was Ivan Marx? A complete hoaxer who was cashing in on the 60s-70s bigfoot craze? A backwoodsman who believed in bigfoot, but liked to take the piss out of the gullible public? Was he mad at other sasquatch researchers and "experts" who scorned him? Was he "anything-for-a-buck" Ivan Marx, or really a serious researcher into bigfoot who

318

decided to perpetrate a few (or many, as the case may be) hoaxes? Later in his life Marx even to claimed that a bigfoot attacked him. Naturally, he got film footage of that, too.

༖ —ᴡᴠ— ༖

Ivan Marx: Bigfoot Hunter

As alluded to above, Marx's big break was the sensational discovery of a set of highly unusual giant footprints that became known as the Bossburg Cripple footprints, named after the area of Washington State where they were found. The Bossburg Cripple footprints were first discovered in October 1969 by a local butcher named Joe Rhodes. The sighting was reported to Ivan Marx, whose interest in the sasquatch was well known, and who happened to live in the area. Marx made casts of the footprints. Subsequently, in the same area, Marx and the Canadian sasquatch researcher Rene Dahinden discovered a set of tracks and followed them for half a mile. Dahinden told researcher Dr. John Napier that he had counted 1,089 prints in all. The remarkable feature of the Bossburg tracks to Napier, Dahinden and Marx was that the sasquatch had a deformed right foot.

Said Dr. Napier on examining the casts:

> The left foot appears normal, and in every respect is similar to a modern human foot—similar, that is, until one considers the matter of size. The Bossburg tracks, large even for a Sasquatch,

measure 17-1/2 inches by 7 inches. Apart from satisfying the criteria established for modern human-type walking, the Bossburg prints have, to my way of thinking, an even greater claim to authenticity. The right foot of the Bossburg Sasquatch is a club-foot, a not uncommon abnormality that labors under the technical name of talipes-equino-varus. The forepart of the foot is twisted inwards, the third toe has been squeezed out of normal alignment, and possibly there has been a dislocation of the bones on the outer border (but this last feature may be due to an imperfection in the casting technique). Club-foot usually occurs as a congenital abnormality, but it may also develop as the result of severe injury, or of damage to the nerves controlling the muscles of the foot. To me, the deformity strongly suggests that injury during life was responsible. A true, untreated, congenital talipes-equino-varus usually results in a fixed flexion deformity of the ankle in which case only the forepart of the foot and toes touch the ground in normal standing. In these circumstances the heel impression would be absent or poorly defined; but in fact the heel indentation of the sasquatch is strongly defined. I conclude that the deformity was the result of a crushing injury to the foot in early childhood.

Marx had earlier accompanied Texas oil millionaire Tom Slick on some of his bigfoot expeditions, and was trusted by many of the early researchers in the

320

field. In 1959, Slick financed the Pacific Northwest Expedition, a group of "professional bigfoot hunters" including Bob Titmus, Rene Dahinden, John Green and Ivan Marx. This seems to be Ivan Marx's first foray into the world of professional sasquatch investigation.

Marx's early career does not seem to be marked with hoaxes. Nor were the Bossburg Cripple footprints thought at all to be a hoax—then or now. On the possibility of the Bossburg Cripple footprints being hoaxed by someone, Dr. Napier said, "It is very difficult to conceive of a hoaxer so subtle, so knowledgeable—and so sick—who would deliberately fake a footprint of this nature. I suppose it is possible, but it is so unlikely that I am prepared to discount it."

Marx, however, apparently decided to go into the bigfoot hoaxing business after this discovery. The reason for this seems to be money. Dahinden returned to Vancouver but was in regular telephone contact with Marx; it seemed that every time he called, Marx had found something—a handprint here, a footprint there, signs of an unusually heavy creature bedding down in the bush—always something to keep the trail warm. Marx was hot on the trail of sasquatch!

Marx phoned Dahinden one evening in October 1970 and proclaimed, "I've got a film of the cripple." The details of the filming were reported in the *Colville Statesman Examiner* under the byline of Denny Striker:

321

On the night of Oct. 6 an unidentified person called the Marx home, leaving a vague message that either a car or a train had struck a large upright creature on the highway about seven miles north of Bossburg. Marx was away at the time but when he received the message... he left immediately for the area with a hunting dog he hoped would follow the spoor of the sasquatch, if indeed that was what it actually was.

Marx was armed with nothing more than a Bolex 16mm movie camera with a 17mm lens, a 35mm Nikon and a two-way radio with which he had contact with rancher Don Byington, who was in the area by the time Marx's dog had located the creature.

The day was heavily overcast with smoke... when Marx jumped the creature in the bottom of a dense draw and began filming. The initial footage shows a large black upright figure moving stealthily but rapidly through the dense growth, but only in silhouette.

Marx pressed the pursuit with his hound, forcing the sasquatch into a clearing where, with his movie camera set at f2.8 he took the remarkably clear footage of an impressive looking creature. On the screen the sasquatch is shown moving from right to left at an angle of about forty-five degrees away from the photographer. Distance from the subject according to Marx ranged from twenty-five feet to more than a hundred feet as it made its way into the heavy underbrush on the far side of the clearing.

Probably the most impressive part of the film, besides its extreme clarity, is the fact that the sasquatch is visibly injured, holding its right arm tightly to its chest and using its long muscular left arm for compensating balance. Also, both ankles of the creature seem badly skinned, the wounds showing plainly raw

One of Ivan Marx's photos of bigfoot—a hoax? **323**

against the black hair of the legs and feet.

The story was released to the wire services and the second siege of Bossburg, Washington, was underway. Film producers made offers for the film and author Ivan T. Sanderson phoned on behalf of *Argosy Magazine*. He offered to buy the serial rights to the story, as he had done with Roger Patterson's famous 1968 film footage.

Then appeared on the scene Peter Byrne, who had been part of some Tom Slick-sponsored expeditions in the Himalayas and northern California. Tom Slick had died in a plane crash a decade before, but Byrne still had a source of financing. He and Marx came to an arrangement: Marx would be paid a monthly retainer of $750 as a sasquatch hunter, and his film would be placed in Byrne's safety-deposit box as security. This arrangement carried through to the spring of 1971, Marx being comfortably subsidized to pursue his hunting while at the same time having to make no commitments about the film. But Peter Byrne was considerably less gullible than he might have seemed. The young son of rancher Byington insisted that he knew exactly where the film had been shot, and Byrne listened to him. The child led him and a group of investigators to a spot at the back of the Byington property immediately recognizable as the film site. Ivan's footage was clearly a hoax.

Peter Byrne and The Bigfoot Project
Peter Byrne, the former head of The Bigfoot

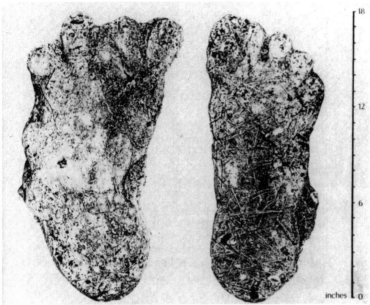

A photo of the Bossburg Cripple footprint casts.

Project, had this to say about Ivan Marx in 2003:

Some bumbling statements have recently been made via Internet lists about the original Ivan Marx 1971 Bigfoot film footage and my association with it. The origin of the statements, the person who made them, is unimportant. But in them the footage is described as an actual film and it is suggested that at the time Marx produced it, I am guilty, with the end in view of commercial gain, of exhibiting it to local "dignitaries" in Bossburg, northern Washington, where Ivan Marx lived at that

325

time and of making, as a result, "Lord knows how much money." The statements, like others that emanate from this same petulant source on a boringly regular basis are, as I can prove, blatantly untrue. Firstly, let's set the record straight. When I was associated with Ivan Marx, which was for the brief three months that he worked for me in early 1971, there was no film. There was a short piece of 16 mm film footage made by him, of what he said was a Bigfoot, that ran for about 30 seconds. That, truly, is all there ever was. Ivan Marx, an amateur cine photographer (and a mediocre woodsman), shot the footage in late 1970—or so he said—and when I came on the scene in early 1971 my job, as the primary focus of a new Bigfoot research program, was to examine the footage, determine its authenticity and then, like my work as designer and director of the original northern California Bigfoot project, follow up with full time research.

When I first met Marx at the start of the 1971 Bigfoot Project—at which time I recruited him into my team as a salaried, full-time employee and provided him with camping gear, outdoor clothing, a snowmobile and a new International Scout—he told me that his BF encounter began with an early morning call from a railway train driver who said that his engine had hit a Bigfoot the night before; the man, Marx said, gave him the location of the accident and so the same day, without delay, he set out to track and find the Bigfoot. There was a blood trail, he stated, that led him up into some 4000/4500 high foothills, roughly six miles north and east of Bossburg, Washington. About midday, in bright sunshine and under a clear sky, close to the deep snowline of the upper hills, he caught up with the Bigfoot, which, he said, was limping and appeared to be injured. The creature, he stated, weighed at least 650 pounds, was covered with thick, dark brown hair and stood a minimum of eight feet in height.

Marx said that as soon as he saw the creature he turned his 16 mm movie camera on and shot about 30 seconds of footage, in three ten-second sequences, and then, dropping the camera, which he apparently carried on a shoulder strap, he quickly and with seconds to spare, pulled out his still camera and took half-a-dozen pictures. The Bigfoot then disappeared and so he left the area and walked back down to a main road. There, coming out of the woods, he met several people, among them Norm Davis, the owner operator of the Colville Radio Station, Bill Harper, a Department of Immigration and Naturalization officer and Don Byington, a local rancher who later joined my research team; he told them that he had caught up with the Bigfoot and had been able to get footage and still pictures of it. Discussing the event

327

with Marx, he told me that the place where he got the footage definitely had more Bigfoot living in it. He had, he said, seen several sets of fresh footprints while tracking the injured one and that as soon as it was spring and the snow drifts melted off, he would lead me in there and we could get more footage.

In the meantime, the area being too rugged for snowmobile access, he suggested we wait for the snow to clear; I agreed and in turn told him that in the interim he could work for me on full salary, with all expenses, on general research in the Bossburg and Colville area. As to the footage itself, which he wanted to sell to the Bigfoot Project's sponsors for $25,000, I guaranteed him this amount, to be paid after we had thoroughly examined it and were satisfied with its authenticity; in return, as a guarantee of good faith, he agreed to let us hold the master copy. He gave this to me in a sealed metal film container and I immediately sent it by registered mail to Washington DC, to the offices of my attorneys there, to be held in trust, unopened, until such time as we made a positive decision about the work. He also gave me, on request, a working copy of the footage, for study and analysis, allowing me to take selected 8x10 prints from this for the same purpose; in addition, he gave me enlargements of the still pictures he said he had taken of his film subject.

328

The first cracks in the authenticity of the footage appeared when I was about two and a half months into the project, in late March 1971 and they surfaced one evening during a study showing of the working copy of the footage at the home of Don Byington at his ranch about a mile to the east of Marx's Bossburg home. Present at the showing were Don, his young son Stephen—about eight at the time, Don's wife, Alta, Dennis Jensen, a veteran Bigfoot researcher who had worked with Roger Patterson and was now a member of my research team, Bill Harper and Norm Davis with his wife. (These, incidentally, were probably the local "dignitaries" referred to by the accusatory source mentioned at the beginning of this article; at the least, I feel sure, they would all have been delighted to be have been given this elevating title.) When the showing was over, I heard young Stephen whisper to his father that he recognized the place seen in the footage, the place that Marx said was the site of his Bigfoot encounter; the boy was puzzled, he said, because the place was not six miles north of Marx's house, in the hills, as Marx had stated, but actually at the edge of the forest that bordered the northern boundary of their ranch.

Stephen's remarks were heard by others but were discounted at the time as the imagination of an impressionable young boy. But later that

329

night, lying in bed in my research base house at Evans, a scattering of small houses about halfway between Colville and Bossburg, and listening to the bitter winds of the end of winter howling in the frozen trees, I kept thinking about what the boy had said; and I found myself bothered by it. Next day I went to see Don and his wife and a little later that morning, accompanied by Don, Bill Harper, Dennis Jensen and Norm Davis, young Stephen led us on a search for the place he thought he recognized as the footage site. Sure enough, we soon found it and, using the two sets of 8x10 enlargements from the footage and the still pictures, were very quickly able to positively identify it via objects clearly seen in both the pictures and at the site itself. These latter included large rocks, stones, dead branches, frozen cow droppings, a rusting piece of metal from an old tractor and, most important, a small tree past which Marx's "creature" is seen moving in the footage, a tree with a horizontal branch under which it walks, without stooping, just before it disappears. The branch, it was noted by all, measured six feet from the ground; to walk under it, without stooping, the subject of the

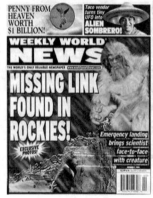

330

footage could only have been a maximum of five feet eleven inches in height.

We said nothing to Marx about our discovery, which was plainly that he had misled us about the site of the footage, but continued to employ him, his principal job being to search for footprints. (He reported finding several sets over the course of some weeks but for various reasons was never able to lead us back to them.) In the meantime we pondered on our discovery, and privately discussed it, and it worried us. In the last days of March I got a call from Norm Davis. He said that he had made an important discovery about the footage and that I should come quickly to his offices at the radio station in Colville. I did so and there found Don Byington, Bill Harper and Dennis Jensen waiting. Norm sat us down around his desk, on which he had laid out the aforementioned two sets of enlargements. He brought us all coffee, waited while we examined the pictures and then said, "So, do you see it? Do you see what I've discovered?"

We could not see whatever it was he wanted us to see and so he leaned forward and pointed. The film subject, in both sets of pictures, photographed in bright sunshine, had a distinctive shadow. And the shadow angles of each set were different, clearly indicating that the two phases of photography—the movie photography, and the still shot—had been carried out at different times and not, as Marx had told us, seconds apart. We had a brief meeting and then decided that it was time to have a serious talk with Mr. Ivan Marx to ask him, among other things, how he could have been mistaken—to put it kindly—about the site of his filming and how it was that the movie footage and the still pictures appeared to have been taken at different intervals. And so next morning, at six am—to confront our enigmatic employee while he was still drinking coffee, so to speak, we all went to Marx's rented home, a dilapidated tar paper shack just off the highway at Bossburg, to find out what he had to say about the little discrepancies in his story.

Alas, we were too late. In the night—as was clearly indicated by the discarded personal belongings strewn across his front yard—our quarry had got wind of our plans and, as they say, had upped and run for cover. And in a hurry he left a veritable river of trash running from the open, flapping-in-the-wind front door of the shack to where he parked his Volkswagen Bug, one that included ancient and tattered magazines and newspapers, old patched and re-patched gum boots, torn cotton towels, plastic rain coats, ragged shirts, woolen hats, ripped up, oil and grease stained work shirts and trousers, empty motor oil containers, rusting baked bean and soup cans, stained and ragged

332

blankets, mayonnaise and jam and pickle jars and dog food cartons and half filled trash bags. (In answer to the unspoken question, no, the abandoned garbage did not contain a fur suit.) Marx headed, as we heard later, for Burney, a town in northern California where he lived before coming north to make his Bigfoot film and find fame and fortune in the Bigfoot world and, yes, as was to be expected, we never saw or heard from him again.

Meanwhile, back in Washington DC, Marx's original footage supposedly lay in the office safe of my attorneys and that posed a question... in the light of our discovery of the fact that the footage was obviously a total fabrication, were we justified in opening the sealed canister that he had left with us in good faith, pending its purchase by us for an agreed $25,000? I consulted with the members of my team and then made a call and told my attorneys to go ahead and open it. They did this, to find that the canister did indeed contain probably a hundred feet of neatly coiled film. Original Bigfoot footage of Marx's immortal achievement? Alas no, or if you like, laughingly no... for what the wily Mr. Ivan Marx had given us was about a hundred small cut pieces of old Disney, black and white Mickey Mouse footage from the fifties and sixties.

The Marx "film" from which we all made "Lord knows how much money?" — There

333

never was a film. And there certainly was never any money made from it. How could there be, when it never existed? Later, I understand, Mr. Marx went on to make several full-length Bigfoot films, which he distributed commercially. Some of them, I have been told, are quite extraordinary—hilarious might be a better word—and show Bigfoots swimming, running and jumping, bathing in a river, playing kick-the-can, climbing trees and, in one case, actually waving at the photographer! But this was later, and not while we were associated with him. Nope. All we got for our honest efforts was Mickey Mouse and, darn it, not even in color.

There was a sequel to Marx's venture in cinematography in the fall of 1972. On Saturday Oct. 21 he appeared on "You Asked for It," a U.S. television show that pursues odd and interesting items at the request of its entranced audience. This time Marx appeared with the show's host, clutching a sealed container of movie film of a creature he said he had photographed during a snowstorm in northern California. Marx's never-ending search for the truth had once more culminated in his seeing a sasquatch, this time a white one.

He had followed it through the deepening snow until he realized he could predict its route and, as he quaintly put it, "head it off at the pass." This he did, having enough time to set up his camera, tripod and

334

all, before the thing lurched into view. The TV host then explained that Marx had brought the film straight from the camera, undeveloped, and that the show's producer would process the film under the strictest of supervision and would then examine it. Following a commercial break we were flashed ahead in time to where the film had been processed, and then the film was shown.

It was marvelously clear footage. A primate expert whom the TV people had co-opted for an opinion said it best: "I think it's a man in a beast's suit." It certainly looked like someone in a beast's suit. Great folds of the suit swung around like an old army blanket amid the California snows as might happen if one were running through deep snow in an overcoat. The thing cavorted before the camera, now running comically toward it, now turning about and gallivanting off through the drifts, flipping its clumsy feet backwards and sideways as it went. Marx had clearly hoaxed the footage and most of the audience had little doubt that they were watching a snow job in a blizzard.

Grover Krantz and the Ivan Marx Handprints

Longtime sasquatch researcher Grover Krantz began examining evidence from Ivan Marx starting in 1970 and found Marx to be a credible investigator. Though he had some doubts about Marx and his motives, Krantz was particularly impressed with

335

handprints that Marx claimed to have discovered in the summer of 1970.

Says Krantz:

> During the summer of 1970, handprints of two of these animals were photographed and plaster casts of them were made by Ivan Marx, a game guide in northeastern Washington State. Marx loaned the original casts to the writer who then made latex molds from them in order to produce exact duplicates for further study.
>
> The authenticity of these casts is impossible to demonstrate by any direct means. That they were not faked is strongly indicated by the fact that these are only the best two out of several prints that were cast, and that photographs of many more were taken. For a hoaxer to have made them all would have involved a considerable amount of difficulty.
>
> The two good prints described here are both of left hands which were imprinted flat into soft ground showing all digits and outlines of the palms. The longer print shows all digits somewhat flexed and their tips were well indented into damp ground. It measures 292 mm. in actual length to the end of digit III, but the hand would be closer to 300 mm. long if fully extended.
>
> The hands which supposedly made these imprints can be compared and contrasted with

those of recent man in several particulars. Most obvious is their immense size—in linear dimensions they are more than half again greater than an average European's hand. My own hand, of average proportions but quite large, measures 205 mm. in length and 95 mm, in breadth. The Sasquatch hands are thus 46.4% and 29.3% longer than mine, and 83.2% and 94.6% broader, giving a mean of over 63% greater in these two dimensions. This is at least commensurate with claimed stature estimates.

Probably the most unexpected feature indicated for these hands is the apparent non-opposability of the thumb, which is clearly evident in both individuals. In the short hand the *palmar* surface of the thumb is quite flat and is in the same plane as all of the fingers. In the larger hand the thumb flexion parallels that of the other digits in digging into the ground. Still, these thumbs both separate from near the base of the palm and extend out to the side in a quite human direction.

There are many other irregularities in the cast's surfaces which cannot be identified in terms of human anatomy. Most of these irregularities no doubt resulted from unevenness in the dirt into which the hands were pressed, and also from various particles which fell into the impressions before the casts were made.

The *thenar* pad, or eminence, at the base

337

of the thumb is virtually non-existent. In this eminence would be found the major muscles (abductor pollicis brevis, opponens pollicis, and flexor pollicis brevis) which in man pull the opposable thumb in various ways across the palm. Since in this case the thumbs do not oppose, it is consistent that the *thenar* area is not thickened. It would require someone quite familiar with the anatomy of the human hand to make the connection between a non-opposable thumb and an absence of a *thenar* eminence. This tends to support the authenticity of these handprints. Ivan Marx has no known training in human anatomy, and no other person could have planted the many impressions without leaving his own track for Marx to observe.[83]

Ivan Marx was clearly a respected hunter and trapper, as far as Grover Krantz was concerned. In fact, Krantz considers the possibility that Marx may have hoaxed the handprints and decides that he did not. Some of the Bigfoot evidence that Marx is associated with seems quite authentic. But other "evidence" is clearly hoaxed by him.

Ivan Marx was a complicated man, as far as I can tell. He was a genuine outdoorsman, one who fought cougars bare handed and drank with the best of them. He had clearly learned to tell a tall tale around the campfire with the best of them, too. Given the bigfoot craze waxing in 1969, there was money to be made if some hunter could bag himself a real-life abominable snowman. Marx was determined to be that person (at least he said so in his movie)!

Though Marx may have genuinely believed in bigfoot, and occasionally gathered some slim evidence for the creature's existence, he decided he needed better evidence. Evidence that paid better—evidence that would make him rich and famous.

So, here's to Ivan Marx, may he rest in peace. While bigfoot rolled in his grave, Ivan was laughing all the way to the bank, even if the payoff was meager in the end. Marx seems to never have gotten truly rich off his sasquatch photography. *The Legend of Bigfoot* looks to be a spoof of bigfoot hunters, one told with the straight face of a real backwoodsman with a piece of jerky and a hip flask in his pocket.

⁂ ⸺⟿⸺ ⁂

Bigfoot Central

One amusing incident, almost out of a B-horror movie, was the Sycamore Flat Campground incident that took place near Palmdale, California in the summer of 1971. During that summer, three local students (Brian Goldojarb, Richard Engels

339

and Willie Roemerman) were driving along an area known as The Flat, which is really just a narrow strip of camping area with picnic tables on the edge of the road, on the western edge of the Antelope Valley in the Angeles National Forest, southwest of the town of Pearblossom.

The three boys were in Willie's pickup truck with Willie driving. Richie and Brian were riding in the truck's bed. As they drove past the campground late at night a huge creature suddenly bolted from the campground and followed the men in their pickup. After running (seemingly) after the truck for about 50 feet, the dark-colored creature suddenly veered off the road and plunged into a swamp. The whole episode lasted for about 20 seconds.[76]

As it veered, according to the witnesses, its head brushed an overhanging tree branch that was nearly 10 feet off the ground. The height of the cardboard cutout in their famous photograph was based on the tree branch. The Creature of Sycamore Flat was later dubbed "Big Ben" by locals and it made continual appearances in the area. It had a habit of standing straight-backed, arms akimbo, on high ridges at night as if surveying the action down below.

One of the better photographs of a sasquatch was released in 1996. According to an article in *Fortean Times*[51] (No. 93, Dec. 1996), a forest patrol officer from Tacoma, who wishes to remain anonymous for fear of losing his job, had an encounter with a giant ape-like creature and was able to take a series of 35mm photos. The ranger then called Cliff Crook

340

at the sasquatch-monitoring group named Bigfoot Central.

Bigfoot Central is located in Cliff Crook's living room in Bothell, Washington. Crook held a news conference on December 9, 1995 to satisfy the mounting interest over the photos. Crook told the conference that the ranger had taken 14 photographs of the sasquatch but eight of them were dark because fleeting clouds blocked the sun on his 50mm telephoto lens. The ranger said that he heard a splashing noise to his left while hiking along a ridge in Washington state's Snoqualmie National Forest. He went to investigate the noise. Then, from a high bank, he observed the eight foot creature just 30 yards away in a swampy lagoon. He use up what remained of his roll of film.

The photos are sensational, clearly depicting a hairy bigfoot creature with its head low on a pair of massive shoulders. Not the sort of creature one wants to tangle with in a back alley or backwoods swamp. The photos have a certain Frank Frazetta look to them that makes their authenticity seem doubtful. One photography analyst declared that he had found tiny diamond shapes in the image indicating that it was a digitally created image. Cliff Crook countered that the analyst was examining a laser-copied print and not an original.

Skeptics believe that the photo was digitally created, probably in Photoshop, while some think that it is genuine. Genuine bigfoot photos would be welcome by all cryptozoologists, but fakes occur

341

from time to time.

Another encounter of note also occurred in the summer of 1995 when several ex-Forest Service employees claimed that they had had an encounter with a bigoot in the Pacific Northwest of the USA. An Associated Press story released from Walla Walla, Washington on Aug. 10, 1995 carried the headline "3 Men Claim Bigfoot Sighting." The story went on to say:

> A man who has frequently claimed to have encounters with a legendary creature dubbed Bigfoot says this time he's got witnesses.
> Paul Freeman, a former U.S. Forest Service employee, said he and two other men saw a tall, hairy creature on Saturday in the Blue Mountains, about 25 miles east of Walla Walla in the Mill Creek watershed.
> Freeman, who claims to have spotted a similar creature four other times, brought back part of a tree he says Bigfoot twisted, some hair samples and two plaster footprint molds.
> Freeman went on the expedition with Walla Walla resident Wes Sumerlin and former state game department employee Bill Laughery. The trio said they first saw signs of the creature's presence: a strong odor, small, twisted trees with clumps of long, black hair, and large footprints, 15 inches and 7 inches wide.
> Then on Saturday, through the dense timber, they saw bigfoot, nearly 8 feet tall and a hairy

342

tan-brown, Laughery said.

Stories of encounters with bigfoot in Canada and the USA continue to this day. Bigfoot encounters even occur in Arizona and southern California. In the next chapter we will examine some of the most recent encounters that have made the news.

Above and Opposite: Two of several photos allegedly taken of a sasquatch in Washington state on December 9, 1995. Courtesy of Cliff Crook.

CHAPTER 9

MODERN SASQUATCH REPORTS

Clearly the sasquatch does not constitute a new order of mammals like the elephant. Almost certainly it is not even a distinct family like the giraffe. Its physical distinctions from known primates would most likely rate a new genus, nothing higher. And that genus is quite possibly one that is already known in the fossil record; it might even be a known fossil species.
—Grover S. Krantz

The fairest thing we can experience is the mysterious.
—Albert Einstein

Yetis, bigfoot, hairy giants and skunk apes will continue to crop up in the news for decades to come. There is no sign, as yet, that these creatures are extinct. Perhaps they need protection, but they seem to be able to take care of themselves. Indeed, rather than the reports of sasquatch becoming fewer, they are becoming more common and widespread. Recent reports from Arizona, New Mexico and Colorado indicate that bigfoot is still tromping around a wide swath of the United States.

Sasquatch in Arizona

The Arizona sasquatch, sometimes called the Mogollon Monster, made the news on September 2, 2006, when newspapers in Arizona reported on bigfoot activity at the White Mountain Apache Nation which comprises a large part of east-central Arizona. This area of the state is heavily forested and lies along what is known as the Mogollon Rim, which stretches from Flagstaff, Arizona, through small towns to the south like Pine and Strawberry, into Payson, Show Low and the White Mountain Apache Nation and then to the Mogollon Mountains in New Mexico. This area contains the largest ponderosa pine forest in the world and is the sort of habitat the sasquatch is said to prefer: dense forest with plentiful rivers and streams, and a near complete lack of human towns and cities. Indeed, this vast area, larger than many eastern states, could contain many hundreds of sasquatch. Areas around Flagstaff, Stoneman Lake, and the tiny towns of Pine and Strawberry have had bigfoot reports for many years, and I personally know several people who have told me that they have briefly encountered

348

bigfoot in this area.

The White Mountain Apache Nation reports were particularly interesting because a number of Apache Nation police officers were involved and reports were made to the police department that tended to show the seriousness of the encounters. Local television news crews were dispatched to interview witnesses and this story appeared on Tucson's Channel 3 website, azstarnet.com, under the headline, "Apaches go public with Bigfoot Sightings":

Footprints in the mud. Tufts of hair on a fence. Ear-piercing screeches in the night. These are only fragments of the stories now coming from the White Mountains in Eastern Arizona.

For years the White Mountain Apache Nation has kept the secret within tribal boundaries. "We're not prone to easily talk to outsiders," said spokeswoman Collette Altaha. "But there have been more sightings than ever before. It cannot be ignored any longer."

It is a creature the world knows as "Bigfoot".

"No one's had a negative encounter with it," said Marjorie Grimes, who lives in Whitewater, the primary town on the reservation. Grimes is one of many who claim to have seen the creature over the last 25 years. Her first sighting was in 1982. Her most recent was in the summer of 2004, driving home from the town of Cibecue.

349

She becomes more animated as the memory comes forth. "It was all black and it was tall! The way it walked; it was taking big strides. I put on the brakes and raced back and looked between the two trees where it was, and it was gone!"

Grimes' son Francis has a story. Their neighbor Cecil Hendricks has a story. Even police officers have had strange encounters. Officer Katherine Montoya has seen it twice. On a recent Monday night dozens of people called into the tribe's radio station, KNNB, to talk about what they'd seen. Others came in person.

...Tribal police lieutenant Ray Burnette puts it in terms of public safety. "A couple of times they've seen this creature looking through the windows. They're scared when they call."

As in all alleged sightings of a bigfoot creature, tangible evidence is scarce. The "Patterson film" from 1967 is the most-often-seen video. It shows a tall hairy figure striding through the woods of the Pacific Northwest. For nearly 40 years this film's authenticity has been debated; it has never been discredited.

In the White Mountains last year, investigators found footprints, several tufts of hair and other material at the scene of a sighting. Tribal police made plaster casts from the prints and sent hair and plant samples to the Department of Public Safety for analysis in its state-of-the-art crime lab. Test results showed the hair was not human, but animal in origin. Further testing to determine what kind of animal was not done.

...Back on the reservation, Lieutenant Burnette wants outsiders to realize that the department takes these calls seriously, and so should you. "The calls we're getting from people—they weren't hallucinating, they weren't drunks, they weren't people that we know can make hoax calls. They're from real citizens of the Fort Apache Indian Reservation."

Another report came from the same area on November 6, 2006, published by *The Arizona Republic* with the headline "Ft. Apache reports spur Bigfoot hunt." In the article it was mentioned that a police report had been made by White Mountain tribal Officer Katherine Montoya, who responded to a call at 2:30 a.m. on August 14 when Barry and Tammy Lupe of Whiteriver called 911 to report an un-humanly large prowler peering through their window. Officer Montoya reported what she witnessed when she arrived at the Lupe residence:

It stood approximately 6'7" tall. It appeared to be about 220 pounds or more. It had exceptionally long arms; it did not appear to be wearing any clothes, and just appeared black. When it turned towards me, the most

351

obvious feature was its eyes. The skin around his eyes was a lighter color than the rest of the face. It appeared almost white while the rest of the suspect was black. I could smell a distinct odor, like a stinkbug. You know, when you squish a stinkbug it smells. It never made any sounds until it crashed through the fence [while running away].

Apparently, Officer Montoya had never heard of skunk apes or the Fouke Monster from Arkansas. Her suspect was, by her own admission, a large, hairy, stinky apeman. She had just met the Mogollon Monster.

In the same area, with the nearest town being Strawberry, Arizona, a man named John Johnson reported on July 10, 1999 to Oregonbigfoot.com that he had camped with a friend a few days earlier, and they had a sasquatch visit their camp. Johnson claimed that they heard strange screaming noises like a banshee's one night. On the next night he and his friend heard what sounded like pounding on a hollow log. This occurred off and on through the night and the next morning they discovered an old tree that had been torn into pieces by some powerful being. Said Johnson, "You would have to be Hercules to do this to a tree." (Oregonbigfoot.com file #00503)

A doctor posted a story on the Unexplained Mysteries forum (UnexplainedMysteries.com) about an encounter in the same area in 2006:

I'm a doctor in Northern Arizona. On a trip from Show Low to Concho on the afternoon of Thursday, October 26th, 2006, I saw a sasquatch about 1/2 a mile in front of my car. It entered the road from the right, ran across the road, down the shoulder on the other side and into the brush. My first thought/comment was "What the hell was that!" thinking that it certainly did look like a sasquatch, but I didn't believe that they might be in Arizona of all places. Perhaps in the Pacific Northwest or even in the mountains of the eastern US, but Arizona? That certainly would have never crossed my mind! ...until my wife looked up this site on the net which contained several references to sasquatch by the local White Mountain Apaches.

...The interesting thing is that no matter how much a person doubts the existence of something, no matter how much other people try to explain it away as your eyes playing tricks on you, no matter how much people try to rationalize somebody else's experiences, once you've seen something crystal clearly on a bright, clear day yourself, you know. You realize that the comments of others is simply their ignorance and need for denial. It no longer matters to me what anybody says about sasquatch, there will never again be a single doubt in my mind. Once you see one, it takes it out the realm of possibility and firmly into the realm of knowing. I don't consider myself a "believer." It's not a matter of believing. I now know.

Many more stories of the Mogollon Monster have surfaced over the past decade and there is even a website devoted to the creature. In a feature article in *The Arizona Republic* on April 3, 2009, reporter Clay Thompson told of hearing stories of the Mogollon Monster as a Boy Scout at a camp near Pine, Arizona in the 1960s. He also reported that a friend of his, Don Davis, who died in 2002, claimed that he encountered the monster at a Boy Scout camp near Payson in the 1940s. Davis had reported:

> The creature was huge. Its eyes were deep set and hard to see, but they seemed expressionless. His face seemed pretty much devoid of hair, but there seemed to be hair along the sides of his face. His chest, shoulders and arms were massive, especially the upper arms; easily upwards of 6 inches in diameter, perhaps much, much more. I could see he was pretty hairy, but didn't observe really how thick the body hair was. The face/head was very square; square sides and squared-up chin, like a box.

The Mogollonmonster.com site also records a sighting near Springerville, Arizona by a woman named Donna who reported her encounter on

December 25, 2008:

We spotted it on the old Bigelow homestead. It was walking down the treeline along the Little Colorado River on the south side of the creek. It was huge—about 8 feet tall. It didn't seem too worried about us either. We were on the road a good 100 yards from the creature, and we were in our truck. We had just dropped down off the plain on the South Fork access road. We wanted to look at the old abandoned house. Then we spotted it. It was large, looked black. There was no clothing, so it was not a man. We watched it until it moved back into the tree line. A good 4 minutes, but we had no cameras with us. It was about daybreak.

Another report, this one submitted to BFRO (bfro. net), was about an incident that occurred in 2005 at the Lo Lo Mai Springs Campground by Page Springs, which is near the New Age Mecca of Sedona, and also very near the northern Arizona home of John and Cindy McCain. Said the report:

I was in Page Springs Arizona on Oak Creek in July 2005 with my kids, camping, and my daughter and I saw something. I saw it twice. Also, a friend of mine and myself had some bad feelings in a particular area there. He was camping further down the creek. What I saw was odd. It was grey, 4'-5' tall, slender, fast

355

moving, able to hide, and made a screeching noise twice, once when I think it hit something while moving and again, far away when tons of dogs were barking. Could hear stones clicking, walking and breathing nearby after I went into my tent for the night. Our peaceful camping trip turned into us being frightened.

It is interesting to note how close this incident was to the home of Senator McCain. One might think that the Secret Service would be especially vigilant in protecting him if they suspected that a bigfoot was somehow on the property!

ༀ —៳៳— ༀ

The 2003 Colorado Sasquatch Sighting
Bigfoot was big news in Colorado in early 2003 when *The Denver Post* featured an interesting story about sasquatch in its Sunday, January 5th edition. A former instructor at the University of Colorado Law School named Julie Davis claimed she met bigfoot one morning while camping.

The article was headlined: "Camper Says She was 12 Feet from Curious Giant." The article then says: "When Julie Davis burst from her tent in a remote part of the San Juan National Forest late on the afternoon of Aug. 5, 2000, the 54-year-old musician expected a confrontation with a hungry bear. What she got was the surprise of her life."

Julie goes on to say, "It was gigantic—it must have

356

been 8 feet tall. My first thought was, 'I'm looking at something I've never seen before,'" she said. "I didn't even think about bigfoot. The notion that these animals were out there in Colorado never crossed my mind."

Davis said she was too afraid to move, and simply stared at the bigfoot standing 12 feet away. Says Davis in the article, "It had very, very broad shoulders — huge shoulders. Its face was almost completely covered in fur but human-like, on the human side of halfway between a human and gorilla."

Davis, according to the article, was an experienced backcountry camper from rural Boulder County and a former volunteer with the Great Bear Foundation; apparently she knew a bear when she saw one. This was not a bear. There was medium-chestnut fur "like an Irish setter's" covering the giant, which stared back at her in apparent curiosity with big brown eyes.

"I've had a lot of time to get to know what bears look like up close," she says in the article. "This animal was bigger than any bear." It uttered a low rumble, and immediately a second animal — slightly smaller and lighter in color — peered at her from behind the big one. Suddenly, the two turned, ran back into the forest, and disappeared. Davis did not leave her remote campground near Jarosa Mesa until the next day.

For two years, Davis kept quiet about her encounter, sharing it with only a handful of friends and the Bigfoot Field Researchers Organization (BFRO).

The article goes on to say that Davis' account is one of 54 sasquatch sightings, tracks or vocalizations reported in Colorado during the past 40 years that are listed on the BFRO website.

⚡ —᷈ᴠᴠᴠ— ⚡

Yukon Sasquatch Sighting in 2004

On June 10 of 2004 the Associated Press reported out of Whitehorse in the Canadian Yukon that two men traveling down the Alaska Highway had witnessed a large sasquatch along the road.

The AP story quoted a Conservation Officer named Dave Bakica who said he was convinced that whatever the two men saw early on June 6, a Sunday morning, "shook them up." Bakica said that

A photo of bigfoot allegedly taken in 2005 in northern Idaho with a motion-sensitive camera. Little else is known about this photo.

Marion Sheldon and Gus Jules were traveling out of town along the Alaska Highway on an all-terrain vehicle between 1 and 2 a.m. when they passed what resembled a person standing on the side of the highway. Said the story:

> Thinking it was a person from their small community who might be in need of a ride, they turned around. As the two lifelong Teslin residents and members of the Teslin Tlingit Council approached to within 20 feet, they noticed the figure was covered in hair, but standing upright the entire time.
>
> Though natural light was dusky, Jules saw what he believed to be flesh tones hidden beneath the mat of hair, he told Bakica.
>
> "I have no doubt they saw something, and are convinced it was not a bear or anything in the ordinary," Bakica said. "They are convinced this was something out of the ordinary… And they are pretty shook up over it."
>
> Bakica stated that Jules is an experienced hunter and described the figure as standing about 7 feet tall, but hunched over. They could see it was not a person. As the two parties went their separate ways, the dark-haired figure crossed the highway in two or three steps.
>
> Bakica said ground conditions mixed with rainfall made it impossible to pick up definitive tracks and there was no hair on branches or other vegetation. Also, by the time he went to

359

the scene Monday morning, half the town had been out to the site, he said.

The AP story mentioned that Jules launched a search for evidence that could document his experience.

"I have no doubt in my mind that they believe what they saw was a sasquatch," said Bakica. "Whether it was or not, I do not know. Just because you can't prove something was there, does not mean it was not there."

According the story, other sasquatch sightings have occurred in the area. In April 1991, three Pelly Crossing residents reported seeing a sasquatch while driving between Pelly and Stewart Crossing. The creature fled back into the woods as the vehicle passed. The residents took a photo of what they claim were footprints measuring 15 inches long in the melting snow.

꙾ ——ᨑ— ꙾

The Sangre de Cristo Mountains, New Mexico Sighting

The Taos News 2007 carried a story on January 18, of a sasquatch sighting in northern Taos County, in the Sangre de Cristo Mountains near the New Mexico-Colorado border. A Costilla, New Mexico man named Arturo Mart'nez, age 67, and a friend (who wished to remain anonymous) had an encounter on September 27, 2006. Said the article:

360

Mart'nez and friend returned to another area several miles away from where they had been earlier in the day. This time, while driving on another fork of the rough road, they found many tops of aspen trees cleanly broken off that were strewn over the road.

"We decided to investigate who was breaking the trees and throwing them on the road. I asked my friend, 'Who would want to do this?'" Mart'nez explained, "These were aspens ranging in size from 3 to 4 inches to 6 to 8 inches in diameter, cleanly broken about 13 to 15 feet up the trunk of the trees. There were no tracks of bear or elk, or human tracks—no tracks of any kind, no sawdust at the bottom of the trees and what was strange, it was as if they were thrown several feet away from where they were broken. There were two big aspens completely uprooted and thrown away from where they had been growing. If bears had broken them, they would have left claw marks. Bears leave a smell on trees they scratch or break.

"Elk in rutting battles leave the ground very disturbed. It wasn't, and seeing many broken trees we continued on to investigate who or what was breaking them. The broken treetops were lying in the road as if something or someone wanted to say, 'Nobody is welcome here.' Rounding a curve, my tire blew out and things started getting very scary," he continued.

"We could hear elk bugling up higher and we decided to walk back down since it was late afternoon," Mart'nez said. "We needed to get a spare, and come back to change the tire. We were taking our time checking out more broken trees, and there was easily over a hundred broken the same way. That's when I heard the scariest noise I have ever heard in my life.

"It started at first, sounding like an elk bugling, then turned into a scary roar so loud it kept echoing through the canyon," he continued. "The elk up high stopped bugling. It kept making that noise at us. It reminded me of the noise the devil made in *The Exorcist* movie. Whatever was making the noise started breaking trees and throwing them in our direction a few seconds later.

"Then I saw a huge creature moving through the edge of an aspen grove, about 30 to 40 feet from me. It walked upright, but hunched over, maybe 6 feet tall bent over, and standing straight was 7 to 8 feet tall with very dark fur all over. It was not a bear. Bears don't walk like humans. I am convinced I saw what many call Sasquatch. Even with my gun, I was very scared and we left in a hurry. It seemed to be following in the edge of the trees, breaking more, throwing them toward us and making that awful noise. It was almost dark and we had to get out of there," he recounted.

The two men fled down the mountain, and Mart'nez said every time the creature roared the noise continued reverberating through the entire area. "I felt like at any moment something was going to grab me from behind all the way out of there."

They arrived on foot in Costilla well after dark, deciding no matter how scared they felt, it was necessary to return to the canyon, change the blown tire and bring Mart'nez's vehicle back. The two men returned to where the vehicle was parked, and by the time they changed the spare it was after 2 a.m. on Sept. 28.

"We decided to stay until daylight and try to find out what it really was we had experienced," Mart'nez continued, "It was deathly quiet the whole time, nothing moving, no elk bugling, not a sound at all. At sunrise, we checked around, found more aspens broken the same way. Nothing else happened to us. There was no sign of anything out of the ordinary except more broken trees."

Not finding any other evidence of their frightening experience of the afternoon before, Mart'nez and his friend returned home. "Like I said, I know what I saw. I know it is not a bear or any other of the wildlife I have seen around here all my life. I decided to tell my story because America, wake up, these creatures exist," he said. "Every time I go into the mountains anywhere from now on I will have a camera and an audio recorder with me. I have had other people tell me that even though they wish to remain anonymous, they have had similar experiences over the years, but don't say much because they get ridiculed. I know what I saw and heard."

Similar bigfoot encounters were reported in the San Luis Valley area, on the Colorado side of the Sangre de Cristo Mountains, in the winter of 1993-94. The events were originally reported in the February edition of the *Crestone Eagle* and later the events were featured the 1996 television show *Strange Universe*. During the last week of December into the first week of January, seven sasquatch encounters were reported to local authorities along the Colorado-New Mexico border in the San Luis Valley. A niece of the undersheriff called to tell him that she had found some tracks that he'd better come look at. She told him that they were huge, human-looking, barefoot tracks.

On the morning of December 31, he followed her to the remote location with a video camera to document the scene. Descending for hundreds of yards down a cow trail were two sets of human-looking tracks. One set measured 20 inches in length, while the other was 18 inches long. They descended over a variety of terrain, in snow and bare ground.

364

The undersheriff's niece told him that on the eve of discovering the tracks, she had heard her dog barking furiously outside. She went out to see what the commotion was all about when she heard huge footsteps go running by the house. Outside, she found her dog cowering inside the fenced yard. The dog had originally been locked out of the yard and she put him back outside the fence. A short time later, he started barking again, and once more she heard the huge running footsteps and a twang of something hitting the barbwire fence. After going outside again she found her dog once again inside the fence and shaking with fear!

The following morning, while stalking a herd of deer to take photos, she happened to stumble on the giant barefoot tracks. She called her uncle to report the possible encounter and the tracks.

Christopher O'Brien reports in his book *The Mysterious Valley*[92] that the undersheriff related several other recent Accounts. One found a mother and son driving back from the mountains just after sunset on the southern part of the San Luis Valley near the New Mexico border. As they rounded a curve, their headlights revealed a sasquatch in the middle of the road with large glowing eyes and pointed ears. The mother slammed on her brakes and put the car in reverse and backed up. The bigfoot then dropped down on all fours and ran away like a dog!

The mother and son proceeded directly to the sheriff's office to report what they had seen. According to the undersheriff, "They were real upset about

it." This impressed the authorities enough for them to mount a search for the creature.

O'Brien mentions two additional reports that were subsequently filed by motorists who had spotted large hairy humanoid creatures, at night, next to the highway. One report was made by a trucker who claimed the hairy giant he saw was "all white."

Yet another report was filed by a man who claimed he witnessed a pair of bigfoot "stalking a herd of elk" on the side of a mountain. He was close enough to see them "signaling to each other" while watching them through his binoculars.[92]

O'Brien also mentions a New Mexico Cattle Inspector who lives in Rancho de Taos, New Mexico, who said that he had used binoculars to watch "a white bigfoot" clamber up a rocky slope during the late fall of 1993. It ascended the seemingly-impossible slope in minutes. The inspector became even more impressed with the creature's agility when he tried to make the same climb the following day. It took him over two hours.[92]

To me it is always interesting to hear stories of white-haired sasquatch. Perhaps the white hair would help it blend in with the abundant snowdrifts that blanket Colorado in the wintertime. Or, perhaps the white sasquatch is an older sasquatch, whose hair was once reddish-brown, but is now white or grey—like

366

the changing of pigment that happens in aging apes and humans. More on that later.

🙚 —ᴠᴠᴠ— 🙙

Bigfoot in the Upper Peninsula 2007

Bigfoot got into the news in Michigan when he suddenly was spotted near Manistique. Located in the Upper Peninsula at the eastern edge of the Hiawatha National Forest, Manistique is a major fishing, hunting, boating and camping area with large sections of uninhabited forest to the west, north and east of the lakeside town. So it may come as no big surprise that the Associated Press reported on June 26, 2007 that sasquatch had been sighted repeatedly around the town.

Under the headlines "Scientists set to prove 'Bigfoot' is no myth," and "Bigfoot Field Researchers say almost every expedition yields a sighting," the story said:

> Researchers will visit the Upper Peninsula next month to search for evidence of the hairy manlike creature known as "Bigfoot" or "Sasquatch."
>
> The expedition will center in eastern Marquette County, following the most recent Bigfoot eyewitness account, said Matthew Moneymaker of the Bigfoot Field Researchers Organization.
>
> "We'll be looking for evidence supporting

367

a presence. ...We hope to meet local people who might have seen a Sasquatch or heard of someone else who had an encounter," Moneymaker told the *Daily Press* of Escanaba.

Most experts consider the Bigfoot legend to be a combination of folklore and hoaxes, but there are a number of authors and researchers who think the stories could be true.

Among all U.P. counties, Marquette County has logged the most reported Bigfoot sightings with four, Moneymaker said. Bigfoot encounters also have been reported in Ontonagon, Baraga, Dickinson, Luce and Schoolcraft counties.

In all but three of 30 expeditions in the United States and Canada, BFRO investigators have either glimpsed Bigfoot or gotten close enough to hear the creature, Moneymaker said.

Indeed, it seems that Manistique and the Hiawatha National Forest would be good places to search for sasquatch, though no reports of bigfoot being captured in Upper Michigan have so far been reported by the local media. A seven-second clip of a sasquatch walking through the woods near Bay City, Michigan was posted on Youtube.com on July 23, 2008. It very clearly shows a white-haired sasquatch walking through the woods, swinging its arms by its sides as it disappears behind a tree. The clip, which

368

is short and without any voice over, is so sharp that it would seem to be a hoax, though it seems like a lot of trouble to go to, including making the fake sasquatch suit (a white one, at that), for a seven-second video for Youtube. The absence of any explanation or provenance for the clip seems suspect. As with many videos of bigfoot, we will probably never know if this is an authentic sighting or just another fake.

Kentucky Backyard Bigfoot 2009

Newspapers carried a bigfoot story that ran locally in Kentucky and nationally (*Weekly World News*) and internationally (*The Telegraph* in Britain) on September 8, 2009. The story featured photos from Kenny Mahoney of Fairdale, Kentucky who had set up a motion-sensitive camera in his backyard to take photos of any passing wildlife. Mahoney said that he was expecting to get photographs of squirrels, raccoons and other small animals, but instead got photos of a "gorilla-like creature" in his backyard.

Said Mahoney, "It looked like it had the outline of a head, and like, gorilla-type shoulders, and then the arms crossed is what it looks like to me."

He told reporters that he is very doubtful that the creature in the photo is bigfoot, yet he has no idea what it could be. His wife showed it to a local wildlife expert who thought it might a bear. Certainly, the photo was of a fur-covered animal, but the expert could not say what it was.

Some newspapers, like *The Telegraph,* said it was "one of the clearest ever photos of Bigfoot." Mr. Mahoney, like many people, does not want to seem to be gullible and a believer in sasquatch, so he cautiously contends that the photo is a mystery. No one has made the accusation yet that he is trying to pull off a bigfoot photo hoax, so the conclusion of many researchers, including myself, is that this is a genuine photo of sasquatch.

It is interesting to note that hairy apemen, even ones with white hair, are being seen every month or so across the U.S. and Canada. If more would-be photographers would put automatic cameras in their backyards, we might get more and more pictures of bigfoot and his smelly kin the skunk ape. As I have suggested before: with the prevalence of cell phones and digital cameras and other new technologies, we should be getting more and photos of sasquatch—and we have been! I predict that more and more people will be surprised to find that there is a gorilla-like creature creeping into their gardens at night!

And what of the strange tales of white-haired sasquatch? While yetis, sasquatch and bigfoot are generally said to have reddish-brown hair, there are many—too many— reports of white-haired sasquatch and yeti. Are they old sasquatch that have gone "rogue"? As with many animal

Ken Mahoney's backyard photograph.

370

species, there may be a tradition that older, once dominant males are outcast from standard sasquatch society (presumably in deep wilderness somewhere) and are forced to fend for themselves. They may become "loner sasquatch" and, like rogue lions, tigers or bears, venture closer to human society in order to raid garbage dumps, gardens, chicken coops and such.

Indeed, in an earlier chapter we learned about yeti breaking the necks of powerful yaks and eating their brains—something that a normal yeti would probably not do, but a starving rogue yeti might take the chance of raiding a yak pasture and coming close to humans.

Is this why there are so many sightings of the unusual white-haired sasquatch? Is it because he is old, and has been forced to roam away from the remote mountain forests or river swamps into areas where roads, trailer parks and rural towns lay dotted across the vast North American continent?

Another curious feature of many yeti-sasquatch encounters is a sexual element. Often, teenage women seem to be of interest to bigfoot intruders. In most cases where bigfoot has peeped in windows or tried to get into a shack or trailer, a young woman was inside, as in the case of the Fouke/Boggy Creek Monster and the recent incident at the White Mountain Apache Nation where the police had been called because of a Peeping Tom bigfoot.

Indeed, bigfoot has a keen sense of smell. A sasquatch can smell humans; he can smell sex; and he can smell if a woman is menstruating. A menstruating woman, or a teenager girl who is going through puberty, might be of special interest to young male sasquatch—and there is evidence that this is so. We even have the older tales of females being kidnapped by lonely sasquatch or yeti.

In fact, in at least one of the Du Pont Monster sightings, reported in the Ottawa, Illinois *Times* on July 21, 2005, there was a menstruating woman involved in an encounter. A couple had been having sex in the backseat of a car, and a used tampon had been tossed out the window. This apparently attracted the well-known bigfoot of the area. The Du Pont Monster had also been seen by campers in the area. In one incident related in the Ottawa *Times* story, campers smelled a strange musky, pungent odor, like an old mop, and could see the creature vaguely in the light of their campfire.

The strange bigfoot-like beast involved in these sightings is known as the Du Pont Monster to locals because it is often sighted aound the sprawling dynamite factory and grounds, formerly owned by Du Pont, along the south bank of the Illinois River just east of the town of

Weekly World News headline.

372

Seneca. In the thick forests and hills is a special bend in the road and a hollow at the bottom of a ravine. At this special spot, favored as a lover's lane for the Seneca area, folks seem to encounter the Du Pont Monster most often.

In August of 2007 I stood at that spot late one night with some friends and someone who had encountered the monster while looking for snakes in the forest. At this bend in the road, he had seen bigfoot from the waist up, looking at him from a distance. At night, he claimed, the sasquatch would throw small pebbles at him and his friends if they camped in the area.

"They're apes," he told me. "They're like gorillas. They live in nests back in the dense forest along the river. No one goes back there."

I looked around the dark hollow with its steep hillsides going up in into the forest where folks had often encountered the sasquatch. The forest was silent and still. I waited to be pelted from the forest. Nothing happened. Eventually, we got into our car and left.

The Du Pont Monster was only about 40 miles from my home in Kempton, Illinois. I had traveled across the world—to Nepal, Mongolia and Tibet—looking for yeti, and I was to have my closest encounter less than an hour away from my house.

It seems incredible, but the reality of the hairy giants—the apemen that live on the fringes of civilization, curious about our lifestyles, and ready to steal our women at any chance—seems hard to deny when faced with what seems an overwhelming

373

amount of evidence. Could all of the stories that have come down to us for nearly 200 years in North America be cases of misidentification of bears, or the occasional escaped circus gorilla? Or hoaxes? That, to me, would be very difficult to swallow.

Indeed, if playing the skeptic, I would have to be skeptical that there can be so many stories, photos and footprints (even frozen bodies) for it all to be a fabrication of imaginative hunters, miners and policemen (and women). One thing that we have learned in this book is that people in general are cautious about their encounters with yeti and sasquatch, and in many cases do not want to report them because they think—they know—that their friends and the general public will ridicule them for the experience that they claim they had.

No, they did not get a photograph. No, they didn't stop their car and chase after the animal that they spotted briefly in their headlights. No, they didn't report their sighting to anyone, except a few close friends that they could trust. I personally know many people exactly like that who have had encounters with bigfoot in various places around the United States, but are reticent to talk about it or have their names published. They feel that "normal" folks will ridicule them, accuse them of lying, and even question their professional standing (as a doctor, lawyer or engineer) after hearing their story. They might lose their jobs, their friends—and even their sanity. How can they have seen something that doesn't exist?

Fortunately, we have a few people who "know

what they saw." There are those folks, often residents of remote rural areas, who had an encounter with a giant hairy apeman and aren't afraid to talk about it. I say, "hurray for them."

So what is the reality of yetis, sasquatch and hairy giants? It is for you to decide. Whether a believer or skeptic, hopefully you are open-minded and willing to honestly look at the evidence, such as it is. Why not try what Kenny Mahoney in Kentucky did: buy a motion-sensitive camera and put it at a good spot near your house. Maybe, like lucky Kenny, you might find out that you have more and stranger late-night visitors than you have ever imagined!

Yetis, Sasquatch & Hairy Giants

WHITE MOUNTAIN APACHE
Game and Fish Department

Law Enforcement
Investigation Report
Phone (520) 338-4385
Fax (520) 338-1712

Case # 0507070419
Date 7-22-05 Time 1000 A
Received GF-8
How Received Page out

COMPLAINT

Nature of Complaint: Sighting of a large unidentified primate.

When Occurred, Day of Week: TUESDAY   Date: 7-19-05   Time: 700 P.
Exact Location of Occurrence: R78 AND 78H JCT.
Suspect (s) Name (s): N/A
License # and Description of Vehicle: N/A
Complainant: N/A

Name   Address   Phone

Witnesses: ▓▓

INVESTIGATION

Details of Investigation: On 7-19-05, I WAYNE B. Amos, received a phone call from ranger Raymond D. Valentino requesting assistance with traffic in the area of Paradise Creek. A report was made by a male subject of seeing what he believed to be something that look like Bigfoot. Upon arrival I made contact with male subject John Morris. ▓▓▓ began to tell me that he and his wife were driving down the R78 road heading west, when they saw what appeared to be a large hairy animal step out of the tree line walking like a human. As they stopped their vehicle the animal noticed them and went down into a squat position and began to look back and forth several times. At this time ▓▓▓ ▓▓▓▓ told her husband that it was a gorilla. ▓▓▓▓ tells his wife, "NO" and then observes the animal stand up and begin to run east. He describes the run as right hand and right leg moving forward together and left hand and left leg moving forward together. ▓▓▓▓ states he exited his vehicle and started walking south of the road to

Report Given to:

07-24-05
0933

Sworn Affidavit

On this date; __8/21/2006__ , I, ▓▓▓▓▓▓▓▓▓▓▓▓▓▓
                     _{Today's Date}   _{Print name}

of, __P.O. Box 218   WR.   Az. 85941__
      _{Address}   _{City}   _{State}   _{Postal Zip Code}

do subscribe and swear to the following;

During the time period of; __Summer   Summer   2004 1982__
                             _{Month(s)} _{Day(s)} _{Year} _{Approximate hours}

and at the following location(s) __Reservation Lake area__
                                  _{State} _{City/Town} _{General Location/Description}

__on ow. Ft Apache Reservation in Arizona.__
_{General Location/Description Cont..}

did experience and/or witness the following: ▓▓▓▓▓▓ *On way*
time from work on Whiteriver Reserve
@ appro. 2:30 pm @ Cowboy @ the
open range area @ ease. On the
Crossing was on big tall black hairy
being walking (strides) with arms
pumping. His arms @ his side.
when my vehicle he saw he
froze in place. I was traveling @
55 m.p.h. and acknowledged what
it was Big Foot. He I reversed the
vehicle but when I got in the
position the Being (Bigfoot) was
Gone. next day I went back.
to check for foot prints but was grazing
area ▓▓▓▓ *_____ one _____ only.*

_{If additional space is required for this description, the additional pages will be attached to this statement only.}

Certification: ▓▓▓▓▓▓
I, ▓▓▓▓▓▓▓▓▓▓▓▓ , **have given this statement of my own free will
and certify under oath and under penalty of perjury that the statement written
above is true and complete to the best of my recollection and ability**

This Page and Opposite: Official documents from the 2005 sasquatch
encounters at the White Mountain Apache reservation in Arizona.

Above: A photo of a Texas bigfoot given to Donna Shelton at the Kountry Kubbard Restaurant in Lamar, Texas in the summer of 2009.

BIBLIOGRAPHY

1. **Lore and Legend of the Yeti**, Kesar Lall, 1988, Pilgrims Book House, Kathmandu.
2. **On the Yeti Trail**, M. Gupta & T. Nath, 1994, UBSPD Publishers, New Delhi.
3. **Yeti Accounts**, Ram Kumar Panday, 1994, Ratna Bandar, Kathmandu.
4. **Yeti: Fact or Fiction**, Know Nepal Series No. 8, T. Majupuria & R. Kumar, 1993, Indra Majupuria, Kathmandu.
5. **Tom Slick & the Search For the Yeti**, Loren Coleman, 1989, Faber & Faber, London & Boston.
6. **There Are Giants in the Earth**, Michael Grumley, 1974, Doubleday & Co., Garden City, NY.
7. **Mount Everest: The Reconnaissance: 1921**, C. K. Howard-Bury, George Leigh-Mallory, et al. 1922. Longmans, Green and Co., London. (reprinted by Pilgrims Books, Kathmandu)
8. **Everest**, Walt Unsworth, 1989, Grafton Books, London.
9. **Abominable Snowmen: Legend Come To Life**, Ivan T. Sanderson, 1961, Chilton Book Co., New York. Reprinted 2006, Adventures Unlimited Press.
10. **The Sherpa & Snowman**, Charles Stonor, 1955, Hollis & Carter, London.
11. **The Story of Everest**, W.H. Murray, 1953, Dent & Sons, London.
12. **Bhutanese Tales of the Yeti**, Kunzung Choden, 1997, White Lotus, Bangkok.
13. **Still Living?**, Myra Shackley, 1983, Thames & Hudson, London.
14. **The Major Mysteries of Mainland China**, Paul Dong, 1984, Prentice Hall, Englewood Cliffs, NJ.
15. **Bigfoot: The Yeti & Sasquatch in Myth & Reality**, John Napier, 1973, E.P. Dutton, New York.
16. **Do Abominable Snowmen of North America Really Exist?**, Roger Patterson, 1966, Franklin Press, Yakima, Washington.

17. **Tales of the Yeti,** Kesar Lall, 1988, Pilgrims Book House, Kathmandu.
18. **An Encounter with the Yeti,** Kesar Lall, 1991, Ratna Pustak Bhandar, Kathmandu.
19. **Nepal: Off the Beaten Track**, Kesar Lall, 1992, Ratna Pustak Bhandar, Kathmandu.
20. **Yeti Mystery**, Ram Kumar Paday, 2007, Ratna Pustak Bhandar, Kathmandu.
21. **Mysterious Australia,** Rex Gilroy, 1995, Nexus Books, Mapleton, Queensland.
22. **The Locals,** Thom Powell, 2004, Hancock House, Surrey, BC.
23. **Meet the Sasquatch,** Christopher Murphy, 2004, Hancock House, Surrey, BC.
24. **Mysterious Creatures,** 1988, Time-Life Books, Alexandria, Virginia.
25. **The History and Lore of Freaks**, C.J.S. Thompson, 1930, Senate Books, London.
26. **Buccaneers of America,** Alexander O. Exquemelin, 1678, reprinted 1967, Penguin Books, London and 2000, Dover Books, Mineola, NYC.
27. **The Aquatic Ape**, Elaine Morgan, 1982, Stein & Day, New York.
28. **Beyond the Andes,** Pino Turolla, 1980, Harper & Row, New York.
29. **The Morning of the Magicians**, Louis Pauwels & Jacques Bergier, 1960, Stein & Day, NYC.
30. **Bigfoot**, Ann Slate & Alan Berry, 1976, Bantam Books, NY.
31. **High In the Thin Cold Air**, Desmond Doig & Sir Edmund Hillary, 1962, Hodder & Stoughton, London.
32. **On the Track of Unknown Animals**, Bernard Heuvelmans, 1955, MIT Press, Cambridge, MA.
33. **Gigantopithecus**, E.L. Simons & P.E. Ettel, Scientific American, January, 1970.
34. **The Mysterious Monsters**, Robert & Frances Guenette, Sun Classic, Los Angeles.
35. **The Yeti**, Odette Tchernine, 1970, Neville Spearman, London.
36. **Weird America**, Jim Brandon, 1978, E.P. Dutton, NYC.
37. **The Elusive Monster**, Maurice Burton, 1961, Rupert Hart David, London.

380

38. **Shambala**, Andrew Tomas, 1977, Sphere Books, London.
39. **Strange Abominable Snowmen**, Warren Smith, 1970, Popular Library, NYC.
40. **The Snowman and Company**, Odette Tchernine, 1961, Robert Hale, London.
41. **That Untravelled World,** Eric Shipton, 1969, Charles Scribner & Sons, New York.
42. **Tibet**, Thubten Norbu & Colin Turnbull, 1969, Penguin Books, NYC.
43. **Giants: The Vanished Race of Mighty Men**, Roy Norvill, 1979, The Aquarian Press, Welllingborough, UK.
44. **The Historical Bigfoot**, Chad Arment, 2006, Coachwhip Publications, PA.
45. **Enigmas**, Rupert Gould, 1945, University Books, NYC.
46. **Buffalo Bill** (Autobiography), William Cody, 1879, Frank Bliss Co., Hartford, Connecticut, reprinted 1978, University of Nebraska Press.
47. **The Neandertals**, Erik Tinkaus & Pat Shipman, 1970, SBS, NYC.
48. **The Mountain Gorilla**, George Schaller, 1963, Chicago University Press, Chicago & London.
49. **Men and Apes**, Desmond & Ramona Morris, 1968, McGraw Hill, New York.
50. **The Abominable Snowman**, Ralph Izzard, 1955, Doubleday & Co. Garden City, NY.
51. **Fortean Times**, No. 93, Dec. 1996, John Brown Publishing, London.
52. **Stranger Than Science**, Frank Edwards, 1959, Bantam Books, NYC.
53. **Strange World**, Frank Edwards, 1962, Bantam Books, NYC.
54. **The Complete Guide to Mysterious Beings**, John A. Keel, 1994, Doubleday & Co., New York.
55. **Trail of the Abominable Snowman**, Gardener Soule, 1966, G.P. Putnam & Sons, New York.
56. **More Than a Legend**, Constance Whyte, 1952, Hamish Hamilton, London.
57. **Magic and Mystery in Tibet**, Alexandra David-Neel, 1929, Dover, NYC.

58. **Lost Cities of China, Central Asia & India**, David Hatcher Childress, 1985, AUP, Kempton, IL.
59. **Lost Cities & Ancient Mysteries of the Southwest**, David Hatcher Childress, 2009, AUP, Kempton, IL.
60. **Lost Cities of North & Central America**, David Hatcher Childress, 1994, AUP, Kempton, IL.
61. **A Kino Guide**, Charles Polzer, 1974, Tucson.
62. **Baja California: Vanished Missions, Lost Treasures, Strange Stories Tall and True**, Choral Pepper, 1973, San Diego.
63. **Desert Lore of Southern California**, Choral Pepper, 1994, Sunbelt Publications, San Diego.
64. **The Sacred Myth of Shangri-La**, Peter Bishop, 1987, Athlone, London.
65. **The Lovelock Cave**, Llewellyn Loud & Mark Harrington, 1929, University of California Press, Berkeley.
66. **Bigfoot Encounters in Ohio: Quest for the Grassman**, Christopher Murphy, Joedy Cook and George Clappison, 2006, Hancock House, Surrey, BC, Canada.
67. **Sasquatch: The Apes Among Us**, John Green, 1978, Hancock House, Surrey, British Columbia.
68. **Ivan Sanderson's Book of Great Jungles**, Ivan Sanderson, 1965, Simon and Schuster, New York.
69. **Things and More Things**, Ivan T. Sanderson, 1970, reprinted by Adventures Unlimited Press, 2007.
70. **Spaceships in Prehistory**, Peter Kolosimo, 1975, University Books, NYC.
71. **Timeless Earth**, Peter Kolosimo, 1973, Bantam Books, NYC.
72. **Out of the Shadows**, Tony Healy & Paul Cropper, 1994, Macmillan Australia, Melbourne.
73. **Giants: The Vanished Race of Mighty Men**, Roy Norvill, 1979, Aquarian Books, Northhamptonshire, England.
74. **The Field Guide to Bigfoot, Yeti, and Other Mystery Primates Worldwide**, Loren Coleman and Patrick Huyghe, 2006, Anomalous Books, New York.
75. **The Land of the Lamas**, W. Rockhill, 1891, London (reprinted 1975, New Delhi).
76. **The Bigfoot Casebook**, Janet & Colin Bord, 1982, Granada, London.
77. **Bigfoot: Man, Monster or Myth?**, Peter Byrne, 1975, Acropolis

382

Books, Olympia, Washington.

78. **Encounters With Bigfoot**, John Green, 1980, Hancock House, Surrey, British Columbia.

79. **On the Track of the Sasquatch**, John Green, 1980, Hancock House, Surrey, British Columbia.

80. **Sasquatch/Bigfoot**, Thomas N. Steenburg, 1990, Hancock House, Surrey, British Columbia.

81. **Bigfoot Memoirs**, Stan Johnson, 1996, Wild Flower Press, Newberg, Oregon.

82. **Sasquatch/Bigfoot**, Don Hunter with René Dahinden, 1993, Firefly Books, Buffalo, New York.

83. **Big Footprints**, Grover S. Krantz, 1992, Johnson Books, Boulder, Colorado.

84. **World of the Odd & Awesome**, Charles Berlitz, 1991, Fawcett, NYC.

85. **The Book of the Damned**, Charles Fort, 1919, Ace Books, NYC.

86. **Mysteries of Ancient South America**, Harold Wilkins, 1946, Citadel, NYC. (reprinted by Adventures Unlimited Press)

87. **Secret Cities of Old South America**, Harold Wilkins, 1952, Library Publications, Inc., NYC. (reprinted by Adventures Unlimited Press)

88. **Rumors of Existence**, Matthew Bille, 1995, Hancock House, Surrey, British Columbia.

89. **The Goblin Universe**, Ted Holiday, 1986, Llewellyn, St. Paul, Minnesota.

90. **The Six Mountain-Travel Books**, Eric Shipton, 1985, Diadem Books, London.

91. **My Quest for the Yeti**, Reinhold Messner, 1998 (Austria), 2001, St. Martin's Press, New York.

92. **Lost Cities & Ancient Mysteries of South America**, David Hatcher Childress, 1984, Adventures Unlimited Press, Kempton, Illinois.

93. **The Mysterious Valley**, Christopher O'Brien, 1996, St. Martins Press, New York.

94. **Mysteries of Time and Space,** Brad Steiger & Ron Calais, 1974, Prentice Hall, Inc. Englewood Cliffs, New Jersey.

95. **Bigfoot: America's Abominable Snowman**, Elwood Baumann, 1975, Franklin Watts, Inc., New York.

96. **The Bigfoot Film Controversy**, Roger Patterson and Chris Murphy, 2004, Hancock House, Surrey, BC.

97. **The Making of Bigfoot**, Greg Long, 2004, Prometheus Books, Amherst, NY.

98. **Sasquatch: Legend Meets Science**, Jeff Meldrum, 2006, Forge Books, New York.

99. **Cryptozoology: Science & Speculation**, Chad Arment, 2004, Coachwhip Publications, Landisville, PA.

100. **Strange Indiana Monsters**, Michael Newton, 2006, Schiffer Publishing, Atglen, PA.

101. **Lost Cities & Ancient Mysteries of the Southwest**, David Hatcher Childress, 2009, Adventures Unlimited Press, Kempton, IL.

102. **Montezuma's Serpent**, Brad Steiger and Sherry Hansen-Steiger, 1992, Paragon House, New York.

103. **Arizona Cavacade**, edited by Joseph Miller, 1962, Hastings House Publishers, New York.

104. **Lost Cities of North & Central America**, David Hatcher Childress, 1994, Adventures Unlimited Press, Kempton, IL.

105. **"The Yeti: A Rock After All?"**, Anthony B. Wooldridge, *Cryptozoology*, 6:135, 1987.

106. **In the Footsteps of the Russian Snowman**, Dmitri Bayanov, 1996, Pyramid Publications, Moscow.

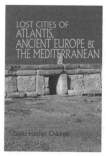

LOST CITIES OF ATLANTIS, ANCIENT EUROPE & THE MEDITERRANEAN
by David Hatcher Childress

Atlantis! The legendary lost continent comes under the close scrutiny of maverick archaeologist David Hatcher Childress in this sixth book in the internationally popular *Lost Cities* series. Childress takes the reader in search of sunken cities in the Mediterranean; across the Atlas Mountains in search of Atlantean ruins; to remote islands in search of megalithic ruins; to meet living legends and secret societies. From Ireland to Turkey, Morocco to Eastern Europe, and around the remote islands of the Mediterranean and Atlantic, Childress takes the reader on an astonishing quest for mankind's past. Ancient technology, cataclysms, megalithic construction, lost civilizations and devastating wars of the past are all explored in this book. Childress challenges the skeptics and proves that great civilizations not only existed in the past, but the modern world and its problems are reflections of the ancient world of Atlantis.

524 PAGES. 6x9 PAPERBACK. ILLUSTRATED. BIBLIOGRAPHY & INDEX. $16.95. CODE: MED

LOST CITIES OF ANCIENT LEMURIA & THE PACIFIC
by David Hatcher Childress

Was there once a continent in the Pacific? Called Lemuria or Pacifica by geologists, Mu or Pan by the mystics, there is now ample mythological, geological and archaeological evidence to "prove" that an advanced and ancient civilization once lived in the central Pacific. Maverick archaeologist and explorer David Hatcher Childress combs the Indian Ocean, Australia and the Pacific in search of the surprising truth about mankind's past. Contains photos of the underwater city on Pohnpei; explanations on how the statues were levitated around Easter Island in a clockwise vortex movement; tales of disappearing islands; Egyptians in Australia; and more.

379 PAGES. 6x9 PAPERBACK. ILLUSTRATED. FOOTNOTES & BIBLIOGRAPHY. $14.95. CODE: LEM

LOST CITIES & ANCIENT MYSTERIES OF SOUTH AMERICA
by David Hatcher Childress

Rogue adventurer and maverick archaeologist David Hatcher Childress takes the reader on unforgettable journeys deep into deadly jungles, high up on windswept mountains and across scorching deserts in search of lost civilizations and ancient mysteries. Travel with David and explore stone cities high in mountain forests and hear fantastic tales of Inca treasure, living dinosaurs, and a mysterious tunnel system. Whether he is hopping freight trains, searching for secret cities, or just dealing with the daily problems of food, money, and romance, the author keeps the reader spellbound. Includes both early and current maps, photos, and illustrations, and plenty of advice for the explorer planning his or her own journey of discovery.

381 PAGES. 6x9 PAPERBACK. ILLUSTRATED. FOOTNOTES. BIBLIOGRAPHY. INDEX. $16.95. CODE: SAM

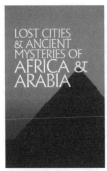

LOST CITIES & ANCIENT MYSTERIES OF AFRICA & ARABIA
by David Hatcher Childress

Across ancient deserts, dusty plains and steaming jungles, maverick archaeologist David Childress continues his world-wide quest for lost cities and ancient mysteries. Join him as he discovers forbidden cities in the Empty Quarter of Arabia; "Atlantean" ruins in Egypt and the Kalahari desert; a mysterious, ancient empire in the Sahara; and more. This is the tale of an extraordinary life on the road: across war-torn countries, Childress searches for King Solomon's Mines, living dinosaurs, the Ark of the Covenant and the solutions to some of the fantastic mysteries of the past.

423 PAGES. 6x9 PAPERBACK. ILLUSTRATED. FOOTNOTES & BIBLIOGRAPHY. $14.95. CODE: AFA

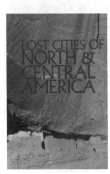

LOST CITIES OF NORTH & CENTRAL AMERICA
by David Hatcher Childress

Down the back roads from coast to coast, maverick archaeologist and adventurer David Hatcher Childress goes deep into unknown America. With this incredible book, you will search for lost Mayan cities and books of gold, discover an ancient canal system in Arizona, climb gigantic pyramids in the Midwest, explore megalithic monuments in New England, and join the astonishing quest for lost cities throughout North America. From the war-torn jungles of Guatemala, Nicaragua and Honduras to the deserts, mountains and fields of Mexico, Canada, and the U.S.A., Childress takes the reader in search of sunken ruins, Viking forts, strange tunnel systems, living dinosaurs, early Chinese explorers, and fantastic lost treasure. Packed with both early and current maps, photos and illustrations.

590 PAGES. 6x9 PAPERBACK. ILLUSTRATED. FOOTNOTES. BIBLIOGRAPHY. INDEX. $16.95. CODE: NCA

LOST CITIES OF CHINA, CENTRAL ASIA & INDIA
by David Hatcher Childress

Like a real life "Indiana Jones," maverick archaeologist David Childress takes the reader on an incredible adventure across some of the world's oldest and most remote countries in search of lost cities and ancient mysteries. Discover ancient cities in the Gobi Desert; hear fantastic tales of lost continents, vanished civilizations and secret societies bent on ruling the world; visit forgotten monasteries in forbidding snow-capped mountains with strange tunnels to mysterious subterranean cities! A unique combination of far-out exploration and practical travel advice, it will astound and delight the experienced traveler or the armchair voyager.

429 PAGES. 6x9 PAPERBACK. ILLUSTRATED. FOOTNOTES & BIBLIOGRAPHY. $14.95. CODE: CHI

TECHNOLOGY OF THE GODS
The Incredible Sciences of the Ancients
by David Hatcher Childress
Popular *Lost Cities* author David Hatcher Childress takes us into the amazing world of ancient technology, from computers in antiquity to the "flying machines of the gods." Childress looks at the technology that was allegedly used in Atlantis and the theory that the Great Pyramid of Egypt was originally a gigantic power station. He examines tales of ancient flight and the technology that it involved; how the ancients used electricity; megalithic building techniques; the use of crystal lenses and the fire from the gods; evidence of various high tech weapons in the past, including atomic weapons; ancient metallurgy and heavy machinery; the role of modern inventors such as Nikola Tesla in bringing ancient technology back into modern use; impossible artifacts; and more.
356 PAGES. 6x9 PAPERBACK. ILLUSTRATED. BIBLIOGRAPHY. $16.95. CODE: TGOD

VIMANA AIRCRAFT OF ANCIENT INDIA & ATLANTIS
by David Hatcher Childress, introduction by Ivan T. Sanderson
Did the ancients have the technology of flight? In this incredible volume on ancient India, authentic Indian texts such as the *Ramayana* and the *Mahabharata* are used to prove that ancient aircraft were in use more than four thousand years ago. Included in this book is the entire Fourth Century BC manuscript *Vimaanika Shastra* by the ancient author Maharishi Bharadwaaja, translated into English by the Mysore Sanskrit professor G.R. Josyer. Also included are chapters on Atlantean technology, the incredible Rama Empire of India and the devastating wars that destroyed it. Also an entire chapter on mercury vortex propulsion and mercury gyros, the power source described in the ancient Indian texts. Not to be missed by those interested in ancient civilizations or the UFO enigma.
334 PAGES. 6x9 PAPERBACK. ILLUSTRATED. $15.95. CODE: VAA

LOST CONTINENTS & THE HOLLOW EARTH
I Remember Lemuria and the Shaver Mystery
by David Hatcher Childress & Richard Shaver
A thorough examination of the early hollow earth stories of Richard Shaver and the fascination that fringe fantasy subjects such as lost continents and the hollow earth have had for the American public. Shaver's rare 1948 book *I Remember Lemuria* is reprinted in its entirety, and the book is packed with illustrations from Ray Palmer's *Amazing Stories* magazine of the 1940s. Palmer and Shaver told of tunnels running through the earth—tunnels inhabited by the Deros and Teros, humanoids from an ancient spacefaring race that had inhabited the earth, eventually going underground, hundreds of thousands of years ago. Childress discusses the famous hollow earth books and delves deep into whatever reality may be behind the stories of tunnels in the earth. Operation High Jump to Antarctica in 1947 and Admiral Byrd's bizarre statements, tunnel systems in South America and Tibet, the underground world of Agartha, the belief of UFOs coming from the South Pole, more.
344 PAGES. 6x9 PAPERBACK. ILLUSTRATED. $16.95. CODE: LCHE

ARKTOS
The Polar Myth in Science, Symbolism & Nazi Survival
by Joscelyn Godwin
Explored are the many tales of an ancient race said to have lived in the Arctic regions, such as Thule and Hyperborea. Progressing onward, he looks at modern polar legends: including the survival of Hitler, German bases in Antarctica, UFOs, the hollow earth, and the hidden kingdoms of Agartha and Shambala. Chapters include: The Golden Age; The Northern Lights; The Arctic Homeland; The Aryan Myth; The Thule Society; The Black Order; The Hidden Lands; Agartha and the Polaires; Shambhala; The Hole at the Pole; Antarctica; more.

220 Pages. 6x9 Paperback. Illustrated. $16.95. Code: ARK

SECRETS OF THE HOLY LANCE
The Spear of Destiny in History & Legend
by Jerry E. Smith
Secrets of the Holy Lance traces the Spear from its possession by Constantine, Rome's first Christian Caesar, to Charlemagne's claim that with it he ruled the Holy Roman Empire by Divine Right, and on through two thousand years of kings and emperors, until it came within Hitler's grasp—and beyond! Did it rest for a while in Antarctic ice? Is it now hidden in Europe, awaiting the next person to claim its awesome power? Neither debunking nor worshiping, *Secrets of the Holy Lance* seeks to pierce the veil of myth and mystery around the Spear.

312 PAGES. 6x9 PAPERBACK. ILLUSTRATED. BIBLIOGRAPHY. $16.95. CODE: SOHL

THE CRYSTAL SKULLS
Astonishing Portals to Man's Past
by David Hatcher Childress and Stephen S. Mehler
Childress introduces the technology and lore of crystals, and then plunges into the turbulent times of the Mexican Revolution form the backdrop for the rollicking adventures of Ambrose Bierce, the renowned journalist who went missing in the jungles in 1913, and F.A. Mitchell-Hedges, the notorious adventurer who emerged from the jungles with the most famous of the crystal skulls. Mehler shares his extensive knowledge of and experience with crystal skulls. Having been involved in the field since the 1980s, he has personally examined many of the most influential skulls, and has worked with the leaders in crystal skull research. Color section.

294 pages. 6x9 Paperback. Illustrated. $18.95. Code: CRSK

THE LAND OF OSIRIS
An Introduction to Khemitology
by Stephen S. Mehler
Was there an advanced prehistoric civilization in ancient Egypt? Were they the people who built the great pyramids and carved the Great Sphinx? Did the pyramids serve as energy devices and not as tombs for kings? Chapters include: Egyptology and Its Paradigms; Khemitology—New Paradigms; Asgat Nefer—The Harmony of Water; Khemit and the Myth of Atlantis; The Extraterrestrial Question; more.

272 PAGES. 6x9 PAPERBACK. ILLUSTRATED. COLOR SECTION. BIBLIOGRAPHY. $18.95. CODE: LOOS

THE MYSTERY OF EASTER ISLAND
by Katherine Routledge

The reprint of Katherine Routledge's classic archaeology book which was first published in London in 1919. The book details her journey by yacht from England to South America, around Patagonia to Chile and on to Easter Island. Routledge explored the amazing island and produced one of the first-ever accounts of the life, history and legends of this strange and remote place. Routledge discusses the statues, pyramid-platforms, Rongo Rongo script, the Bird Cult, the war between the Short Ears and the Long Ears, the secret caves, ancient roads on the island, and more. This rare book serves as a sourcebook on the early discoveries and theories on Easter Island.

432 PAGES. 6x9 PAPERBACK. ILLUSTRATED. $16.95. CODE: MEI

IN SECRET TIBET
by Theodore Illion

Reprint of a rare 30s adventure travel book. Illion was a German wayfarer who not only spoke fluent Tibetan, but travelled in disguise as a native through forbidden Tibet when it was off-limits to all outsiders. His incredible adventures make this one of the most exciting travel books ever published. Includes illustrations of Tibetan monks levitating stones by acoustics.

210 PAGES. 5x9 PAPERBACK. ILLUSTRATED. $15.95. CODE: IST

DARKNESS OVER TIBET
by Theodore Illion

In this second reprint of Illion's rare books, the German traveller continues his journey through Tibet and is given directions to a strange underground city. As the original publisher's remarks said, "this is a rare account of an underground city in Tibet by the only Westerner ever to enter it and escape alive!"

210 PAGES. 5x9 PAPERBACK. ILLUSTRATED. $15.95. CODE: DOT

MYSTERY CITIES OF THE MAYA
Exploration and Adventure in Belize
by Thomas Gann

Gann was close friends with Mike Mitchell-Hedges, the British adventurer who discovered the famous crystal skull with his adopted daughter Sammy and Lady Richmond Brown, their benefactress. Gann battles pirates along Belize's coast and goes upriver with Mitchell-Hedges to the site of Lubaantun where they excavate a strange lost city where the crystal skull was discovered. Lubaantun is a unique city in the Mayan world as it is built out of precisely carved blocks of stone without the usual plaster-cement facing. Gann shared Mitchell-Hedges belief in Atlantis and lost civilizations (pre-Mayan) in Central America and the Caribbean. Lots of good photos, maps and diagrams.

252 PAGES. 6x9 PAPERBACK. ILLUSTRATED. $16.95. CODE: MCOM

MAPS OF THE ANCIENT SEA KINGS
Evidence of Advanced Civilization in the Ice Age
by Charles H. Hapgood
Hapgood has found the evidence in the Piri Reis Map that shows Antarctica, the Hadji Ahmed map, the Oronteus Finaeus and other amazing maps. Hapgood concluded that these maps were made from more ancient maps from the various ancient archives around the world, now lost. Not only were these unknown people more advanced in mapmaking than any people prior to the 18th century, it appears they mapped all the continents. The Americas were mapped thousands of years before Columbus. Antarctica was mapped when its coasts were free of ice.
316 PAGES. 7x10 PAPERBACK. ILLUSTRATED. BIBLIOGRAPHY & INDEX. $19.95. CODE: MASK

PATH OF THE POLE
by Charles Hapgood
Hapgood researched Antarctica, ancient maps and the geological record to conclude that the Earth's crust has slipped in the inner core many times in the past, changing the position of the pole. *Path of the Pole* discusses the various "pole shifts" in Earth's past, giving evidence for each one, and moves on to possible future pole shifts. Packed with illustrations, this is the sourcebook for many other books on cataclysms and pole shifts.
356 PAGES. 6x9 PAPERBACK. ILLUSTRATED. $16.95. CODE: POP

MYSTERIES OF ANCIENT SOUTH AMERICA
Atlantis Reprint Series
by Harold T. Wilkins
Wilkins digs into old manuscripts and books to bring us some truly amazing stories of South America: a bizarre subterranean tunnel system; lost cities in the remote border jungles of Brazil; cataclysmic changes that shaped South America; and other strange stories from one of the world's great researchers. Chapters include: Dead Cities of Ancient Brazil, The Jungle Light that Shines by Itself, The Missionary Men in Black: Forerunners of the Great Catastrophe, The Sign of the Sun: The World's Oldest Alphabet, The Atlanean "Subterraneans" of the Incas, Tiahuanacu and the Giants, more.
236 PAGES. 6x9 PAPERBACK. ILLUSTRATED. INDEX. $14.95. CODE: MASA

SECRET CITIES OF OLD SOUTH AMERICA
by Harold T. Wilkins
The reprint of Wilkins' classic book, first published in 1952, claiming that South America was Atlantis. Chapters include Mysteries of a Lost World; Atlantis Unveiled; Red Riddles on the Rocks; South America's Amazons Existed!; The Mystery of El Dorado and Gran Payatiti—the Final Refuge of the Incas; Monstrous Beasts of the Unexplored Swamps & Wilds; Weird Denizens of Antediluvian Forests; New Light on Atlantis from the World's Oldest Book; The Mystery of Old Man Noah and the Arks; and more.
438 PAGES. 6x9 PAPERBACK. ILLUSTRATED. BIBLIOGRAPHY & INDEX. $16.95. CODE: SCOS

LOST CITIES & ANCIENT MYSTERIES OF THE SOUTHWEST
By David Hatcher Childress

Join David as he starts in northern Mexico and then to west Texas amd into New Mexico where he stumbles upon a hollow mountain with a billion dollars of gold bars hidden deep inside it! In Arizona he investigates tales of Egyptian catacombs in the Grand Canyon, cruises along the Devil's Highway, and tackles the century-old mystery of the Lost Dutchman mine. In California Childress checks out the rumors of mummified giants and weird tunnels in Death Valley—It's a full-tilt blast down the back roads of the Southwest in search of the weird and wondrous mysteries of the past!
486 Pages. 6x9 Paperback. Illustrated. $19.95. Code: LCSW

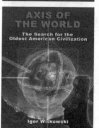

AXIS OF THE WORLD
The Search for the Oldest American Civilization
by Igor Witkowski

Witkowski's research reveals remnants of a high civilization that was able to exert its influence on almost the entire planet, and did so with full consciousness. Sites around South America show that this was a place where they built their crowning achievements. Easter Island, in the southeastern Pacific, constitutes one of them. The Rongo-Rongo language that developed there points westward to the Indus Valley. Taken together, the facts presented provide new proof that an antediluvian civilization flourished several millennia ago.
220 pages. 6x9 Paperback. Illustrated. $18.95. Code: AXOW

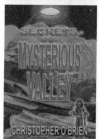

SECRETS OF THE MYSTERIOUS VALLEY
by Christopher O'Brien

No other region in North America features the variety and intensity of unusual phenomena found in the world's largest alpine valley, the San Luis Valley of Colorado and New Mexico. Since 1989, O'Brien has documented thousands of high-strange accounts that report UFOs, ghosts, crypto-creatures, cattle mutilations, and more, along with portal areas, secret underground bases and covert military activity. Hundreds of animals have been found strangely slain during waves of anomalous aerial craft sightings. Is the government directly involved? Are there underground bases here?
460 PAGES. 6x9 PAPERBACK. ILLUSTRATED. BIBLIOGRAPHY. $19.95. CODE: SOMV

STALKING THE TRICKSTERS:
Shapeshifters, Skinwalkers, Dark Adepts & 2012
By Christopher O'Brien

Manifestations of the Trickster persona such as cryptids, elementals, werewolves, demons, vampires and dancing devils have permeated human experience since before the dawn of civilization. But today, very little is publicly known about The Tricksters. Who are they? What is their agenda? Known by many names including fools, sages, Loki, men-in-black, skinwalkers, shapeshifters, jokers, *jinn*, sorcerers, and witches, Tricksters provide us with a direct conduit to the unknown in the 21st century. Can these denizens of phenomenal events be attempting to communicate a warning to humanity in this uncertain age of prophesied change?
354 Pages. 6x9 Paperback. Illustrated. Bibliography. $18.95. Code: STT

ORDER FORM

10% Discount When You Order 3 or More Items!

One Adventure Place
P.O. Box 74
Kempton, Illinois 60946
United States of America
Tel.: 815-253-6390 • Fax: 815-253-6300
Email: auphq@frontiernet.net
http://www.adventuresunlimitedpress.com

ORDERING INSTRUCTIONS

✓ Remit by USD$ Check, Money Order or Credit Card

✓ Visa, Master Card, Discover & AmEx Accepted

✓ Paypal Payments Can Be Made To:
   info@wexclub.com

✓ Prices May Change Without Notice

✓ 10% Discount for 3 or more Items

SHIPPING CHARGES

United States

✓ Postal Book Rate { $4.00 First Item / 50¢ Each Additional Item

✓ POSTAL BOOK RATE Cannot Be Tracked!

✓ Priority Mail { $5.00 First Item / $2.00 Each Additional Item

✓ UPS { $6.00 First Item / $1.50 Each Additional Item

NOTE: UPS Delivery Available to Mainland USA Only

Canada

✓ Postal Air Mail { $10.00 First Item / $2.50 Each Additional Item

✓ Personal Checks or Bank Drafts MUST BE US$ and Drawn on a US Bank

✓ Canadian Postal Money Orders OK

✓ Payment MUST BE US$

All Other Countries

✓ Sorry, No Surface Delivery!

✓ Postal Air Mail { $16.00 First Item / $6.00 Each Additional Item

✓ Checks and Money Orders MUST BE US$ and Drawn on a US Bank or branch.

✓ Paypal Payments Can Be Made in US$ To:
   info@wexclub.com

SPECIAL NOTES

✓ RETAILERS: Standard Discounts Available

✓ BACKORDERS: We Backorder all Out-of-Stock Items Unless Otherwise Requested

✓ PRO FORMA INVOICES: Available on Request

ORDER ONLINE AT: www.adventuresunlimitedpress.com

Please check: ✓

☐ This is my first order   ☐ I have ordered before

Name

Address

City

State/Province   Postal Code

Country

Phone day   Evening

Fax   Email

Item Code	Item Description	Qty	Total

Please check: ✓

☐ Postal-Surface

☐ Postal-Air Mail (Priority in USA)

☐ UPS (Mainland USA only)

Subtotal ▶	
Less Discount-10% for 3 or more items ▶	
Balance ▶	
Illinois Residents 6.25% Sales Tax ▶	
Previous Credit ▶	
Shipping ▶	
Total (check/MO in USD$ only) ▶	

☐ Visa/MasterCard/Discover/American Express

Card Number

Expiration Date

10% Discount When You Order 3 or More Items!